The Woman

I Was Not

Born To Be

The *Woman*
I Was Not
Born To Be

A Transsexual Journey

ALESHIA BREVARD

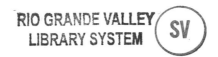

TEMPLE UNIVERSITY PRESS
Philadelphia

Temple University Press, Philadelphia 19122
Copyright © 2001 by Aleshia Brevard
All rights reserved
Published 2001
Printed in the United States of America

♾ The paper used in this publication meets the requirements of the American National
Standard for Information Sciences—Permanence of Paper for Printed Library Materials,
ANSI Z39.48–1984

Library of Congress Cataloging-in-Publication Data

Brevard, Aleshia, 1937–
    The woman I was not born to be : a transsexual journey / Aleshia Brevard.
        p. cm.
    Includes index.
    ISBN 1-56639-839-8 (cloth : alk. paper) — ISBN 1-56639-840-1 (pbk. : alk. paper)
        1. Brevard, Aleshia, 1937– . 2. Transsexuals—United States—Biography. I. Title.

HQ77.8B74 A3 2000
305.9′066—dc21
[B]   00–032568

Contents

Photographs follow page 126

The Woman
I Was Not
Born To Be

CHAPTER 1

Just for a Change

MOTHER NEVER said I was not different. She knew I was not like other boys and realized the suffering that dissimilarity caused me. Unfortunately, she was powerless to make my pain go away.

"If everyone were the same," she'd say to stem the flood of my youthful tears, "what a boring world it would be." I wasn't sure my mother knew what she was talking about. Nothing could possibly be better than being exactly like everyone else!

My reverie was broken as the nurse suddenly strode into my hospital room.

"That makeup has to come off!" she barked. Shaking her head, she left just as abruptly, slamming the door.

I did not like this woman. From the moment I was put in her care, my night-shift nurse had been the personification of a junkyard dog. Now she was proving herself a bitch, to boot. At twenty-three, my reckless quest for understanding and acceptance made me vulnerable to such hostility. I wanted to be universally loved. For this reason, I convinced myself that my nurse's hatred was not directed toward me personally.

"Stupid, stupid, stupid," I berated myself. "It isn't you that's upsetting this nurse—it's your makeup. That's why she wants you to take it off. You've chosen the wrong lip color!"

Flights of fancy were part of my survival technique in those last presurgery months in San Francisco. As quickly as I could snap my fingers, I'd create a scenario with which I could live comfortably. Self-deception had always been my mechanism for coping. I was good at it.

For example, there was the every-Monday-morning-after-leaving-electrolysis illusion.

Weekly I braced myself in the chair of an electrologist who had the unlikely name Ange'l. I'd grit my teeth and grimace as she pushed a small needle into the follicle of my offending facial hair and gave the root a sharp jolt of electricity. It hurt like hell—but I loved Ange'l for doing it. As soon as one little hair was electrocuted, she would declare war on its partner. My upper lip and jawline were areas especially sensitive to her painful invasion. To endure sessions with the electrologist, I needed more than self-deception. I took Percodan. Before leaving her office, I would swallow my second pain pill. Thus fortified, I would undertake my walk home to the Victorian on Steiner Street.

In a Percodan haze, I would promenade. Toe first, then heel. One foot placed purposefully in front of the other. Toe. Heel. Toe. The shoulder placement was of major consequence. Was my walk more enticing with Garbo's slightly sloping shoulder or with a calculated Dietrichesque strength? I would glide by storefront windows and check my reflection. I could also judge the power of my strut by watching my shadow on the sidewalk before me. I dismissed pedestrians sharing my sidewalk; it was too embarrassing to acknowledge their presence. My face looked like ground beef, with some sort of greasy salve liberally spread upon it for preservation. I was a mess. So, in my head, I created a beautiful scenario. I was in the preliminaries of the Miss America Pageant.

Toe. Heel. First, one foot. Now, the other. Each placed purposefully in front of the foot before. Head held high, knees slightly bent, I would glide up Market Street toward home.

At a red light, waiting for the pedestrian signal to flash, I would pose in third ballet position—right heel pulled tightly into the curvature of the left foot. In my imagination, the red light represented the pageant's preliminary judging sequence, and I waited with nervous anticipation. The stoplight always turned green, the crossing sign always flashed "Walk," and I always passed into "the final phase of competition."

"Well?" the night nurse snapped. "Are you going to do what I told you, or not? You can't wear makeup to surgery."

So much for being crowned Miss America. I gave in.

Wearing makeup to surgery was a ridiculous hang-up; even I understood that. I was scared. I was holding onto the familiar, and my face was the only thing of which I was confident. If I were to die during surgery, I wanted to be beautiful when I departed this earth. All I wanted from this disgruntled nurse, my surgeon, and the Westlake Clinic was a little gender reassignment. That was all.

It was 1962, and I was one of a mere handful undergoing transsexual surgery in America. The procedure was in its infancy, but I was prepared to take advantage of everything medical science knew about altering gender. I hoped it knew enough.

I wasn't sure of my doctor. During an earlier meeting in his office, my surgeon had offered to take measurements of my future husband's private parts. He said it would ensure a proper fit. I thought his suggestion twisted and disgusting. I'd wanted to scream at him, but I knew no one else who did the surgery in this country. I smiled, cast my eyes toward the floor, and said nothing.

"He's only a means to an end," I cautioned myself. "This doctor doesn't have to be polite. You need his expertise, so keep your mouth shut, let it pass, and don't make waves." It was hard advice to follow.

The evening before my operation, the good doctor stopped by my room. "I'm going to carve a hole in you the size of that roll," he said, pointing a long, slender surgeon's finger at my dinner tray. I didn't want a vagina the size of a large dinner roll! Still, I smiled at his sexual allusion. I knew the drill. My destiny, as I saw it, was to accept whatever a more powerful male said or did. It was simple. Everything revolved around the penis. Men accepted theirs; I refused to acknowledge mine.

"You will have a wonderful future," the doctor assured me. "You know what it's like to be a man." And he swaggered out of my room.

"What the hell did he just say?" I asked aloud. My physician believed my future as a woman would be rosy because I understood what it was like to be a man? Only a male could possibly believe that. I had *no* concept of what it was like to be a man. Why did this doctor think I needed gender-altering services? But I swallowed my feelings. I couldn't complain. I valued this operation more than I valued my own life. It was clear, however, that there would be no violins sweetly playing in the background as my not-so-understanding surgeon worked his trans-gendering magic. I bit my tongue. I reacted as I always had when threatened—I turned everything inward.

Wisely, I decided to concentrate on my lip gloss. In only twenty-three years, I'd turned the safe haven of superficiality into an art form.

In the early 1960s, I wasn't alone in accepting superficial values. The whole world seemed to accept that life was, indeed, totally about how one looked. The Beat Generation had their dark, somber presentation. Allen Ginsberg, poet; Bob Dylan, musical spokesman for the generation; and England's shaggy-haired musical phenomenon, the Beatles, all had their own look. My image was a decidedly femme presentation, but it was a look. Projection of an image is, after all, a statement of how one wants to be perceived: self-identification is in the look.

In my very early twenties, I understood nothing beyond the planes of my face. Enlightenment was too much to expect. Sequins didn't come in that color! By the age of twenty, I'd become a drag queen. Queen? Hell—I'd become a goddess. I looked fabulous.

It was onstage at San Francisco's world-famous nightclub, Finocchio's, that people found me exciting. I found approval when dressed as a woman. Offstage, I was merely a sissy boy afraid of the world and trying not to be noticed.

Finocchio's featured "the world's greatest" female impersonators, and big-name celebrities such as Bette Davis, Lana Turner, and Sal Mineo came to sit ringside. Nightly, Grey Line Tours filled the club with audiences of predominantly upper-middle-class heterosexual tourists. The celebrated club was also Mecca for many of our country's predominantly closeted homosexuals. Partly this was because our impersonators were glamorous, openly queer entertainers—and gay and lesbian audiences shared a sense of pride in our mainstream acceptance. For me, Finocchio's offered the first sense of true acceptance I'd ever known. As Lee Shaw, drag diva, I was notable, and nothing was demanded except that I look incredible—and have a modicum of talent. As the blonde ingenue of the San Francisco nightspot, I was almost complete.

For the first time in my life, I was sought after. One major comedy star and his wife, both with hands steepled in front of them, were hanging around anxiously—hoping for a ménage à trois. Several straight men wanted to date me; a few luckless female strippers wanted relationships; and more than a few intrigued military men were willing to dismiss the fact that I was a boy. The prurient attention was disconcerting, but the lifestyle was certainly exciting. I wasn't sure what I had, but seemingly I had it in ample proportions. I'd found what looked like love and felt like acceptance.

I was at loose ends as to how to explain this newfound acceptance to my parents. So I didn't. I wrote that I was working as a male dancer in a review. It wasn't a total lie. For the moment, I was happy, young, a semi-sensation, and . . . onstage, I was myself.

After a year and a half at Finocchio's, I remained the only blemish on an otherwise perfectly charming existence. In spite of the sparkling, protective veneer I'd learned to apply to my face and my professional persona, inside I was still the frightened, insecure kid I'd always been. I was still the problem. Offstage, I didn't belong. I was applauded by gay society, but they didn't accept me as one of their own. I was too feminine to be attractive to most gay men. "If I wanted a woman, I'd find one" was a familiar phrase. I didn't belong in straight society either. Society was apparently divided into two distinct sexual groupings, and I didn't fit in either one. It was as though one foot was forever wedged into a sequined, spiked heel while the other was firmly planted in a dingy sneaker. I spent my evenings in designer gowns, but during the day, society demanded I live as a man. It was a confusing way to live. In public, I generally wore jeans and lumberjack shirts and prayed I would pass as a lesbian.

From my earliest years I'd known that something was wrong with me. It wasn't about my body. That wasn't it at all. It was about who I was, about the boy I was presumed to be. I'd been subjected to all the traditional male training and none of it took.

There had been despised trips to the barbershop, after which I went home and cried. There were years of unflattering clothes in masculine, muted tones; summers at boys' camp; boxing lessons; dance class, where I learned to lead with my left hand elevated while guiding strongly with the right. I'd been carefully trained to make proper introductions, to rise to my feet when my elders or women entered the room, and certainly to offer men a firm handshake while looking them squarely in the eye. But the worst trauma was an introduction to every sport known to mankind and the subsequent misery of disrobing in the boy's locker room. That was the worst. Very early I developed elaborate ploys to escape that locker room—the most terrifying of the traditional male rituals. There was never any real escape. There were subtle pressures from every corner of my universe to turn me into the proper little man I was said to be.

I felt that people kept treating me improperly. They did. They insisted on treating me as though I were a boy. That was the problem, and I didn't see any way around it. That problem could never be fixed.

I was wrong, of course. I was going to be "fixed." Rebuilt! A nip here, a few tucks there, and I would be perfect. All the waiting was over. This very day I would be transformed/reborn/made whole. In the parlance of the early 1960s, I was having a "sex change."

Bless you, Christine Jorgensen.

When, in 1952, Christine Jorgensen's gender reassignment became headline news all over the world, I was mortified. I feared that people would now watch me too closely. Miss Jorgensen's public spotlight might spill over onto me. I didn't yet understand that Christine and I were akin, but I knew I differed from the male standard. I was in danger of being stained by her transsexual notoriety.

"Buddy caught the same thing that Christine Jorgensen got!" I intercepted the note being passed around my freshman class. I pretended to drop the scrap of paper before reading the message, but I was devastated by it. I had always been ashamed of being noticeably different, but I made no conscious connection with the gender event of the century. In high school, I was clinging to rigid male definitions and identities even as the current of my life was washing them away.

Because sexual reassignment was a new surgical procedure, there was little postsurgical data available. There were certainly no self-help books. Even the prerequisites for the procedure itself were rather sketchy. Applicants were required to have psychotherapy. That was a firm requirement. Not even the professionals, however, seemed quite sure what questions to ask.

When I made my decision to transition, I saw a psychiatrist once for about an hour, maybe less. He asked me if I thought I was a woman. I did. That was pretty much that. He asked no clever questions to suggest that gender issues stem from Oedipal struggles—those opposing arguments would come later in the transsexual movement. In my day, *Oedipus Rex* was merely a Greek tragedy. In my personal drama, Mother gave me life and then sustained it by becoming my best friend. She encouraged me to feel. Being intimate with another soul is a privilege, and I was blessed by having a mother who always tried to comprehend my emotional turmoil. My doctor viewed that relationship as a healthy coexistence between a mother and her daughter. Becoming a woman was easier in the old days.

The shrink, as an aside, did say he found me extremely manipulative. He also thought I was pretty. For that insight I paid him fifty dollars.

It could be I'm a full-fledged, governmentally stamped and certified woman because my particular psychiatrist had a manipulative wife—or mother—or both. More likely, he considered all women manipulative. No matter; I passed his test. Additionally, there was irrefutable proof that I should be a woman: I was engaged to marry a card-carrying man. In the 1960s, desiring to be a housewife carried a lot of weight. The fact that a man wanted me as his legal wife probably cinched my claim to womanly status.

I'd passed the medical world's inspection with the encouragement and guidance of Dr. Harry S. Benjamin. A renowned endocrinologist and the world's leading authority on the transsexual phenomenon, Harry led me through the maze to my day of deliverance. I'd filled out all the proper forms releasing the surgeon from legal responsibility should he goof. I'd faced my parents, releasing them from all moral responsibility, in case they'd goofed. I'd plunked down the required twenty-five hundred dollars. I was grabbing for the gold ring. After today, the gold ring could be on my lefthand ring finger and not beyond my grasp.

Nothing else mattered. Beatniks had turned North Beach into their own personal Times Square; Kubrick's *Lolita* was raising eyebrows in movie houses; Jackie Kennedy was in her pillbox hat, and I . . . was totally self-absorbed.

My time had finally arrived.

The pre-op injection was administered by a friendly technician who, without doubt, was sent directly from God.

Secretly, I had been a bit concerned as to how a patriarchal God would react to my changing his genetic blueprint. I'd grown up a God-fearing child of the South. I often felt my family lived inside the Church of Christ.

There was Sunday school, Bible school, worship on Sunday, Sunday night, and Wednesday night. There were church sings and tent revivals. My hometown was the very buckle of the Bible Belt—and, in the southern regions, male genitals were the next thing to holy.

Having been raised in the shadow of the church, it's amazing that I grew up wanting to be a woman. Women are not the movers and shakers of southern Christianity. In our churches as in our lives, men set the rules and women follow them. Disobedient women, biblically speaking, are generally stoned to death.

In spite of my fundamentalist upbringing, if not because of it, I discovered my soul in San Francisco's subculture. Drag was, is, and shall always be a subculture . . . and I took to it with a religious vengeance.

My eyes were beginning to get very heavy. The presurgery injection was kicking in. I must remember to add pre-op medication to my "Bless you" list. "Oh yes," I smiled, "and bless you, MM." There was a blonde goddess I'd come to worship.

Newspaper columnists touted me as Marilyn Monroe's double. That was flattering, but it was only good publicity. Mr. Finocchio paid for such fanfare. I was young, professionally blonde, and sang, "My Heart Belongs to Daddy," in a red knit sweater, but that does not a legend make. I knew the difference. Marilyn was the epitome of everything I wanted to become.

The nation's favorite sex symbol came to Finocchio's to catch my act. She must have read the publicity.

"Marilyn left after your number," I muttered to myself.

That was true. I might be reacting to the pre-op medication, but I wasn't hallucinating. Miss Monroe had watched me perform her song from *Let's Make Love*—and fled.

"Well, I wouldn't be sittin' my famous ass in some nightclub watching a drag queen sing my number," I mused. "Not if I was Marilyn Monroe! No way, darlin', I'd have better things to do with my life."

Soon I, too, would have better things to do with my life.

After hours of surgery, Alfred Brevard Crenshaw would legally become Aleshia Brevard Crenshaw. Aleshia was my chosen name. It was a combination of my first and last stage names, Lee and Shaw.

Alfred would become A Lee Shaw. It was a haphazard way to choose a name, but it served the government's requirements that a transsexual's initials stay the same.

Damn, I loved this suspended state of being.

"Oops!" What was going on here? They were wrapping my hair in a towel, or something. It seemed like a towel.

"Looks like a towel, feels like a towel . . . must be a towel," I cackled as they rolled me from my room. These orderlies had me confused with Carmen Miranda. "If you'll just put a little fruit on this turban, I'll look better," I quipped.

The aides were not a good audience. No one laughed. They continued to roll my gurney down the hospital corridor. Men!

"Darling, men are rats. They're either rats, or they're superrats," Holly Golightly whispered from deep inside my considerable memory of movie memorabilia.

Holly Golightly from Truman Capote's *Breakfast at Tiffany's* was another of my heroines. I adored Audrey Hepburn's Holly! I agreed with her that men were rats, yet I'd been known to settle for a good-looking rodent or two.

"That flamenco dancer wasn't even good-looking," a nasty voice inside my head chided.

"Yeah?" I said aloud, "Says you. Did you get a look at the buns on Jose? Remember, honey, you can't drive a spike with a tack hammer. And, don't forget, Jose was famous."

"Star fuck!" the hostile voice shot back.

Then everything was quiet. Suddenly I found safety in a drug-induced euphoria. The random voices subsided. The panic was over. I felt like I was caught in an amber glow. It was like being center stage in my special Bastard Pink spot. I was in a grand state.

"Mr. de Mille, I'm ready for my close up," I said, giggling to myself. Where was I? Was I still in San Francisco?

I was being rolled into the operating room. That took all the good feelings out of the lovely medication. The panic returned.

Seeing nurses in green masks and surgical gear sobered me right up. Their look was not fetching.

This wasn't a dress rehearsal. These people were ready to begin the show, and like it or not, I was headlining the bill.

I was acutely aware of the lighting. Bright lights. People in the room were something of a blur, but the operating table and the harsh lights above were very, very distinct. As a famed female impersonator, my appeal had been enhanced by flattering illumination. In this surgical arena's fierce glare I lay exposed. In such bright light, someone might see that I was not emotionally prepared for what was happening to me. It would become evident to everyone that my certainty was merely an act, just as it had always been. They'd decide I had no right to control my destiny. If people really saw me, they could never love me.

"Somebody put out the lights," I pleaded.

For the first time since taking the first female hormone pill, I questioned my decision to become a woman.

I had not been this frightened when I did my own castration. Emasculating myself was something that simply had to be done.

If I was to have surgery in this country, first I had to get a castration. That was that. Otherwise, the testicles would be placed inside my body during the operation. The ol' testosterone would keep right on pumping. That was the standard practice in America. On this issue, American doctors seemed to agree. For some reason known only to man, testosterone was sacrosanct. In the United States, it was unlawful to tamper with that particular part of the reproductive system.

I could get around that. No problem. I'd do my own castration.

I convinced a doctor I intended to castrate my cat. I didn't own a cat, but no need for the doctor to know that. It had reached a point where I had to take life into my own hands. So, while the doctor drew me a how-to-neuter-your-pet diagram—I stole Novocain and a syringe from his medical cabinet. If I botched my castration, the blame would be mine, but there was no reason for the procedure to hurt more than necessary. The worst-case scenario would be severe genital mutilation. That, after all, was the point. With serious enough mutilation, doctors would be duty bound to correct the damage. In contrast, if my castration was successful, minus testicles I could have surgery in this country without those hormone-producing organs being inserted inside me. For that, anything was worth the risk.

With a castration diagram in hand, the next step was to ensure a sterile operating theater.

I stuck my sheets in the oven after spraying them with Lysol, the first step in preparation. Heat and pine-scented disinfectant would surely sterilize anything. Next, I took a healthy dose of Percodan and waited for numbness to take over my body. While I waited, I put on *Thurber Carnival*. Maybe my favorite comedy album would take my mind off what was happening to me. My best friend and I then scrubbed for surgery.

"How bad could it be?" I joked, trying to bolster my surgeon's spirits. Stormy and I were both nervous. After my friend clipped and disposed of my testicles, I was going to get off the operating table and return the favor.

"Farmers castrate pigs and calves all the time. There's nothing to worry about. Farmers don't even worry about sanitary conditions."

All did not go as planned.

Stormy made the initial cut, saw blood, and went outside to throw up. In mid-operation, I was left alone on a kitchen table draped with Lysol-scented sheets. I sat up and finished my own castration.

Once the scrotum was split, the testicles were pulled from the sac and unceremoniously severed with a razor blade. They were gone . . . now what? Should the sac be left open to drain, or should it be closed? The diagram gave no clues—there was no one to call for help. This procedure was illegal. There was also the problem of blood. That came as a total surprise. I'd helped perform a castration or two in a high school agriculture class that I abhorred but had never noticed any blood. I should have paid more attention.

Once Stormy returned to our makeshift operating room, we decided that being 50 percent right was better than being 100 percent wrong. We closed one side of the empty testicle sac and let the other side stay open to drain.

The messy deed done, and with my testicles flushed down the commode—I passed out.

The following morning, scared, swollen, sore, yet delighted to still be alive, I dragged myself to Haight Street. It took thirty painful minutes to climb the steps to my doctor's office on the second floor. He was not glad to see me. "This is a strong antibiotic," he growled, giving me an injection, "but you're to tell no one that I saw you today. I could lose my license for not reporting what you've done." I went home, fell into bed, and slept for a week before returning to work.

Now I was facing my final surgery, the operation that would physically change me into a woman. It was possible that I might not be so lucky again. This time, I might not wake up.

Even if I wanted to, I couldn't call a halt to this procedure. What would I tell my parents? Mother and Daddy had come from Tennessee to be by my side at this moment of gender transition. They were both crushed, of course, but they were resolutely being supportive.

Neither parent had any concept of how or why this terrible thing had happened to their only son. The mere idea was beyond their understanding. Such things simply did not happen in their world.

Even though Dr. Harry Benjamin, the world's leading authority and originator of the term *transsexual*, telephoned them and explained, they still didn't understand. I couldn't blame them. A strange doctor calls from the other side of the world and says someone needs to cut off their only son's penis! It was a shock. Sure, I'd written a letter saying I was going to become a woman and marry Hank, the man I loved—but that only convinced my family I was crazy. It was my doctor's call that made them nervous. He'd explained everything in great detail, but my parents still could not understand how God could let such a thing happen.

That I, too, had some trouble understanding.

My parents promptly went to see their minister. Surprisingly, he'd read something, somewhere, about the transsexual phenomenon. My parent's spiritual leader shared what little he understood of the matter.

"Well, Brother Crenshaw, who can judge these things?" the preacher asked. "Some people love only one person in their entire life. Who knows this isn't true for your son, Sister Crenshaw?" That was the deciding factor for my mother. Daddy still had doubts.

I was reasonably sure that Daddy came west under protest. It didn't matter. Whatever pushed him there, he'd crossed a continent to be with me. Surprisingly, Daddy also accepted my future husband. Hank was about to steal "Daddy's little girl" right off the assembly line, and yet my father liked him. My intended had the two qualities that, traditionally, southern fathers expect in a son-in-law. Hank knew about football; Hank knew about fishing. In short, Hank acted as a male was supposed to act. He looked like a man, strong and tall and proud. There was none of that damn embarrassing sissy stuff. Hank was the son my daddy never got. If my father were to question Hank Foyle's masculinity, then he would have to examine the entire gender curve and societal assignment of power. That could not happen. Real men know a man when they see one.

"Oh, my! What about Hank?" I gasped, mentally lurching back to the surgical arena.

He'd be so disappointed if I got up and ran.

Could I run? Could I get up?

"He might leave me if I don't go through with surgery," I shuddered. I wouldn't blame him. He certainly wouldn't marry me.

"Men marry women—not freaks."

Freak! Where had the word come from? That ugly, hurtful word has a life of its own. People didn't call me that—it was how I thought of myself.

Hank had never looked at me as a freak of nature. He thought I was beautiful. He had loved me from the beginning.

"Maybe he only allowed himself to love me because of my promised gender change," I sobbed.

That's when I saw the anesthetist. I'd spoken to him the day before, but I hadn't noticed his eyes. They were beautiful. Now, standing there looking down at me, he seemed to be smiling. He looked somehow benevolent. He looked like the pictures of Jesus on the back of the fans they passed out in the summertime at our Christian tent revivals. I breathed a sigh of relief. I was going to be all right. I had panicked for a moment, but I was going to be fine. I was doing the right thing. Suddenly, I knew I would be taken care of by the charming, smiling man with the beautiful eyes. Jesus in a green mask. The decision was out of my hands.

"Whoever you are," I breathed deeply, "I've always depended on the kindness of strangers."

He asked me to count backward from one hundred. I obediently started counting.

"One hundred."

I felt a sharp spinal prick.

"Ninety-nine. Nine-ty-e-igh-t. Ni-n Ni."

I fell down a kaleidoscopic hole. My life didn't flash past me; I was the one whirling wantonly past colorful bits and pieces of my life.

Suddenly, I could hear voices. It was my grandmother, Miss Minnie Lee Crenshaw, calling me.

"Alfred! Alfred Brevard . . . "

"Nine-ty . . . " I tried to count.

"Ni . . . "

. . . and there stood Gran, telling me again how I was born the year Amelia Earhart disappeared in her plane over the warm Pacific.

"But you fell to earth during a huge snowstorm, December the ninth, 1937," my grandmother was saying.

"Nine-ty-seven . . . "

As my paternal grandmother's story went, it was a storm so fierce that James, my daddy, couldn't get to the hospital. "But Mozelle was okay," Gran said with an edge to her voice.

I can't remember my grandmother ever telling a story in which my mother or her family much mattered. Miss Minnie Lee told stories only about the Crenhaw family. To Gran, my mother's family, the Gillentines, didn't warrant a lot of discussion. Miss Minnie's first words to her son after meeting his new bride were "Well, James, I'll say one thing for you. You've certainly managed to marry beneath yourself." The statement caused a war between the two Mrs. Crenshaws that would divide our family just as surely as the Civil War had divided our nation. The women's fight for my father's loyalty would last the rest of my grandmother's life. That animosity, in large part, ruined my mother's chance at happiness.

I knew my Gillentine relatives and was well aware of their positive influence in my life. In truth, I generally considered myself a full-blooded Gillentine.

"I don't know who you are, but I know you're a Gillentine!" That was a comment I often heard growing up, and it always brought me great pride. The Gillentines were thought to be uncommonly handsome people. I liked having the Gillentine look.

Relatives on my father's side were not uncommonly handsome. Not at all. Most, in fact, were rather pinched around the mouth and took themselves very seriously. I didn't want to be one of them. They had no color in their lives. More important to me was the fact that my mother didn't like them. They weren't exactly fond of her, either.

My mother's family painted life with bold and colorful strokes. An extremely close-knit family, they enjoyed each other. They didn't seem to miss the family tree my grandmother, Miss Minnie, said they needed so desperately.

Daddy had surprised his mother by ignoring her disapproval and marrying into the Gillentine family. Daddy was twenty-seven and my mother was seventeen when they married on a July morning in 1936. My parents exchanged vows at the Gillentine home in Erwin, Tennessee. Marrying Mozelle Gillentine was the only act of rebellion my daddy had in him.

James Upshaw Crenshaw had been born late in his mother's life. Miss Minnie Lee Upshaw purposely waited late to marry. As she would tell it later, there was no shortage of marriage proposals, but she was waiting for a gentleman who would support her well. Miss Minnie was rather attractive, trim, and, as the eldest daughter of a country doctor, had her choice of the available young bachelors in the county. Having the pick of the crop didn't make her desire the pickings. My grandmother was the daughter of an old, well-respected family with pre–Civil War plantations both in Tennessee and in Louisiana. The Tennessee property, where later I would be raised, had been a land grant from the days of the Revolutionary War. Land from the deed had originally filled the entire bend of the Cumberland River just outside Hartsville, Tennessee. Miss Minnie Lee was a small-town elitist.

Over the years, through mismanagement and the Civil War, all but three hundred acres of her family's property had been sold. Still, in the South of her youth, my grandmother was considered landed gentry. Miss Minnie Lee Upshaw could afford to wait for marriage without causing people to snicker.

When Gran married Alfred Brevard Crenshaw, they settled in a home on Church Street in Hartsville, Tennessee. It was there that my father, James, was born and would grow up, raised as though the Old South's aristocracy still remained intact.

"James was raised to be a gentleman," Gran would remind my mother from time to time. "He wasn't raised to work."

Their lives passed fitfully along.

In a barely respectable amount of time, I was born and named for my recently deceased grandfather, Alfred Brevard. Everything appeared normal enough. I had all the appropriate parts. But in the first weeks of life I suffered from pyloric stenosis, a hereditary condition in male children. Pyloric stenosis is a blockage in the esophagus that causes all food to be regurgitated. In short, I was on the verge of starving to death. Steps were quickly taken. I was the first male heir, born to an only son, and my life was very precious. My dad donated his blood for my transfusion; a doctor friend of the family operated; and my young life went on.

It was almost an idyllic life. I grew up on a sprawling farm with fields to roam and animals to be petted. As I remember it, I was happy. I adored the hollyhocks outside my window and the swarming bees that were always busy at the blooms. I loved my goldfish swimming in the horse trough. It was a good, solid lifestyle. At some point, however, I became dimly aware that all was not exactly right. I neither looked nor acted like the other little boys of Trousdale County. People, especially women, were always commenting on my appearance.

"Oh, he's too pretty to be a boy," they'd say. "Just look at that peaches 'n' cream complexion."

I am suddenly in my grandmother's front guest bedroom. It's my favorite room in her rambling old house. I love the scent of lavender that's always lingering in the air. The afternoons are cool and sweet, and I am sheltered from the summer heat by the high ceiling. I spend most of my afternoon visits hidden away in this, my favorite room.

"Alfred Brevard!" my grandmother is calling. "Your Daddy just drove in the yard."

That message always shattered the sweetness of a summer afternoon. In those early years before starting school, I treasured those quiet hours when my grandmother took her midday nap, and I lived freely in my own world. While Gran slumbered in the parlor, I was in the front guest room dancing to the music from the radio. Alone, I could be anybody I wanted to be—and I wanted to be Miss Ginger Rogers, dancing film star.

I danced in Gran's gray crocheted shawl with the rust scalloped trim. Gran's bed shawl was my lovely long skirt. When closed, the one throat button caused the garment to fit snugly around my waist. With my skirt secured, I would twirl and twirl around the guest room, now and then catching a glimpse of myself as I swirled past the chifforobe's full-length mirror. I was a whirling dervish in my grandmother's gray crocheted shawl with rust scalloped trim.

Only in those moments of freedom was I totally happy as a child. My real life existed in the world of my imagination—there I was safe. In the presence of friends and family, I accommodated everyone and tried to escape drawing focus. The boy people accepted as Buddy Crenshaw was an illusion. I was myself only when let alone.

"Alfred Brevard!" Gran would call shrilly. "Your Daddy's here. Get out of that shawl."

I would trip over my own feet getting out of that lovely shawl. Daddy would not like it. No one would like it. Glamorous Ginger Rogers transformed back into hated, skinny, frightened Buddy Crenshaw.

Gran's shawl only signified a larger problem. The older I became, the more I realized how different I was.

The realization occurred innocently enough while visiting my mothers' parents. I loved visiting Mama and Granddaddy Gillentine's big old house on Elm Street. I loved the little railroad town of Erwin in far eastern Tennessee. In Erwin, there was always the smell of pine. The woods of the Appalachian Mountains surrounded the little hamlet on all sides. Fingers of pine forest crept from the surrounding mountains into the town. It was a nice, friendly town with a movie theater only one block from the Gillentine front porch. I went to the movies a lot. At night, exhausted by a day of exploration of the town, I would try to hold back sleep. I liked to lie and listen to the lonesome sound the train whistles made as the Clinchfield Railroad's cars snaked their way through the mountains. Long trains hauling coal were headed for North Carolina. I'd listen to the reassuring sound until it lulled me to sleep.

Mama and Granddaddy's home was a great place to visit. I wished I lived there. I had the misguided sense that if my environment were upgraded, my life would be, too. I also loved the fact that while visiting my mother's family, I had a lot of time to spend with Mother's youngest sister, Bobbie Jean. She was my only aunt. I truly loved Aunt Bobbie Jean. Only seven years older than I, she was more a playmate than an aunt. We'd play school. She was the teacher, and she'd read stories to her class. I was her class. She would read stories for hours. She liked to read, and she liked to read to me. I was an attentive audience, mesmerized by her stories of kings and queens, princes, and fair damsels in distress. She read the standard fare, but it was all wonderland to me.

One day after a reading session, Aunt Bobbie Jean took me to town with her. That was nothing unusual. I was not allowed to go alone, but Bobbie Jean would usually take me with her. This day, as a special treat, Aunt Bobbie Jean took me to Brown's Record Shoppe on Main Street. I really liked it there. If you were old enough, you could pick out records you wanted to hear, go into a little booth, and play them as long as you wanted. Bobbie Jean had lots of records at home, and we would play them over and over again in her room. I liked "Sentimental Journey" best.

As we were about to leave the shop, Bobbie Jean ran into some of her eleven- and twelve-year-old girlfriends from school. Everyone stopped to talk. I was hanging back, trying to disappear behind a counter. I generally was not comfortable with people I didn't know. One of Bobbie Jean's school friends made an effort to be friendly.

"What a pretty little girl you are," she said. She stooped down to my level. "What's your name?"

I didn't say a word; neither did Bobbie Jean. Instead, my young aunt turned a bright red. Nothing else was said. My aunt Bobbie Jean and her friends forgot all about my gender; conversation skipped from one girlish topic to another, and I stood there unnoticed. I was the only one overwhelmed by the incident. I'd always known something was wrong, and now I knew what it was. The way I looked was wrong. I looked like a girl.

Most of the time, when no one was there to cause me to feel otherwise, I was comfortable with my body. It was people outside the immediate family who bothered me most. Outsiders reminded me that I was a disappointment to Daddy. Consequently, I spent a lot of time playing

alone, where neither my looks nor my feminine ways would cause anyone embarrassment. Alone I was totally happy.

From the time I could form sentences, I'd told every adult I knew that
I was going to grow up, go to Hollywood, and become a movie star.
Having no idea that medical science could ever provide an opportunity
for me to fulfill my dream, I didn't say the star would be female. But the-
atrically, I was maturing. I now visualized my stardom as the beautiful
blonde heroine of Paramount Studio's 1942 *This Gun for Hire*. I never
took a bath without draping a towel over my head and admiring my
mirrored reflection from beneath the Cannon peek-a-boo bang. I'd
matured from the tap-dancing, wholesome Miss Ginger Rogers into the
svelte, seductive Veronica Lake.

Living on our farm was a friend who would sometimes come and
play with me. Helen was the daughter of a tenant farmer. Until a few
years later, when my sister was born, Helen Leigh was my only real
playmate. She was about five or six years older than I, but that didn't
matter. Helen was my friend. We'd sit in the swing out under the big
trees. Swinging together, out by the beehives, we played at being grown
up, assisted by a well-worn Sears and Roebuck catalog. I loved my
friend. First, Helen and I would plan a marvelous trip, then we'd turn
to Sears and Roebuck, looking for just the right outfits. Helen didn't
mind that I picked out a woman's ensemble.

My disillusionment came one afternoon when Helen and I were playing in the bedroom she shared with her older sister. There, in the closet,
were her sister's clothes. My friend suggested we both get dressed up.
This wasn't pretend, and I knew Daddy would be awfully mad if he
found out. I was afraid, but Helen kept pushing me to put on her sister's clothes. I didn't like the game anymore. It was moving too fast. I
wanted to go home. Getting angry with me, my friend demanded that
I put on a dress. Timidly, obediently, I did as I was told. Even this was
not enough to suit her. She roughly zipped me up, smeared garishly red
lipstick across my mouth, ran across the room and threw open the bedroom door. There Helen stood with her two grown brothers and her
teenage sister. Together they stood in the doorway, laughing and pointing at me. Everyone laughed.

My five-year-old life suddenly took a swing upward. There was a war going on. Men were now vying for my attention, and Helen Leigh was easily replaced.

Soldiers were living in my backyard. The United States was in the Second World War, and, dressed in my own little sailor suit, I was a patriot of the first order. I could sing every patriotic song I heard on the radio.

"There'll be blue birds over the white cliffs of Dover, some fine day, just wait and see." I had no idea where those white cliffs might be; I'd never seen them on the three-mile drive to town, but I loved the idea that they existed.

I was in love with the armed forces. I worshiped every single dog-face. The die was cast, and I was to remain, in my heart, a camp follower to the end of my days. Draw the tattered veil.

The United States of America's military force was on maneuvers, and when the war effort came to Hartsville, Tennessee, I was ready. I would stand by the side of our country road, among the hollyhocks, resplendent in my sailor suit, saluting those brave young men as they drove by. There were truckloads of them, but as long as the caissons kept rolling along, this little sailor kept saluting.

"Don't sit under the apple tree with anyone else but me, anyone else but me, anyone else but me." The Andrews Sisters were singing their patriotic message, and servicemen were bivouacked in the huge field behind my house. It would have been heaven, were I not strictly forbidden access to those wonderful men. They were just across the fence, almost close enough to touch, but they might as well have been bivouacked in Nebraska. I was not allowed past the wire barrier that separated my backyard from their tents. Going past that fence was definitely a no-no, but restrictions had no effect on me where soldiers were concerned.

I would stand by the fence for hours hoping that one of the soldier boys would notice me and come talk. They never did. Now and then, I'd test my luck with tentative steps into forbidden territory. That rock-encrusted cow pasture was Bali Ha'i. It called to me—but I knew that crossing the fence was wrong. It was probably a sin. I felt the flames of hell licking at my heels every time I crossed that fence, but like a shot I was across no-man's-land and into a tent.

I never failed to get my little fat legs flailed with a switch as Daddy dragged me, screaming, back to the homefront. Yet, in spite of everything, I kept crossing that fence. Switches didn't stop me; the threat of burning forever in hell couldn't stop me.

Pretty soon, one soldier started bringing me back home. He admired my dogged determination. Those return trips astride the shoulders of my smiling new friend were triumphant restorations to my side of the fence. The battle to keep me corralled was lost. I was madly in love with a red-haired soldier.

The soldier of my youth was named Matt. He was from somewhere I'd never heard of. Somewhere far, far away. They all were. They were fresh-faced, young American soldiers off to war. Many were away from home for the first time.

Sometimes, late at night, one or two young recruits would slip away from camp. They'd slip across the fence to our house. There would be a timid knock at our back door. Homesick soldiers had come to sit with my parents. They would sit talking around the oilclothed kitchen table. My parents never turned those young men away. I don't know what they talked about. I guess the boys just wanted company. Maybe they were missing home. In most cases, I guess they were frightened of what lay ahead. No matter how late the soldiers knocked, my parents never turned them away. In retrospect, I'm very proud of my parents for their kindness to those young men.

My Matt was the most special of soldiers. My parents liked him too. Matt would visit and sit with me under the big oak tree. There was no longer a need for me to go to the soldiers' camp. I'd found Matt. My soldier and I would sit for a long time on the oak's large exposed and gnarled roots. Sometimes we'd poke the ground looking for acorns. Sometimes we would just sit.

Matt listened to what I had to tell him. I'd tell him the stories I learned from Aunt Bobbie Jean. I'd tell him about kings and queens, princes and fair damsels in distress. If I didn't have a story to tell, I'd make something up. I'd tell anything to keep Matt's attention. Almost anything. I never dared tell my friend about being Veronica Lake. Even Matt would not want to hear that story. Instinctively, by the age of five, I understood that certain things must remain hidden.

As happened not infrequently in the chaos of preparing young men for the rigors of battle, errors in judgment were made. Early in the spring, pontoon boats full of servicemen were ordered to ford the Cumberland River just below our home. The locals tried in vain to convince those in charge that, in flood stage, the river currents were deadly. Those in charge did not listen. The pontoon boats, full of men, were ordered into the swollen Cumberland.

As predicted by those who knew the river well, the pontoon boats capsized. Scores of young human beings spilled into the river and were swept downstream. Many were drowned. Several, fearing the river, had silently slipped away before the calamity and found their way back to our farmhouse. Those soldiers spent that night and several days thereafter hiding in our attic. Matt was not one of them. The army moved out. The excitement was over. Matt didn't come to say goodbye. I never heard from him again.

Goodbye, Matt.

CHAPTER 2

Farm Boy

RECONCILIATION SURGERY was underway. The technique, called vaginoplasty, included the removal of the penis, the inversion of the scrotal and penile tissue to form a vaginal canal, and reshaping of scrotal tissue to form labia folds at the opening of the vagina. A skin graft would provide additional depth to the vagina. My doctor's technique for transsexual surgery included the resiting of the urethra and the forming of a clitoris using part of the penis. The operating theater was booked for eight hours, but we ran three hours past schedule. That's a long, deep sleep, no matter what size dinner roll your surgeon intends to duplicate.

Dreams flitted wherever dreams are prone to flit during a spinal tap. There is a flash of me at age three squatting by a rotting stump, planting cucumber seeds. I'm wearing a seersucker sunsuit, and my copper corkscrew curls shine in the spring sun. Ah, I remember, Mother was overrun with cucumbers that summer. The image blurs and shifts. Now, a skinny child of ten, I stand removed, watching a group of farmers shear my family's sheep. I am repulsed by the shearer's sweat, the bleating of the sheep, and the barnyard smell. I am ashamed of being a farm boy. A more mature image slowly surfaces. I am seventeen and graduating from high school in my signature sports coat.

In 1955, I went to Nashville to shop alone for the first time. I was a teenager off to buy a jacket for my high school senior year.

Alone and feeling very mature, I followed a shopping pattern learned from my mother. I went to every store in town, then had lunch in order to reflect on what I'd seen. The ritual was ingrained but a wasted effort on this outing. I craved the shocking jacket I'd spotted when first starting my rounds.

The jacket was *pink*—not an acceptable choice. In 1955, pastel was not a popular fashion statement for the white male. The store in which I'd spotted the wonderful jacket wasn't even an establishment frequented by Caucasians. I didn't care. Nothing mattered but that wonderfully wicked, slightly sissy coat.

I wore that damn pink jacket for the rest of high school.

My gender dissatisfaction was growing. With each passing year I grew more impatient with my ascribed male role. I'd reached an age where my identity struggle was demanding attention. I was seventeen, totally self-absorbed, and only peripherally aware that struggles other than my own were going on around me.

Civil rights issues had taken center stage in the South, but being a product of our segregated society, I was oblivious to the inequity around me. I accepted the age-old rhetoric that "coloreds" were a happy people, content to be separate but equal. Even though nurtured by, and dearly loving, the black people with whom I'd grown up, I'd never heard it suggested that life was anything but equitable. I blindly accepted what I experienced as the proper composition of society. Negroes were not like me.

On Nashville's Church Street, I would soon watch in dismay as a riot erupted around me. I was shocked and surprised that coloreds were demanding to eat at Walgreen's lunch counter. That one had rights, or that those rights could be denied, was a new concept to me. The established order was all I knew, and I had trustingly accepted the rightness of all social norms. I was raised to do as I was told. History surged around me as I stood across the street from Walgreen's and watched white policemen bar Negroes access to the drugstore lunch counter. I did not know what to feel, but I admired those Negroes who stood peacefully, persistently demanding equal rights. I envied them their sense of purpose. For many years to come, I would meekly continue to deny myself by attempting to please everyone around me. I did not yet know what it meant to be one of society's outcasts, but I sensed that the civil rights struggle somehow included me, too.

Suddenly, the scene shifts. I fall into the arms of my first boyfriend.

Michael Ray Turner would have been a spectacular catch for a real girl; I didn't even dare to wear his class ring. Instead, for appearance's sake, I went steady with a girl all through high school. Having a girlfriend was a ruse, but going steady made me acceptable. My girlfriend was a beautiful young woman, but it was with Michael Ray I wanted to spend my nights.

On weekends, Michael Ray would take me to a sock hop in adjoining Sumner County. Since boys didn't dance together, we found girls as partners, but Michael Ray and I were dancing for each other. On the way home, my date would pull into a deserted country lane where we'd "make out." It was the classic teenage dating ritual—practically.

Neither of us knew what we were doing, and our mutual attraction was tentative and awkwardly expressed. Our physical exploration had begun in grammar school, but unlike those of most sexually experimenting young males, our relationship had matured. My thrill was in having this masculine farm boy treat me as his girlfriend. I liked being treated that way. I reacted emotionally and blocked out everything else. Gender distinctions were no clearer to us then than they are to me now.

After graduation, Michael Ray Turner married and fathered three children. He has lived a respectable heterosexual life for over forty years.

In high school a number of young football heroes tossed a ball or two my way. I didn't understand why. I did not believe it to be because I was "queer"—certainly not in the homosexual sense. The embarrassing, explicit physical attention baffled me, but I believed their erections were my fault. Something was wrong with me—but I simply could not be queer.

The most persistent ravisher was the son of my mother's best friend. He was one of the local athletes my father idolized. Keith Markham was star of the gridiron, diamond, and court. Any game of prowess was played well by the agile Keith Markham. Daddy loudly praised Keith's weekly triumphs, but always with a tinge of sadness. Daddy wanted an athlete for a son. He didn't have one.

Instead, I was an excellent student. I reputedly had a marvelous singing voice; I painted, wrote, and danced well. In our small community, I was often acknowledged as an outstanding youth. Exemplary, in fact! I led singing in our church. I was chosen to represent our county at Boys' State. Artistically, I was the county's leading teenage citizen. I was, however, a klutz on any playing field known to sportsdom. In the South, you gotta be a football hero to get along.

Keith Markham may have been a football hero and my Daddy's standard for athletic prowess, but Keith wanted my ass in the worst way.

"Please don't make me go to Keith's tonight," I would beg my parents. "I don't want to help him study for the exam."

They never heard me. My mother's best friend had requested personally that I come help her son study. I had to go. To refuse Keith would have been rude. What could I say? "But, Mom, I don't want to 'put out' tonight!" That certainly would have kept me home—but I never said it. I didn't know I had the right to say no. It would be many years before I'd learn that lesson.

By the time I was four, Daddy realized that I needed male role models. It was necessary that his fey son find an acceptable place in the local "guy" group. My father's concern was understandable. I did, after all, still have a predilection for dancing in skirts. Because male identification did not come naturally to me, I was packed off to play with the boys. From that time until my graduation from high school, one playmate or another was crawling on top of me. That was one randy group of little boys. Regularly, in elementary school, the boys would de-pant and threaten to castrate me "like a pig." Having a knife brandished around my genitals was part of my public humiliation for being different. When we were alone, those boys were much more neighborly. We'd play cowboys and cowgirls. I wasn't the one packing the pistol.

In high school the games were different, but the result was the same.

In the operating arena, doctors were busily stitching away to create me a vagina; inside my head, my psyche was doing a little patchwork of its own. I was reexamining my past by hopscotching down the road that had brought me to this point of transition.

It was at Memphis State University that I finally came face to face with overt homosexuality. The campus gay community immediately decided I was one of the girls. Using "gay-dar," they took one look and said, "There she is!" I had yet to acknowledge that I was a *sister*; they were positive.

"I mean, just look at her, Mary!"

"I know, but she's so far back in the closet, she doesn't even know she's queer. That queen doesn't even cruise in the dorm shower."

They were right. I stayed to myself, didn't cruise, and wasn't campy. I didn't even know there was such a thing as a queer society.

Queer. The word was used to describe the dirtiest and most vile of beings. It was a word generally uttered in hushed asides, whispered to quickly describe the unspeakable. Fortunately, I had never encountered such lecherous molesters of children. I had, however, experienced a strange encounter that caused me to wonder about them—and to question myself.

At about fourteen, I had, while my parents were otherwise occupied in Nashville, gone alone to a movie. My plan was to watch the film, over and over, until it was time to meet my parents. I was a film fanatic.

During the second showing of the film, a man took the seat next to mine. He was very fidgety and kept moving in his seat. I thought he was scratching himself.

"Disgusting," I thought.

During the second viewing of any film, I was as riveted as during my first sitting. The second viewing was dedicated to watching the secondary characters, but today the man next to me was disturbing my concentration.

When his leg came to rest against mine, I got up and changed seats.

I moved to the back of the theater. The restless male followed. Inadvertently, I'd chosen to sit in the theater's gay cruising grounds. The implication was lost on me, but the guy took my move as an indication of sexual interest. I was totally oblivious. I was feeling harassed because he wouldn't let me concentrate on the film.

I gave up on the movie and left the theater.

On Church Street, studying Castner Knott's department-store window display, I saw the fidgety man from the movie. He was at the window display next to mine.

He was following me!

Holy Jesus! Suddenly, all at once, I understood what he wanted. It was a revelation. There should have been a blinding flash. This man wanted *me*. I think that moment was the onset of puberty.

It wasn't sexual arousal I felt. I felt power. Sissy little Buddy had power over this man.

I liked the feeling.

Oh, I led that poor soul on a merry chase through the downtown streets of Nashville, Tennessee. That he was homosexual, and certainly a pedophile, didn't occur to me. Instinctively, I was playing a time-honored cruising game. I knew exactly what I was doing. I walked. He followed. I never spoke to him. Yet he understood what I was saying. I had discovered a new language.

He broke our ritualistic silence in the museum of the War Memorial Building. We had a short, nondescript conversation. To me, it was loaded with subtext. I had been schooled for such a clandestine meeting by some of the legendary sirens of the cinema.

"I can't stay," I said coyly, perhaps with a hint of regret reminiscent of Bette Davis in *Dark Victory*.

"If I were to come to your hometown this Sunday, would you meet me?" he asked breathlessly.

"Of course," I said demurely, drooping my eyes. I'd seen Claudette Colbert do that a million times in *It Happened One Night*. "I'll give you directions to my house so you can come pick me up. I'll be home alone."

"What's your name?" he wanted to know.

"Tommy Kylee," I lied.

Here was the perfect way to settle a long-standing school debt. I gave the fidgety man directions to the home of my tormentor, Tommy Kylee.

The same teenage cavalier attitude carried over to the surgery taking place on my body. I approached it emotionally. I had no real understanding of what was being done to me. My doctor had drawn grisly diagrams and tried to alert me to the possible dangers of the procedure. It was a waste of time. I didn't want to hear a technician's rhetoric. Who wanted to know the ugly details?

"Can you fix my problem?" That was all I cared about.

Years later, in what would become a large transgendered community, the argument would develop that there was never anything to fix. "You can't fix something that ain't broke" would become the war cry for an increasingly militant group of gender-dysphoric individuals. It was offensive to many that homosexuals and the transgendered were considered medically ill. At the time of my gender reassignment, I didn't care about such debate. I simply wanted my problem to disappear.

As far as I was concerned, scientists could label me any way they wanted. People like me had realized we were "different" from the very beginning. I'd never heard the term *transgendered* or *gender-dysphoric*. In 1962, we didn't need labels to know who we were. What we needed were not words to identify us but rather the technology to free us.

According to Dr. Benjamin, my particular "problem" likely occurred in the womb, early in pregnancy. All human beings begin their lives female. The hormonal bath that determines the sexual assignment of the child occurs later in the gestation period. In some cases, mine as an example, the external sexual assignment and the mental sexual assignment do not jibe. It was what I'd said all along—my pieces didn't fit. Dr. Benjamin's was a wonderfully scientific explanation as far as I was concerned. My misery was not something I'd caused. I wasn't crazy. Here was a medical standard I could live with. I'd merely had a small mishap during my hormonal bath—big deal. I was the product of a biological accident, and that could be corrected. Dr. Harry Benjamin was my liberator.

In the early 1960s, there were no transsexual support groups. There was no transsexual community. There were damn few houses on the transsexual block. We learned to survive individually, generally through the use of humor. We learn early to mask our pain by putting on a comic face. Dr. Benjamin's transgendered patients were "funny girls" long before Barbra Streisand hit the Broadway stage. Most transsexuals understand well that if you let a "gender bully" know you're wounded by an attack, the next time you might be permanently maimed.

For Benjamin's Girls, womanhood and anonymity were dual goals. One could quietly have surgery, with the promise of a "normal" existence to follow. None of us knew what the long-term physical consequences of our actions would be. Few of us cared. We were interested in living peacefully in the present.

Would such invasive surgery affect our life spans? Ultimately, what were the risks? There simply were no answers available. No one had completed the journey. We were taking the first step of our pilgrimage. A complete transformation had only now become a reality. For those transsexual pioneers who were willing to brave the unknown, the promised land loomed across the horizon. The handful of transsexuals

I met were all exceedingly feminine, caring, nurturing individuals. We were Dr. Benjamin's select few. I was proud to be one of them. We had all taken the same painful journey to reach this point. We were all grateful for the promise of a fulfilling life. I never met a transsexual I didn't like . . . until long after surgery. For those early transsexuals I knew, surgery was not intended as a springboard into a self-aggrandizing spotlight. We weren't public in our discussions. Our unusual history was not used to elicit sympathy or to seek political clout. We had grown to adulthood in emotional pain. We understood what it meant to hurt. We wanted to put that life behind us. In a more perfect world, I might have cared about things such as vaginal depth or sensation. I might have wanted a vaginal canal the size of a dinner roll. I might even have wondered what my surgeon was talking about when using words such as *labia* and explaining that my penis would be used to construct it, thereby ensuring sexual stimulation. I shut out technical explanations. I simply wanted my emotional and physical pieces aligned.

It was not until 1979 that a Standard of Care begun by Dr. Harry S. Benjamin would be formally put in place. The standard would outline medical and psychiatric guidelines for working with the estimated thirty-five thousand to sixty-five thousand gender-dysphoric men and women who would surgically follow in our early footsteps. The Standard of Care stipulated three months of therapy before a client could be recommended for hormones, one year of hormone therapy, one year of cross-living, and two psychiatric evaluations before recommending surgery. Seventeen years after my reassignment surgery, transsexuality would become a regulated big business; but on July 6, 1962, I believed I was alone.

"In the glory of His bosom, Christ transfigured you and me. . . . "

My life was still flashing past, but in *no* linear fashion.

"As he died to make men holy, let us die to make men free. . . . " Now I was singing the damn "Battle Hymn of the Republic." "Our God is marching on."

I'm singing in the tenor section of my high school choir. I wasn't a tenor. At seventeen I was still, embarrassingly for me, a boy soprano.

"I said tenors alone, ladies." Mr. Swenson was rapidly tapping his baton on his music stand. "One time again, please, tenors only."

We started again.

"In the glory of His bosom . . . "

Mr. Swenson stopped us again. He was getting red in the face. The whole choir held its breath.

"Tenors!" Mr. Swenson held up his baton to give the downbeat for the third time. I mouthed the words. The choir practice went smoothly on.

After school, and after Mr. Swenson had cleared the music room of the final overanxious student, I timidly approached him.

"Today . . . " My voice shook. I could barely hold back my tears of shame. I started over. "Mr. Swenson, today when you kept asking only the tenors to sing—it wasn't a soprano. . . . " The tears were under control, but I couldn't steady my voice.

"Yes," he interjected. "It was a soprano."

"It was me, Mr. Swenson. I have a high voice."

I had come to quit choir, but Mr. Swenson wouldn't hear of it. "My boy, a tenor in this town is as scarce as hens' teeth," he reassured me.

Mr. Swenson never acknowledged that the troublesome voice had been mine. To the end he maintained that there had indeed been some disruptive soprano. We both knew the truth.

Finally, my voice did break. I broke it.

In the mid-1950s, "womanless weddings" were popular fund-raising events. They had no relationship to the same-sex ceremonies I'd later attend. These amateur theatricals featured local male dignitaries dressed as women and cavorting around a stage. The sponsors and performers were fraternal organizations. Since my dad was a brotherly Leo, I was asked to join our local Lions' Club in what was, for all practical purposes, a drag show. The local Lions even brought in a professional director from the Big Apple. At our first rehearsal, she immediately expressed delight at my having been cast.

"Oh, you're so pretty," she cooed. "You'll make a beautiful girl." Either this New York director did not understand rural America, or she did not have my best interests at heart. Being pretty is not an advantage to a farm boy.

At every rehearsal, at the director's request, I demonstrated how a woman should walk, sit, and move. It was embarrassing. I already knew I was different—I didn't want the Hartsville Lion enclave made aware of my unique distinction. Some of the burly men were already starting to take notice. Their reaction was not the unbridled wrath I'd expected. The owner of a local car dealership kept pinning me up against the wall and telling me what pretty blue eyes I had. Randy little boys grow up to be randy little men.

The entire town was soon caught up in the spirit of the approaching drag show. My algebra teacher joyfully donated her full-length black lace formal for me to wear in the worthy theatrical event. Who said the Fates have no sense of humor? I knew nothing about algebra, and obviously, Miss Lucy knew nothing about me. I'd worked contentiously at developing a passable male persona, borrowing my shuffling gate from James Dean. The rather casual disregard for those around me was a direct steal from Ronald Coleman. I thought I'd created a passable male, brick by brick. Now I was going to be revealed as the girl-boy I knew myself to be.

Still, show business took hold of my soul. I was secretly thrilled when slated to play Sophie Tucker, the Last of the Red Hot Mamas. I was even to sing her signature song, "Some of These Days." Unfortunately, the score was too low for me.

"My voice is higher than Sophie Tucker's?" I squeaked. This was terrible.

The director sweetly offered to raise the key of my song—in front of our entire male cast. I would've died first! I forced my vocal register low enough to sing the score as written. The voice never went up again. Bid adieu to the boy soprano.

Fast-forward . . .

I'm twenty-one years old with my Finocchio's audition a few moments away. I sit in front of a dressing-room mirror, wondering why I'm here. The house is packed, and the audience has come to see professional impersonators such as La Verne Cummings, Ray de Young, and Stormy Lee. They didn't come to see Buddy Crenshaw! Apart from the Lions' Club fiasco, I've never even been in drag. My life has not been about female garments.

So why am I sitting at a makeup table putting on false eyelashes?

"Mr. Finocchio is going to put your no-talent ass on that stage as part of the show, fool," I whisper to the blonde reflection that stares back at me from the makeup mirror.

This was no small-potatoes audition. I was asking for a job at the top-rated female impersonation club in the country, with no prior experience in show business or in drag. I was out of my league and in over my empty, bewigged head.

"Damn John," I fumed. This was all his fault.

John and I had met over a year ago in a seedy downtown L.A. bar on a Sunday afternoon. We both seemed out of place.

I was in the bar only because Keith, a male model I'd met shortly after hitchhiking across the country to Los Angeles, had dragged me to the bar. Skid row, according to Keith, would give me a much-needed brush with real life.

I'd hitched two thousand miles carrying a sign reading "Hollywood or Bust!" I crossed the U.S.A. in three days. Either it was that placard or the invisible sign I wore around my neck that got me to California and had me sitting in a sleazy downtown L.A. tavern on the Sabbath.

I spent the afternoon feeding quarters to the jukebox for my favorite rhythm-and-blues songs.

"Good Golly, Miss Molly sure likes to ball!"

John Lomond sidled up to me and complimented me on my musical taste. I took him seriously.

"Would you like to go somewhere for dinner?" he asked.

"I can't." I blushed. "Keith and I are out for the evening."

"We'll meet him later," John countered.

I looked to Keith for help. That was like looking to a slave trader for moral consolation. My fashionable friend always looked smashing but generally lacked finances for a night out on the town.

"That's a great idea," Keith chipped in. "You two grab a bite, and I'll meet you later at the Fireside." Keith knew a pigeon when he saw one.

I left the seedy downtown bar with an attractive man wearing jeans and a nicely knit sweater—that was all I knew about him. He could easily take me to the desert and tie me to a cactus—or worse—but, like Scarlett O'Hara, I'd think about that tomorrow. My fashionable friend was right. I needed to develop a few basic survival instincts.

John did not tie me to cacti. Instead, he took me to the Villa Friscottia in Hollywood.

"Good evening, Mr. Lomond." John was greeted warmly by the parking attendant. "Will you be dining this evening?"

"Yes," John replied as he unobtrusively slipped the valet a few bills.

John chose to sit next to me rather than across the booth. No other man in the restaurant was seated so close to a young male companion. I was thrilled by his daring but embarrassed by the obvious attention.

"It's impolite to watch your date chew," he said, noticing my discomfort.

Hollywood in the late 1950s was an exciting town. She was clean. She was bustling. She still retained glittering remnants of her former heyday. On the corner of Hollywood and Vine, I often saw the same overly made-up elderly lady, looking like a long-lost Clara Bow. I suspected she stood, waiting to be discovered, in the same spot where she'd waited since 1922. Her streets had not been paved with gold. I'd pass the aged ingenue and say a silent prayer.

"Bless her, Lord . . . and please don't let me end up the same way."

God wasn't listening. After a short courtship, John moved me across town from my downtown, low-rent, transient hotel room. My lover stashed me in the hills overlooking Silverlake. He even gave me a black Sunbeam Alpine convertible to make the trip more comfortable. I was moving up in the world.

My new home was a charming apartment in the private residence of an elderly widow. John introduced me as his nephew. Both the widow and I were comfortable with his lie. In Hollywood, very soft boys often have an older John in their life, but the landlady never indicated that the older man and his nubile nephew could possibly be anything more than loving relatives.

It was six months before John told me he was a practicing Catholic priest. Only once did he take me across the mountain to his parish house in China Lake, California. The trip was a fiasco. I couldn't sexually perform with all those saints staring down at me—and I wasn't even Catholic.

John Lomond was my first long-term relationship with a mature man, yet I never felt we were a couple. By the time I came into his life, my lover was in his thirties and serving his God in China Lake. He pampered me, but I had no real part in his life. John kept his devout life across the mountain separate and distinct from his secular life in Hollywood. I pouted, preened, and played the role of the perfectly adorable kept boy. John liked it that way.

Finally, John stuck me in Marinella Beauty School to keep me out of mischief while he was not in town. It didn't work. I attended when I had nothing more interesting to do, but John was patient with my excesses. Social naïveté was half of my attraction—youth was the other half. My lover was thirty-seven. He took the responsibility not only for my rent but for my tutelage as well.

"Have you read *Catcher in the Rye*?" he'd ask.

"No."

"What about *A Separate Peace*?"

"No."

John was making a list and banging away at my rough edges as fast as he could whack. Before returning to his parish, alone, he would present me with a stack of books. They were not to be read randomly but in a carefully prescribed order. John saw himself as my benefactor.

"When I get back," he'd say, "we'll go to dinner and discuss what you've read."

True to his word, when John returned we always went to a notable restaurant. Satiated, and with a fine bottle of wine in front of us, we would discuss unifying themes, content, and plot development. John never suggested that my insights might be shortsighted.

"Have you, perhaps, thought of it this way?" he'd gently ask.

Rather than resenting his tutelage, I enjoyed the teacher/student aspect of our partnership. I wish I could have appreciated this man who possessed a law degree from Stanford, had the substantial backing of a prestigious department-store founding family, and, because he wanted to make a contribution to humanity, had joined the priesthood. To an immature teenager, however, he was ancient—a sugar daddy.

My shell was developing, and my life with John was speeding the hardening progress. I didn't know where I was headed, but I sincerely believed that I needed a "john" to get me there. My lover was indispensable, but I blamed him for my loss of innocence and the irreversible changes in my life. I was even more unhappy than I had been on the farm.

Sometimes I'd pick a fight merely to transfer my tension to shoulders broader than my own. One spat led to real problems. John wanted to spend the weekend in Laguna Beach at our favorite little hideaway, a bungalow overlooking the ocean. Generally, I would have been thrilled. This weekend I had plans. John was to install the new carpet I'd purchased . . . with his money. When he complained, I pouted and accused him of no longer loving me. I was infuriated when John didn't fall for the ploy.

"Get out!" I screamed. "And while you're gone, find someone else who'll satisfy you."

John slammed out of the house.

Returning the next day, my contrite lover acted as though nothing had happened the night before. He even bought me a new wardrobe, then flew me to San Francisco to show off my ensemble. The man was being too accommodating—that fact alone should have sounded an alarm.

My man had been trifling.

We rarely left our San Francisco hotel room on that trip, but I did manage to pick up an interesting souvenir. My lover, my friend, my spiritual adviser, gave me gonorrhea! I had "the clap," as the venereal disease was referred to in more hip circles.

"Darling, who ever thought he'd take me at my word and sleep with someone else?" I whined to friends. "He wasn't supposed to go out and catch the ol' clap-your-hands, for goodness sake!" Although I was joking publicly, I was devastated at having a venereal disease. Fortunately, human beings had not yet encountered AIDS or hepatitis C.

Enter, stage left, the muse wearing a dress.

On that, my first visit to the City by the Bay, John took me to "world-famous Finocchio's." We were seated ringside, and I was absolutely enthralled. I had never seen anything so deliciously glamorous. La Verne Cummings left me agog. Elton Paris had me in stitches. The beautiful "Lena Horne" stylings of Lew Person were more than I could possibly stand. What a night! A bona fide movie star, Joan Bennett, was even on hand in the audience. I was overwhelmed by the energy of the club. This was heaven. The place had flair! As usual, John, the bon vivant who took great pleasure in introducing me to new and exotic experiences, was plying me with drinks. I could not get my breath, and it wasn't because of the Singapore Sling John had ordered.

Near the end of the first show Lucien, made his entrance as Sophie Tucker. In my hometown's womanless wedding, my teenage rendition hadn't even touched the hem of this Sophie's gown. I'd worn my algebra teacher's black lace hand-me-down gown, but at Finocchio's, Lucien was wearing red velvet—dress, shoes, and purse! Completing the ensemble was a white fox coat and matching hat. More important, he looked and sounded exactly like Sophie Tucker. I was wowed. Lucien stopped at our ringside table during a portion of his banter with the audience.

"Ladies and gentlemen," Lucien said, "I have a school for talented female impersonators. This is one of my star pupils. Stand up, darling."

Lucien was pointing a sparkling finger at me. I stood up as I'd been told to do. The audience applauded.

"Isn't she beautiful?" Lucien continued. The audience's applause escalated. They were applauding me. This scintillating performer had said two magical words.

She and *beautiful*.

I was in a trance. Lucien's preposterous lie about a *rite de passage* school for impersonators was accepted both by me and by the audience. Those lovely patrons of the arts believed that I was becoming a glamorous gilded youth. I accepted that I could. After the show I turned to John.

"You keep telling me I have to do something with my life. Well, that's what I want to do."

John excused himself, went to the front desk, and asked Mrs. Finocchio how one could become a Finocchio's impersonator.

"Send a headshot and a résumé," she said, dismissing him.

John, Buddy, and the clap flew back to Los Angeles.

I had no headshot. I had no résumé. I did, however, have an idea. While getting a male photo taken for John's Christmas present, I finagled a drag photo for Mrs. Finocchio.

A friend from beauty school came with me to the unusual photo shoot. Jay, born in Jackson Hole, Wyoming, or some equally improbable homophobic place, now lived with his traveling salesman lover on the hill across from me in Silverlake. It was Jay who brought a blonde wig to the photographic studio and, as a favor, did my makeup. He would later have a fabulous career in the cosmetology field, and he certainly deserved it. Jay did a great job on my face. In short order I sent a reasonably professional-looking photograph to San Francisco.

"Here's your lash," said Jackie Phillips, Finocchio's star "comedienne," handing me the elusive, spidery false eyelash he had been hunting on the floor. I stopped trotting down memory lane and applied another layer of loose powder. It was a lesson that would serve me well in the ensuing years. When in doubt . . . fix your face.

"Who did your nose?" I heard from the doorway.

There she stood—the queen of burlesque herself. The club's featured exotic, Stormy Lee, was leaning nonchalantly against the dressing-room door.

Jackie had warned me to stay far away from Stormy Lee. According to my dressing-room mate, Stormy lived up to her turbulent name. The stripper had a mean streak and wasn't fond of young impersonators who auditioned for a dancing slot on the bill. She was the featured exotic, with a body deserving of the spot. Stormy held little truck with interlopers. She had nothing to worry about from me.

"No one," I said, watching her from my mirror.

"Liar!" she spit as she strode across the room. She took my nose in her hand and peered inside for evidence that would confirm her theory. There was no evidence.

Stormy Lee had an amazingly small waistline, and an equally amazing bulbous nose. Even with the nose, she was a raven-haired beauty. Her black hair and eyes were set off by an astonishingly white complexion. She was lithe, graceful, and proud. She stood aside a moment, sized me up, then sauntered back to the door. Mean streak or no, she was truly something to watch. In this light, the cosmetic contouring and shading she laboriously applied to her not-so-dainty proboscis was evident. Her jet-black hair was also cleverly arranged to minimize the protrusion. Onstage, under the lights, she was perfection. The "women" of Finocchio's were past masters of illusion.

If women in the 1950s were allowed to have large noses—drag queens were not. In her life, Stormy was to have three major nose jobs. In her mind's eye she never could get the nose small enough. Perceived imperfections die hard.

"When did you start taking female hormones?" she challenged.

I had no idea what she was talking about. Once again, Stormy strode across the room swishing her silk duster as she walked. This trip she grabbed my bosom. Jay had taught me to tape the fatty tissue up as high as I could get it. From early on I had been cursed with a little too much fatty tissue in that area. For years the kids at camp Hy-Lake for Boys had called me Milk Wagon. Now my little wagons were taped up high with duct tape.

"Humph," Stormy sniffed. "You have a core."

Once I was safely back in Hollywood, I'd be able to sit on a bar stool and hold court for months with this story. I'd be a minor sensation merely for having auditioned at the famed Finocchio's.

Lestra La Monte stopped by the dressing room. Lestra, the papier-mâché fashion plate, was the "mistress" of ceremonies for the club. Years of dragging crepe-paper gowns on and off stages had left Lestra a bit tattered around the edge. When allowed to be yourself only while on the stage, it's hard not to get bitchy. All the impersonators had a less-than-personable side, but at the time I thought they were all chic, savvy, and wonderful.

"What's your stage name?" Lestra asked as though it could not possibly make any difference to anyone he knew.

"Lisa," I replied.

"Too feminine," Lestra croaked. "You'll be Lee Shaw."

That was that.

Cue: drum roll.

"Ladies and gentlemen! It is with great pleasure that the world-famous Finocchio's brings you this evening's guest artist. Please give a warm San Francisco welcome to the long-stemmed American Beauty Rose, Lee Shaw." There was my intro music. I was on.

Where had the "long-stemmed rose" business come from?

I danced around a bit, taking off my gloves and a flowing, sheer, turquoise negligee. It was all part of my rented costume. Once that was done, I had no idea what to do. The band, not knowing I'd reached the end of my tether, kept trying to follow my "Sugar Blues" arrangement. They weren't having much luck, either. With their noses buried in my sheet music, they were unaware that I'd run out of steam. "So much," I told myself, "for finding a musical arranger in the yellow pages!" The music played on, and on, . . . and on some more. I sashayed to the left. I sashayed to the right. I sashayed up—and down. The band doggedly kept playing a reasonable facsimile of "Sugar Blues."

Suddenly, Fate turned another page.

Sitting ringside was a young soldier with his mouth hanging open. His bewilderment struck me as funny. Remember, from my earliest boyhood days I'd been drawn to men in uniform! I made a beeline for his table, posed at the post, and looked at him. That was all I did. I watched him turn a bright, glowing crimson. The audience started to laugh. Poor stooge, he became my act. I wrapped one of those long American Beauty Rose stems around the post and arched my back toward him. The solider did not know where to look. The audience loved it. Suddenly the music was over, and now I didn't want to leave the stage.

I didn't have to. I got an encore.

The real show, however, was going on backstage.

The "mistress" of ceremonies, Lestra La Monte, in his hand-stitched crepe-paper gown, had purposely left me on stage in stark white light. He'd probably learned that trick in vaudeville. La Lestra had been treading the boards a long time and knew every bit of theatrical sabotage ever pulled. Without a softening gel, the lights were too harsh, and Lestra knew it. I was untrained and didn't even know enough to ask for specific lighting. My lack of professionalism was unforgivable. Lestra didn't like "New Nanettes." He wanted me to show up poorly, go back where I came from, and leave impersonation to the professionals.

Stormy Lee, the reputed bitch-on-wheels, coming downstairs to watch my act, immediately knew what Lestra had done.

"Give the kid a break," she chided Lestra. With that, Stormy Lee strode over, took command of the light control panel, and put me in her personal amber and blue lights. That kindness changed my life and bonded me to the exotic for the rest of her life.

Mr. Finocchio had been watching me from the back of the house. He came back for Lestra's opinion.

"Well-a," he inquired, "watta ya think?"

"Hire her," Stormy cut in.

"But, what-ta can she do?" the Mister countered. "She has-a no act."

"She's beautiful," Stormy continued. "She'll learn. I'll teach her."

"You'll a-teach?" He couldn't believe what he'd heard.

"Hire her, or someone else will, and you'll be sorry."

While I was taking my final bow the deal was struck. In a union show, a producer could legally pay a lowly chorus member ninety dollars a week—the bottom of the American Guild of Variety Artists' (AGVA) union scale. I was offered a featured performer's position at a chorus boy's salary.

Finocchio's had no chorus.

CHAPTER 3

Drag Queen

SAN FRANCISCO opened a dramatic new life chapter. I was still stuck with someone else's concept of gender-appropriate behavior, but the conventional path I'd been following had suddenly made a sharp turn to the left. I was a drag queen. Correction! I was a celebrated, union-carded, female-impersonating entertainer. I didn't like thinking of myself as a drag queen.

Drag queens have always gotten a bum rap. Always. Men in women's clothing create a sensation, and their detractors live on both sides of society's sexual barbed wire. Nowadays, possibly the most damning rap against drag comes from inside the gay and lesbian neighborhood—the very community that Stonewall helped create.

On Friday, June 27, 1969, Greenwich Village drag queens ignited the Gay Liberation movement when they united at the Stonewall Inn, stood their ground against New York City's police, and kicked law-enforcement ass with sequined pumps. Shortly after those first angry steps toward homosexual liberation, drag became the gay stigma. Many male homosexuals, terrified that mainstream society would believe all gay men wore dresses, began to shun the more outrageous drag members of the community. Many lesbians were equally repulsed by drag, feeling that what had once been considered chic now made a travesty of womankind. Acceptance in the homosexual community was soon measured by the degree to which its citizens met a heterosexual standard. I didn't realize it then, but I was as prejudiced as those against whom I railed. I used beauty as my yardstick. It was inconceivable to me that nonbeauties of ambiguous gender might also be "real women." I blushingly admit to having been so shallow. It is unfortunate that marginalized members of society often fight one another for any available crumb of acceptance. No one wants to live at the bottom of the social barrel.

A decade before Stonewall, as I began my stint as Lee Shaw, Finocchio's was the most legitimized female-impersonation club in the country. It had been since 1936, when Joe and Marjorie Finocchio opened their doors at 506 Broadway. Prior to opening their North Beach location, "The Mister and Madam," as the Finocchio couple were called by employees, had offered female impersonation in a speakeasy at 406 Stockton Street. Drag came into its own when, in 1936, with lavish production numbers, beautiful impersonators wearing designer gowns and mink and sable coats, and a featured star who entered leading Russian wolfhounds, Finocchio's found a large audience. My future boss was soon known as the "Count di Broadway."

Finocchio's lineup boasted "the world's foremost impersonators," and their commercial success paved the way for drag clubs to proliferate across the country. The 506 Broadway location, however, remained the jewel in the drag queen's crown. At Finocchio's, *drag* was not a derogatory term. We were the elitists of impersonation. In the homosexual community the Finocchio cast was revered, and over the decades, the club's performers often served as champions for much of the gay and lesbian community. Professionalism and good press elevated us above most of the heterosexual world's scorn toward the bending of gender.

In spite of the acclaim, coming to terms with my new identity was troublesome. I did not "feel" that I was queer. I certainly differed from the heterosexual men I knew, but I also differed radically from the young gay drag queens with whom I worked. I wasn't lampooning women; I was trying to find myself. Drag, however, was the closest I'd ever come to feeling that I belonged.

"You're male, you sleep with a man, . . . *you're queer!*" society screeched. Added to this news bulletin was the demoralizing message that, no matter how I dressed it up, I was still a drag queen. Onstage, applauding audiences were marvelous, but on the street a man in women's clothing was considered perverse. Each night after I left the stage, I was forced to leave my real self behind. We were required by law to arrive and leave the club in male attire. Rejoining the "real" world as a man was a jarring experience. I hated it. Finding self-worth while presenting myself as a woman and simultaneously feeling guilt at being considered queer drove me deep into the gay subculture. Perhaps there I would find my true self.

In the late 1950s and early 1960s, strong taboos kept homosexuality underground, in the closet, and off the street. The gays I admired had seen the underbelly of that social beast and lived to laugh in its face. They told of a closed social structure that refused access unless you renounced your basic nature. I never met a queen at ease with her sexuality. The homosexuals I knew all accepted that they must either deny their deviance or be shunned by mainstream America. Their stories were of the world as they knew it, of those who hated and feared variance. In that world of majority rule, the terms labeling those who differ from the sexual norm are interchangeable. *Drag queen, faggot, impersonator, transsexual, queer, gay, sissy, dyke, lesbian*—all are dark synonyms for the word *freak*. They are ugly words used to inflict shame. It is society's language for telling you that you're not welcome. I'd sensed my difference from my earliest days; now I had to deal with the fact that others knew my secret.

My closest friends were those who had no choice in the matter. They were too extreme in their appearance and demeanor to be anything but obvious. Femininity was not something we feigned; it was something we had. My best friend, Stormy Lee, had the grace, style, and beauty of an exotic jungle cat. But Stormy, too, had been raised male. As was a common practice with a "too-feminine" male child, doctors subjected my "sister" to massive doses of the male hormone. It did little to change who she was as a person. Testosterone merely caused her to shave—her face, her legs, her arms, and her back.

Arched eyebrows, limp wrists, and a mincing gait created social havoc during daylight hours. Those who inhabited that daytime world were our sworn enemy. Female shop clerks were especially intimidating. Their disdain for obvious queens was legendary. It was "us" against "them." In our subterranean society, drag queens found acceptance after dark. Despite a constant threat of police harassment and the very real fear of "straight" society's physical brutality, queens ruled the queer ghetto after dark. In secreted Tenderloin bars and in North Beach gay clubs such as Chi Chi, The Black Cat, and Ann's 440, tilts with the "established daytime order" were recounted nightly with great glee. The outside world could hurt, humiliate, and momentarily humble us, but a sense of humor saw us through a lot of pain. The power of public acceptance was not at our disposal, but we certainly knew how to create a glorious spectacle by being society's outcasts.

"Call it what you will, Sweetie," Stormy Lee would often say during a White Russian cocktail break, "to them we're not impersonators. To them we're all female 'n peter tasters."

Because of the professional protection I came to accept as a member of Finocchio's elite lineup, I ended the 1950s with a false sense of security. I recognized, however, the strong dividing lines created by gender disturbance and sexual bent. Many members of my social order were denied access to housing, fair wages, and social positioning. Caught in the midst of my country's adolescence, I, too, believed myself capable of nothing more than being a white, queer, cracked boy soprano, singing for my supper and a little acceptance.

Tourist season in San Francisco translated into nonstop performances: three shows a night, seven nights a week. I was hoofing my brains out as the perennial ninety-dollar-a-week chorus girl/boy trainee. I wasn't stopping the show—but I was getting through it. The first person to take notice was a married man named Carl.

Carl started his pursuit with some degree of finesse. He sent flowers backstage. White orchids.

"What, no diamond bracelet concealed in the foliage?" Stormy asked smugly.

I viewed Carl's interest as harmless. I was, after all, a "married woman"—if I counted my priest. Besides, I still had the clap! My particular strain of gonorrhea seemed to be putting down roots. Penicillin was not doing the job in my backyard garden.

Despite all my good intentions and the club's rules against fraternization, I was not as protected as I assumed.

Since coming from L.A. for my audition, I'd lived in a room over Mike's Pool Hall. The beatnik hangout was a landmark in North Beach, half a block from the famed City Lights Bookstore and located directly across Broadway Avenue from Finocchio's. The furnished upstairs room left a lot to be desired.

Several nights after the flowers (sans diamonds), I found Carl at the street entrance to my lodgings. For a while he made polite small talk;

I profusely thanked him for the flowers and the note. Carl quickly became more specific with his desires. I just as abruptly informed Carl that what he wanted he wasn't going to get. He detonated.

"You cheap piece of trash," he bellowed. "You're nothing but a god-damn drag queen shaking your ass for a living."

I could not push past Carl. He was furious. I was scared.

Why is it that a well-placed knee to the groin never occurred to me in such harrowing moments?

"I'm a well-respected businessman," he yelled. His face was getting even redder than normal. Carl had been cursed with beetlike pigmentation. His anger now only inflamed an already florid complexion.

"I'm not the freak," he shouted. "You are. Freak! I'm a man with a wife and family, you're nothing but a cheap-ass drag queen. Consider yourself lucky that I want to fuck you."

The man had finally called it exactly as he saw it.

My pride wouldn't allow me to show how deeply Carl's words hurt, but I felt them to the core of my being. In my heart, I was afraid he might be correct. My real terror was that he'd alert others to my dark truth. He was creating an embarrassing scene across the street from Finocchio's, the scene of my first success in life.

I let Carl come to my room.

There was no love in the coupling. There was no emotion at all. I held my breath and closed my eyes. Carl could *do his business* and leave. I only wanted this humiliation to end. Until the man was through with me, I lay there. I never moved a muscle. I silently told myself over and over that this meant nothing. I could not succeed in convincing myself.

Carl wouldn't want a return encounter; of that I was sure. Not when he discovered the "geraniums" that were growing in my garden. Carl would have his own bouquet to take home from San Francisco. I knew from experience that those flowers were going to keep on growing until Carl watered them with the right strain of penicillin.

In the following weeks, John took time from his priestly duties at China Lake, came to San Francisco, and found me a small apartment on California Street. I wanted to beg his forgiveness and find absolution in his arms, but I did not mention Carl. No matter how I tried to convince myself otherwise, I knew my defilement mattered. He would matter a great deal to John. I said nothing. I needed my partner's understanding, but if I confessed my sin, John might make me leave show business.

"I put all your stuff in storage," John explained. "When we find a larger place, I'll bring everything to San Francisco."

That seemed logical. As John explained, my tenure at Fin's might not last past the tourist season. Until I had a long-term contract, there was no reason to make San Francisco our permanent home. As I always did, I bowed to John's better judgment. The bulk of my wardrobe, my grandmother's silver, my record collection, everything I owned, including the Sunbeam Alpine, would be safer in Los Angeles. I put my future in my lover's more capable hands.

In spite of John's dire predictions, my work in North Beach did continue past the tourist season. Although I still did not have a contract, I was being groomed for feature billing.

I didn't always realize I was being tutored, but I was. Not only did my coworkers teach me their tricks of illusion; they also taught me about life as they knew it. My fellow artisans had been around the undignified block—and met themselves coming back again. They'd survived in this underworld that I now desperately needed to understand. At some point in their lives, my fellow artisans had also been innocents abroad, and now they shared their hard-learned lessons with me, the neophyte.

"Honey, there ain't no man worth losin' a friend over," Kara Montez would declare as she primped in her mirror.

"Take it while you can, Miss Thing," Elton Paris would chime in from the dressing room next door. "You won't be young forever, Child."

"Every last one of 'em will get you in the end," Kara would giggle, adding more pink glitter to her blond wig.

I wasn't being converted to their lifestyle; I was being schooled in mine. Where I had resisted traditional male training, I was now an eager pupil.

Stormy Lee also shared insights from her world of the pre-op transsexual.

"Drag can be what you are, or it can be merely a means to an end," she'd say in private. "Sweetheart, just remember that nobody loves a fairy when she's forty. Most drag queens are faggots earnin' a living, but a few are real women in male bodies and sequin dresses. You've gotta decide which one you are."

In addition to opening my eyes to gender dysphoria, Stormy ran an ongoing critique of my performances. There were many times when I resented my friend. I idolized her, but I was often vexed by her tenacity. I was annoyed at having my performance pulled apart, analyzed, and redesigned.

Stormy was not only my mentor; she was, in the terminology of our subterranean world, a "married woman." A long-term relationship gave queens extra clout in drag circles, where a "real man" was a highly prized accessory. Stormy took very seriously the role-playing that was typical of gay and lesbian relationships prior to the 1980s. She knew no bounds where her man's creature comforts were concerned and played her subservient role to the queenly hilt. My own mother had not been as deferential. But Mozelle was a working, heterosexual woman with little time for measuring her femininity by male society's subjective scale. My mother wasn't a queen caught in the half-light of gay culture. As a "gay wife" Stormy cooked, cleaned, and waited on her husband, hand and hoof. She was the "femme" in a butch/femme relationship modeled on the heterosexual prototype of the time.

With hindsight I ask, "If that's what a wife is, who wouldn't want one?" In the late 1950s, my greatest fear was that I would never be considered "woman" enough to be a good wife. I had no concept that the terms *feminine* and *independent* could be synonymous. Like much of society, straight and gay, I thought a good woman must also be docile and long-suffering. The women I knew, genetic and generic, all agreed that the nurturing of love and romance was woman's most ennobling endeavor. I would believe that for many years to come.

The end of my first year in San Francisco saw the beginning of my fascination with neon-lit suits. The Italian-cut silk suits of the early 1960s were mostly worn by men who were extravagantly cocksure. Men a little too dapper for my own good. I was fascinated by the cut, the look, and the men. An element of danger surrounded these tough guys, and many men of that sort came to the club. Stormy said it was because "the syndicate" viewed queens as good-luck charms.

"Finally," I thought, "someone who respects drag queens."

After hearing exciting stories of the underworld from impersonators who'd worked East Coast clubs like the Jewel Box Review and Club 84, I believed I was singing for the Mob. I expected to be discovered by my own Mickey Cohen or Bugsy Siegel at any moment. In truth, I was working in North Beach, the heart of Little Italy, and Italian men merely looked the way I believed a mobster should look. The Mafia reputedly had little or no hold in San Francisco.

"Honey, you need to realize how good you've got it," Stormy would scold. "John may be out of town, but Girl, your leash ain't that long." Infidelity was her favorite lecture. When all else failed, she stopped using analogies.

"Bitch, you give one of *those* men gonorrhea and it could prove fatal—to you."

Nevertheless, eventually I did succumb to the neon-lit suit temptation. His name was Lane Erstane. He wasn't even Italian. Instead, he came from San Francisco's Presidio, with a father who was highly polished military brass.

Lane came to Finocchio's with a married couple, Janet and Bill, who were his longtime friends. After that first visit, the threesome returned to the club two or three nights a week. That was not unusual. The club had its regular patrons in addition to the tours that were part and parcel of its success. Individual performers had their own clique of appreciative patrons. I added Mr. Erstane and company to my following.

Going out for breakfast with the trio soon became a ritual. After work I'd climb back into my hated male attire and head off to meet my new friends. After breakfast there was a ritual, too. Lane would take me home, and then he'd drop off Bill and Janet. The routine never varied. It was driving me crazy. In my narrow world, acceptance by a man was the yardstick by which a queen measured her worth.

One night, as we were leaving our usual open-air restaurant, I whispered to Lane: "Tonight take Bill and Janet home first."

I wanted Lane Erstane alone. I needed to know what, if anything, was being left unsaid.

He told me.

"I think maybe I'm in love with you, Lee."

My emotional dams burst. Tearfully and laboriously, I recounted how Father John had broken our trust. I blubbered that, in the bargain, the priest had left me with a very stubborn venereal disease. As I sniveled, all my fears came spilling over the brim. I hated living as a boy, was confused by gender expectations, and was terrified of not meeting societal and parental standards. Panic was my only companion. But Lane was a trouper. He held me tightly for the entire emotional out-burst. This, I believed, was love.

It did not strike me as unusual that a straight man could fall in love with me. Married men had been assuring me of my femininity since I was a youngster, and I'd believed every persuasive word they told me. Why wouldn't Lane love me? I was a "girl"—no matter how I dressed it. I didn't realize it then, but I also had other qualities that made me very attractive to dominant males. I was emotionally dependent, fright-ened, and apparently a fragile being. I was also soft and pretty. A man with a good imagination could get past my minor imperfection—at least for the short term.

The perversely rooted strain of gonorrhea found a new garden plot.

John left me with a curse rather than a gentle, fatherly blessing. "I only hope," he said quietly, "that one day you'll love someone as I've loved you. And that they will hurt you the way you've hurt me."

John Lomond walked out of my life, keeping all my belongings still in his care, including the Sunbeam Alpine and my grandmother's silver. I'd fallen prey to a well-tailored neon-lit suit. A simple black suit with a white backward collar after three years no longer turned my head.

Lane and I struggled along in our love/hate relationship. My gender issues were never discussed, but Lane could not accept what our being together signified. Whether we addressed it or not, my genitalia were male and, in public, I was still legally required to present myself accord-ingly. My gender presented an obstacle both sexually and socially.

Then, one wet winter night, instead of picking me up from work, Lane made a bid for freedom. It caught me completely off guard. Only that afternoon, Lane had presented me with a pair of stunning 9 mm pearl earrings. Pearls were his gift of choice. The earrings, he said, were to symbolize the depth of our love. Not eight hours later, I was left standing alone in the rain.

Lane vanished for over two months.

One night, as I was morosely leaving work, a long-distance phone call came for me.

"Lee? I'm in Seattle, Washington. Without you, I might as well be in Mexico. Without you, I don't know where I am," Lane purred.

Within forty-eight hours, Lane Erstane was back in my bed, and I was proudly sporting a new eighteen-inch string of 8mm's. Thank goodness Lane had a thing for giving cultured pearls.

For the next several months all was joyous in my narrow little world, and respectability seemed just around the corner. Basic black gowns to be worn on safe occasions, pearls, a box at the ballet—what more did an aspiring girl need?

While in Seattle, during his flight from homosexuality, my skittish paramour had met Brian Shaw, danseur noble with the Sadler Wells Royal Ballet Company. When the company came to San Francisco, Lane proudly took me to see the elite corps perform. I'd never seen anything like Margot Fonteyn. Few people had. She put the prima in ballerina. Being extended the privilege of going backstage after her stellar *Giselle* wiped away any doubts I might have had about Lane. The man was thoughtful. The man was generous. The man was not ashamed of me.

Lane, basking in my newfound appreciation, hosted a party for the Royal Ballet Company. He rented a suite at the Mark Hopkins Hotel, and on the night of the soiree, people from all over North Beach came to Nob Hill. Gilda, the world-famous Parisian impersonator, showed up with her entourage. The Royal Ballet corps were there en masse, and—naturally—Finocchio's was well represented. Entertainers overran the suite.

Stormy Lee missed the fete. Her partner, Michael, had come home stoned and in no condition to attend a swell bash. Stormy was livid. She was, in fact, fighting mad—and Michael was in no condition to protect himself. Finocchio's exotic beat her boyfriend's head against the bedroom wall. She slapped him, beat him in the kitchen, and then battered him down the hall. She punched with every step he took. She would trounce him for a while, and when her arms got tired, she'd scream at him. Stormy enjoyed a good party and didn't intend to miss mine.

Their landlady, hearing the commotion, was appalled by such rough-housing. She called the cops.

Stoned or not, Michael should have attended the party. It wasn't the elegant evening I'd envisioned. Having set no perimeters to our guest list, the party was open season, socially. Lane and I were sitting ducks.

"Lane's on the phone, everybody," Elton Paris bellowed, trying to quiet the blaring crowd during one of seventeen complaint calls. "Hey, shut up will you?"

"Don't tell me to shut up, nigger!" a belligerent opera-house stage-hand responded.

Elton, with a glass in his hand, slugged the guy. By the time the house detective arrived, the comic impersonator extraordinaire had stopped bleeding and was standing arm-in-arm with the bigoted stagehand.

With the entrance of the fuzz, the ballet corps pirouetted out of every available exit. Dancers vanished. There was a mass company jeté off Nob Hill and out of scandal's way. I dutifully stayed behind with my man. What had gone wrong? It had all started so nicely. One moment I was having a genteel conversation with the conductor of the Royal Ballet, the next I was in the middle of bedlam! Our party was a fiasco. I suggested we jump from the balcony and take our chances. Instead, Lane gave all his cash to the "house dick" and wrote a check to cover hotel damages.

He should have listened to me.

After clearing the bank, Lane's reparation check went directly to his father. The militaristic senior Erstane was not pleased by his son's escapade. He was less pleased to find out about me.

Lane left my apartment, and for weeks our only contact came through notes. Jackie Phillips, Finocchio's comedienne and now our accomplice, picked up messages from my skittish lover and delivered the notes to the club. I was living a remake of *Casablanca*, but the intrigue outweighed the romance.

One Monday, on my day off, Jackie showed up at my front door. The comedienne's eyes were the size of large saucers.

"Grab your sunglasses," Jackie said. "Lane's outside in the car."

I grabbed the shades.

Lane was ensconced in a black stretch limousine . . . complete with a tinted-glass partition. I didn't need sunglasses. I needed a lorgnette.

As we drove through Golden Gate Park, Lane deposed his version of the Erstane family's history: his militaristic father headed a West Coast drug-smuggling cartel.

Oh, please!

So much for Stormy's theory that drag queens are considered good-luck charms by the syndicate, I thought.

Lane's plan was to flee San Francisco. He would fly to Los Angeles; I'd quit work and follow him. While in Los Angeles, we would stay in separate houses, stay out of sight, and wait for my passport to arrive. The James Bond plot/subplot stuff was scaring me to death, but my lover's fear of his father seemed very real. As soon as my passport was in hand, we'd decamp for France.

Fade in. It's late afternoon in the little city of the pines. The ever-handsome Lane Erstane is enjoying the sunset from a charming bistro's patio far above the azure sea. Bees are buzzing 'round the ol' honeysuckle vine. From our nearby chateau, I, in afternoon pearls, ride my frisky Arabian stallion down to the village. I greet my man with some witty, colorful phrase.

"A la carte," I'll say—or perhaps some other little French maxim I've managed to pick up.

As the sun sets, Lane in one athletic leap is seated behind me on the stallion. We gallop back up the dusty trail toward home, now golden in the sunset.

Fade out.

I liked the imagery, so I went to Mr. Finocchio and quit my job. My excuse for leaving was a sudden death in the family. The lie could come true, I thought, if I stayed in San Francisco.

Men were certainly getting to be a bother, but I never questioned the truth of Lane's story.

In Los Angeles, while I waited for my passport, my unsettled lover spent his time pacing the floor. Certain we'd be tracked down and murdered at any moment, Lane soon quit waiting and flew to France alone. "I'll meet you at Orly Field when you land," he whispered as he quickly kissed me goodbye.

For the next month and a half I held onto the dream. I never left the apartment. I was waiting for Lane's telegram. My pattern was well developed; I had no idea how to survive without a man to guide me. No telegram ever arrived. Lane had skedaddled again, and this time he'd left no pearls behind as a token of his affection.

Finally, I lost my faith, gave up, and left the apartment. An old friend took me to an upscale little nitery just off Hollywood Boulevard. It was a packed Saturday-night house, but we had ringside seats for a great comic duo I knew from Finocchio's audience. The evening was perfect, and then suddenly it got better. Dinah Washington visited La Vivandiere that evening. I adored the sweet, soulful song stylings of "Miss D." Dinah was the voice of contemporary blues, and when she left her entourage to step onstage and sing a few numbers, I thought my evening was complete. It wasn't. Also in the audience that night was Lestra La Monte, "mistress" of ceremonies from Finocchio's.

I saw Lestra across the room and commented on his presence to my friend but remained in my seat. That part of my life was over. I no longer intended to grovel at the crepe-paper hem of Lestra La Monte.

Suddenly, I was in the spotlight. One member of the comic duo was saying, "Also in our audience this evening, ladies and gentlemen, is San Francisco's most glamorous showgirl. Won't you stand up, Lee?" I stood. "Ladies and gentlemen, the beautiful Lee Shaw. Ah, Le Grande Illusion!"

I swear, I do believe Lestra La Monte winked at me.

The next morning, I called Mr. Finocchio to ask if I could return to work. "The Mister," as the queens called him, said he wouldn't front me money to come back, but I had a job once I got there.

My second call was to Stormy Lee. I explained the situation and asked if I could stay with her until I got my first paycheck.

"I'll have to ask Mike first," she said. "Let me get back to you."

A money order arrived that afternoon. It wasn't from France. Stormy and Michael not only agreed to my staying with them, they wired me the money to come home to San Francisco.

I believe Michael was secretly glad for his life partner to have a girl-friend at hand. Stormy and I spoke the same language. It was a language that Mike generally failed to comprehend.

The inimitable Stormy was not my blood sister, but we felt equally bonded.

Hazel Jeanne Crenshaw and I had a sisterhood that preceded my rela-tionship with Stormy by many years. Baby Sister was sent to me by a kind-hearted God. From the time I learned the meaning of prayer, I'd prayed fervently for her: "Now I lay me down to sleep. I pray the Lord my soul to keep. God bless Mother and Daddy, and please send me a baby sister to love. Amen."

On August 10, 1942, my prayers were answered—but the baby wasn't exactly what I'd prayed for. I'd forgotten to specify that my sibling should be beautiful. God sent me a baby that was all red and scrunched up in the face. The answer to my prayers was an ugly baby that got far too much attention.

"What's the matter with her head, Gran?" I asked.

"Nothing's wrong, Alfred Brevard," my grandmother smiled. "Don't worry about the shape of her head. That will change. Just be glad she was born without hair," she whispered. "Only common babies have hair."

I adored my sister, Jeanne, and Gran was right about her head. Within days it started looking less and less like a watermelon.

Almost from the very start, Jeanne was utterly without fear. As a baby, she'd giggle as she crawled after snakes. Later, as a schoolgirl, she was my stalwart defender.

"Leave my brother alone," she'd shriek. In my defense, Jeanne was always swinging her lunchbox at the head of some bully.

I could never quite get the self-defense thing down, but to my sister it came naturally.

"You have to learn to take up for yourself," Daddy would tell me after every confrontation.

I didn't want to fight. Even though I was constantly harassed and my feelings were always getting hurt, I wasn't mad at anybody. I turned every slight inward. What I wanted was to be accepted, and I could not get past my belief that if I loved strongly enough, I'd be loved in return. Finding that devotion does not always elicit affection has been one of life's most difficult lessons.

My sister, Jeanne, accepted me as I was. She loved me.

As children we went everywhere together. Jeanne wasn't a baby sister tagging along; she belonged with me. That my sister had no fear was an embarrassment to me, however. When she would scamper up a tree, I was always far below, shaking on the lowest limb. Jeanne never failed to take a dare. Jeanne's bravery only highlighted my innate timidity. She would try anything.

Then—suddenly—my brave sister was grown and married.

She married her high school sweetheart. No matter what negative statement my parents made about the boy, Jeanne stood by him. She was still courageous. She'd met "Frosty" Towns and never seriously dated again. Jeanne loved him, and no matter what the consequences, she was going to stand by her man. She also gave up her independence for him. His word was law.

It distressed me that my sister would toss her life away for a man.

"She deserves better," I moaned to Stormy and Mike. "She's a real girl."

In those days—after Lane but before surgery—I was disillusioned but far from world-weary. Somewhere, something was waiting for me. Every day in San Francisco was an adventure, and I didn't dare stay home for fear I'd miss something. Who knew what might be around the next corner? I intended to find out. Lane Erstane was yesterday's B-grade movie, and it was time to get on with the theater of life.

My fascination with Marilyn Monroe seemed a natural foundation for creating a new me. I, along with the rest of the world, was spellbound by the siren's vulnerability. I didn't want to create a tawdry drag impersonation of Marilyn Monroe; I wanted to find myself. Still, while I was waiting for my real persona to jell, it was time to create a specialty act for Finocchio's. Okay, instead of applying protective layers, like traditional drag queens, I would strip them away. I'd allow my vulnerable self to show through. In college, I'd been told that coeds saw me not as a gay male but rather as a deer caught in oncoming headlights. Most of my life I'd felt almost paralyzed by fear. Why not put that poor-little-match-girl quality to work for me?

While Stormy and I were doing the weekly grocery shopping, we'd practice dance steps behind our shopping cart. Doing the dishes, we prattled about new lyrics. Making the beds, we'd chatter about wardrobe. We were energetic, creative, and in love with show business. One thing was certain: if I wanted to live like a star, I needed to become one.

"My Heart Belongs to Daddy" was introduced at Finocchio's on a Tuesday night. My act in a red knit sweater, slowly removed to reveal a red lace merry widow, was an instant triumph. Thanks to Marilyn's musical performance in *Let's Make Love,* I'd found my routine. I also had found my following. "Daddy" was a hit. By the following Monday, my salary was increased to headliner status.

Life consisted of work, shopping, and developing a bond with Stormy that was to continue our entire lives. In many ways, we felt closer than real sisters. We shared a special understanding. We had a common covenant.

One night after work, we were together at the bathroom sink removing our makeup. Stormy took down a pill bottle and took a purple capsule.

"What's that?" I asked.

"Premarin," she answered.

"What's it for?" I queried.

"They make your boobies grow" was her answer.

"Give me one," I said, sticking out my hand.

It felt like the right thing to do. I could never go back to being Buddy Crenshaw; I'd come too far. Standing by the bathroom sink in a basement apartment at 860 Gary Street, I made a commitment to becoming myself, fully, as I took my first female hormone. Early the next day, Stormy introduced me to her physician, Dr. Harry S. Benjamin. After a physical examination, he accepted me as his newest transsexual patient.

I was slightly disconcerted by the famous doctor's initial excitement over my pubic hair. He found the growth pattern very female in appearance, and for his studies that held great significance. I was sorry to disappoint him, but I shaved the pubic area for just that appearance.

The year that followed meeting Harry Benjamin represents the zenith of my gender quest. It was a period of transition, both on and offstage.

Generally, for several years prior to surgery, male gender-reassignment patients are required to live their daily lives as women, but this testing period was waived for me. I was not able to live full time as a woman. Due to my professional status at Finocchio's, I was too recognizable in San Francisco. It was professionally necessary that on the street I continue to appear in the despised male garb and the hated skullcap I wore to cover my long hair. My doctor, believing I was learning the fine art of feminine mystique onstage, made an exception in my transitioning process. Nightly audiences did pay to judge my femininity, but my doctor had overlooked the fact that customers were applauding a theatrical illusion. Ultimately, his decision to waive my daily, comprehensive experience as a woman made my transition much more difficult. "Passing" for female was not my dilemma. Ensuring a comfortable passage into the real world of women could only come with exposure to their daily experience. The world of most genetic women is made up of the little things, not the glamour. While my daytime "real girl" sisters toiled for unequal pay, rocked society's cradle, and struggled for complete emancipation, I waited impatiently for twilight hours when I could pose and preen.

Now that I knew I had a surgical way out, I was no longer content in the gay bars and restaurants of the city. I wanted to live my life as a woman. On those nights when I felt I could no longer tolerate my male persona, I'd remove *most* of my makeup after my last show, powder my face, stick my shoulder-length hair up under a navy knit skullcap, and hail a cab. I was off to dance with the merchant marines at a notorious club called the Streets of Paris.

The name did not do this after-hours, smoke-filled, low-rent establishment justice. The *Sewers* of Paris would have been more apt. I loved the joint. I convinced myself that here I was living life as a true girl.

I carried with me at all times, in case of arrest, a letter of medical explanation from my doctor. Letter or no letter, had the men with whom

I danced and flirted suspected that I was technically male, there would have been no time for clarification. That, as they say, would have been that. Splat! Smeared all over the tawdry Streets of Paris. The danger was part of the intrigue. I was testing my wings of wax.

Legally, at that time, one was required to wear at least three-gender appropriate articles of clothing. Otherwise you were subject to arrest. Few heterosexuals were aware of the law. The archaic ruling was of major consequence only for the queens of the queer community. For my late-night forays, I generally wore two socks and a silky, if male, tank top under my very feminine slacks and top.

My outer garments had for years been very non-gender specific: velvet tops over stovepipe-cut slacks; oversized shirts over tight, tight jeans. I did not, however, hit the streets in cute little skirts and cashmere sweaters. I was conscious of the dress code and the fact that I was known to every cop on our block.

The city's finest were often found kibitzing with the owners at the club. In the years leading up to San Francisco's "gay-ola" scandal of the early 1960s, it was common practice for the owners of gay clubs to "grease" the legal system. Financial consideration in the right blue pockets allowed talented "fairies" to work and play without constant police harassment. The cops on Broadway knew who I was, and I knew them for what they were. Like everyone familiar with gay life, I carried a healthy fear of our law-enforcement officials. I played by the rules and only slightly bent the dictate that you arrive and exit the club . . . male.

"I know you think you're real, Girl," Stormy would fret, "but you're still almost six feet tall and bear a striking resemblance to that popular drag queen Lee Shaw. Don't think you're invisible to the police."

My friend was concerned for my safety, but her primary fear was not of the men with whom I danced at the Streets of Paris. She knew how badly I would be treated if picked up by the police. I would be unceremoniously tossed into jail, if not worse.

Frustrated by the limitations of my maleness, I increased my oral doses of both Premarin and Provera. I also doubled my injections of estrogen.

Stormy had not lied when she told me the little purple Premarin pill would make my "boobies grow." Lee Shaw quickly became an impressionist with impressive cleavage. My body softened in contour as the weekly ingestion of estrogen layered an extra padding of protective fat beneath my skin. The physical changes could not happen fast enough for me. Nausea, emotional fluctuations, and hot flashes were minor side effects, considering the physical results. A sore, burgeoning bosom was a wonderful daily reminder of the miraculous changes occurring in my body. Rounded hips and pubescent breasts, however, were difficult to conceal under the male clothing I was still forced to wear on public outings. In the 1950s and early 1960s, a well-dressed woman in San Francisco did not appear downtown without her hat and gloves. I hated being forced to stuff my developing body into jeans and sweatshirts. Being caught between genders was, at best, an embarrassment.

I wasn't the only one disturbed by my public appearance. A tax audit of Alfred Brevard Crenshaw caused one federal employee more consternation than *his* summons had caused *me.* As later reported in a *San Francisco Examiner* article focusing on unusual tax audits, the IRS agent said my gender was more perplexing than my 1959 tax return. I was in his office with my habitual skullcap hiding my long hair, no makeup, and wearing a man's sweatshirt. It was my untethered bosom that caused the interrogator's confusion. He couldn't take his eyes off my tits. After an awkward interview, he allowed my claim for sequin and lace deductions. He was more concerned that Alfred B. Crenshaw had perky little breasts.

Although I was committed to my physical development, I sometimes lagged far behind emotionally. I still fully believed anyone who indicated that my very existence was shameful.

When Stormy and Michael decided to move to a lovely Victorian on Steiner Street, they asked me to join them. Stormy and I would continue to split all expenses down the middle.

After work, Stormy and I stayed up all night packing, and on the actual day of the move, we certainly did not look or feel our best. We were tired, dirty, and more than a little disheveled. Michael's concern, however, was that a moving man might think we were less than feminine. The man of our house was tense with fear that a stevedore might question his mate's and her best friend's gender. That could prove the ultimate blow to his masculinity. The two paying members of the household were not at their glamorous best, ergo we were not acceptable.

Neither Stormy nor I was shocked when Michael suggested we hide in the closet while movers were in the house. We were programmed to accept such homophobic reactions. We accepted that our existence was a legitimate cause for shame, so when the movers arrived, we willingly hid. We lived our lives in the shadow of society, and now we shut ourselves away rather than prove an embarrassment to anyone. It's hard to disappear much deeper into shadows than when hiding in a closet.

The dreams, the hormones, the surgery were all a desperate attempt at an acceptable life. The journey is a serious one. We joke. We sometimes cavort outlandishly. Each transsexual follows his or her own ritualistic path, but finally, we all try to desensitize the pain. Ultimately, ours is a journey born of anguish. We make that journey in order to live as we are . . . without having to hide from anyone.

CHAPTER 4

A Man in the House

IN THE final moments of my sexual reassignment, it was my fiancé, Hank Foyle, who waited with my parents on the floor above the surgical arena. Together they anxiously awaited news of the surgery's outcome. My parents waited for their daughter; Hank awaited his future wife. We were a century past the mail-order brides of the Old West, but I'd been ordered to my man's specifications nonetheless.

That no one ever understood the obsessive attraction that bound me to this man did not lessen my need for him. In the thirty-seven years since I fell in love with Hank, I have heard him called a gigolo, a ne'er-do-well, and a louse. Actually, he was a godsend.

On the night of December 3, 1960, the man who would imprint my life forever was seated ringside center for my third show. He sat with a young man and woman watching the evening's performance. Backstage, I heard my introduction and, as usual, made my entrance with "My Heart Belongs to Daddy." The number had been in the show for months, and it was set. I knew exactly what I was doing at every moment.

I opened center stage with the chorus. "While tearing off a game of golf, I may make a play for the caddy. But if I do, I won't follow through 'cause my heart belongs to Daddy. . . . " When I finished the chorus, I vamped down the stairs and went into the dance portion. Here, with heavy drum backup, I slowly, seductively removed my red sweater to reveal a red lace merry widow. Thus exposed, I turned and undulated back up the steps. With my back to the audience I would pause, pivot sharply, and toss blonde wisps of hair onto my face. Then, with puckered lips, I lazily blew the strands from my eyes. That bit of business cued a reprise of my song. I finished the number center stage: up-tempo, bows, and off.

That was the standard routine.

On December 3, all went according to plan until the pivot. I tossed my blonde hair, puckered, and . . . saw Hank Foyle.

Electricity flashed between us. Nothing existed except his eyes. Everything else was lost. The music played on, but I didn't. I forgot the words to my signature song. I couldn't get my breath. I made a complete and utter fool of myself in front of the capacity crowd. My stomach felt as though it had, quite literally, turned over in my body.

I stood there mesmerized.

Suddenly, I turned and abruptly left the stage. Our mistress of ceremonies tried to cover my un-ladylike exit while I ran up the back stairs to Stormy's dressing room.

"There's a man in the audience," I panted.

"God, I hope so" was her jaded response.

"You don't understand," I sputtered. "There's this man . . . "

"Honey! When we start playing to all-female audiences, I'm getting out of the business," Stormy smirked as she applied a finishing swirl with her mascara. My friend used her Revlon wand as though she were conducting an orchestra.

Stormy left her makeup table and started to zip herself into her *Gone with the Wind* strip costume—complete with fluorescent crinoline hoop skirt and pantaloons.

Undaunted, I continued to blather as I chased her around the dressing room.

"But he's going to be waiting for me after work!" I wheezed. "What should I do?"

Stormy turned sideways, easing Scarlett's afternoon-barbecue-at-Twin-Oaks gown through the dressing-room door, and headed for the stage.

"First wait and see if he's there," she drawled as she floated down the stairs.

He wasn't waiting when the club closed.

For the second time that evening my stomach did flip-flops. How could I have so misread those dark eyes? He'd done nothing other than look at me, yet I'd understood that this man saw me as the embodiment of everything he'd ever wanted. I'd left stage convinced that, at long last, I'd found someone who could understand and love the individual beneath the blonde wig. Now, I had made a fool of myself over someone who wasn't even interested in me. I must be losing my grip.

For the next five nights Hank Foyle sat ringside. He came alone and sat in the same seat each evening, watching my every move. His expression never changed. He sat through all three shows and watched.

On the eighth of December, his birthday, I arrived at work to find a note waiting on my dressing table.

"If you feel about me, like I feel about you . . . shame on you."

It was signed "Hank."

During my third show I passed his ringside table, towing my sweater behind me.

"Hank?" I whispered.

He nodded.

"Meet me after work."

It was slightly into the ninth of December when I left the club. It was now *my* birthday. I was twenty-two.

While the club's doorman hailed my taxi, I murmured a discreet "Hello" to Hank. As we shook hands, I passed him my phone number.

"I'll be home in fifteen minutes," I murmured before slipping into the waiting cab.

The telephone was ringing as Stormy and I entered our front door. Mr. Foyle was invited to come celebrate my special day.

The mysterious man's quick acceptance to my impromptu fete stimulated a flurry of activity in our apartment. All evening my dark auburn hair had been pin-curled under a blonde wig. Now my naturally curly hair was frizz. While Stormy tried to straighten the mess, I reapplied makeup. Michael's birthday gift was the rosy glow that soon emanated from a roaring fire in the fireplace. With my image somewhat restored, Stormy frantically started ripping through her closet. She tossed me a light blue chiffon and lace peignoir. The garment was transparent, but what the hell—it was my birthday. As my best friend thoughtfully set out two brandy snifters, I dimmed the living room lights, then; with the stage set for seduction, Stormy and Michael discreetly retired for the evening.

The doorbell rang and, calmly, I buzzed to let Hank Foyle enter my life.

He never took his eyes off me as he ascended those steep Victorian stairs to the landing where I stood waiting for him.

"Thank God," he said taking my hand. "I was afraid that offstage you'd be different."

We walked, hand in hand, into the living room and stood gazing at each other.

"May I do something I've been wanting to do for five nights?" he asked.

Our first kiss was so comfortably familiar that there remained no need for further conversation. We made love in front of the roaring fire and later, in the glow of the embers, fell asleep melded like two cherubs in a sugar-spun dream.

The next morning Hank and I went to the doctor's. I had a rectal tear.

"Looks like you ran into more than you could handle," my physician said as he examined me.

"He's sitting in your waiting room, if you'd like to meet him," I quipped. "When you're falling in love, Doc, there's not always time for lubrication."

That first afternoon together we went for a long walk in the rain. I was wearing—funny how you remember—a black wool coat and had a silk scarf tied, Audrey Hepburn-style, behind my neck. The day was magical—like something straight out of *Roman Holiday.* San Francisco was never more enchanting. Passing the San Francisco Opera House, Hank pulled me into each little alcove and kissed me. I had never felt more desirable or loved. Even with a painful rectal tear, I had a great twenty-second birthday.

Hank never left my bed after that first encounter. Overnight, he became an integral part of my life. It was as though, having been shut away from love and much human interaction, I'd now burst full-blown into a world of total acceptance. I saw Hank as the personification of what every little boy was expected to grow into, and I loved him without reservation. Hank Foyle was the center of my small universe.

At six feet, three inches, with his broad shoulders and tapered waist, he was my romantic ideal. Hank was physically perfect. The fact that he was also kind, considerate, and loving humbled me greatly. I couldn't believe such a wonderful heterosexual man accepted my flawed being. I lived for Hank Foyle. Overnight I changed roles, from the disinterested sexual sacrifice into the lustful lover. I craved his body. So in love was I that it pained me to think other couples might share similar sexual expressions. To correct any romantic duplication, Hank and I became extremely creative. The ritualistic exchange of saliva, from every imaginable position, was our sensual attempt at uniqueness in lovemaking. Initially, we were equally ingenious in the sexual concealment of my gender. As we became comfortable with each other, we no longer needed to hide my penis. We successfully ignored it.

Soon Hank and I found an apartment on Pine Street. The move into our own home immediately caused a major rift with Stormy.

It was not only that my exodus left her to pay all the rent; Stormy likely also felt I had deserted her. That I was madly in love did not mean our friendship was in jeopardy—it did mean she could no longer be the most important person in my life.

With the rent issue, she had a very valid point. The move to Steiner Street had been possible because I was along to pay half of everything. Stormy and Michael were livid when I left. Yet, had there been no Hank, I still would have needed to move. There were mitigating circumstances. Michael was too affectionate toward me, and had been for some time. When Hank showed up as a fixture in my life, Mike's attentions only escalated.

One chilly afternoon, after returning from a walk with Hank, I went to hang up my coat. As I crossed to the closet, I saw Mike sprawled across the bed. He was smoking marijuana. As I passed on my way to leave the room, he grabbed me.

"Let me show you what a real man is like," he slurred.

I pulled away and ran from the room. That night, as I lay safely in Hank's arms, I told my lover what had happened.

I told, partly, because I wanted to share my every emotion with Hank. I told because there was no line of demarcation between us. I also wanted to feel protected. For whatever reason, I shared information that would have best been kept secret. Hank immediately became enraged. Having caused a potentially dangerous situation, I became scared. In tears, I begged him to let it pass. I pleaded with him not to create a scene. Hank reluctantly agreed, but with one stipulation. We would immediately find our own space.

The next afternoon we moved into our apartment on Pine Street. It was a furnished one-bedroom apartment approximately ten blocks from Finocchio's. We would both be able to walk to work: Hank to his daytime shoe-selling job in Union Square, and me to my evening drag gig in North Beach. With combined salaries, we could afford the apartment and still save money toward my surgery. Although I earned almost triple Hank's salary, I refused to see that as important. Stormy, although she was sending Michael to beauty school, promptly labeled my man a cheating leech. My heterosexual friends also looked at Hank with wary eyes. Everyone, even Hank, was concerned that I carried over half our monthly financial obligations. Everyone, that is, but me.

That Hank was less than an enterprising, upwardly mobile young man was a fact not lost on me. I couldn't have cared less. What he brought to our relationship and to me was worth more than a portfolio of blue-chip stocks. Hank gave his love and his unconditional support. I had no idea what I'd done to deserve such a man, but I had found someone who apparently worshiped me. For the first time in my life, I was free to be my real self—a woman—for more than just a few hours a night on a stage.

On my free nights, we would scamper off to a nearby fruit stand. Loaded down with our groceries, we'd rush home to sit cross-legged in bed, feed each other fruit, and bemoan the emptiness of our lives before we met. With each piece of fruit we shared another secret previously hidden from the world.

Hank grew up a "stray" in North Carolina. After his mother died when he was fifteen—his father had deserted them both years before—Hank finished high school with the aid of his friends and their families. He would stay with one friend until his welcome wore out, then move on. After high school followed a hated hitch in the navy. Hank never developed the skills to survive in a world of expectations; he just lived.

Prior to my surgery, while taking massive doses of estrogen and progesterone, I was highly emotional and volatile. Still, Hank was always there for me. He would hold me while I cried uncontrollably and for no apparent reason. With a wry grin, he'd wipe my tears away and say a prayer for more normalcy in our future life together, after surgery. His optimism always calmed my fears.

At times, Hank would shed his own tears.

"Mama would have loved you very much, Lee," he would often say as he cradled me in his arms. I was always very moved.

I had found the person with whom I wished to share the rest of my life. Except for the fact that I still wore my cursed skullcap to cover my hair, dressed in male drag, and tried to evade gender recognition, I had found contentment. The fact that I was soft and pretty enough to pass as a female did not eliminate my fear of discovery. There were even a few occasions when someone would yell, "Hey, man, is that a boy or a girl you're with?" At those moments my heart stopped beating, as Hank's temper flared. I was very aware that the female course I had charted must soon become a reality. If I did not owe it to myself, I owed it to Hank. There was no turning back.

Living with this man did not allow room for the perpetuation of my stage persona or the cultivation of my feminine mystique. It was not unusual for my lover to barge into the room as I dressed, eager to tell me something. To my total embarrassment, as I waxed the remaining beard not yet removed by electrolysis, he'd walk into the bathroom with some bit of news. Hank loved to brace against the door frame, talking, while I applied makeup. Keeping an illusion alive was impossible with such a talkative man. That made me anxious. I harbored the fear that I'd be desired only as long as an illusion of beauty existed, but Hank seemingly saw the real me. He adored the androgynous person he saw.

Hank secretly started his own stash toward my gender transformation. He hid money each week under the carpet in the corner of the bedroom. I, of course, found it immediately. It was with great tenderness that I counted the money's weekly growth. Even though, in very intimate moments, he embarrassed me by insisting I whisper slang words describing the genitalia I'd soon have created "just for him," I unashamedly loved the man with every fiber of my being. Our time spent together, no matter what the undertaking, was joyous. Working on our apartment was a special passion. We hung curtains. We kidded and played like kids while cleaning every nook and cranny of our new home. We spent hours together rearranging furniture. It was newlywed bliss—until we decided to completely repaint the apartment.

Everything except for the bedroom was to be Navajo white. For that very special room we chose a very, very pale baby blue. Oops! The bedroom was located immediately off the living room, separated by a sliding wood panel. That roomdivider became a major obstacle. I was adamant on painting it Navajo white. Hank was equally inflexible on his choice of baby blue. We considered compromising, with one side white and the other side blue. The only thing on which we could agree was that the compromise did not work.

The painting of our apartment quickly became a contest of wills. Put two hard-headed Sagittarians together, and any response is going to be emotionally charged.

When we reached the room divider, all painting came to a standstill. We could not agree on how to proceed. Already late for work, and with Hank starting on a six-pack of beer, I was miffed as I rushed out of the apartment.

"And when I get home, that damn divider had better be Navajo white!" I yelled, slamming the door behind me.

Dragging in from work, I was immediately confronted by an announcement: "Zorro was here!" The divider had indeed been painted my prescribed Navajo white, and painted over it, in a beautiful baby blue, was Zorro's communiqué. Hank, speckled with paint, sat with his arms folded defiantly in front of him, his black eyes firing sparks.

I started to laugh. That night we made love on a Navajo white and baby blue paint-covered drop cloth.

Stormy was not equally bewitched by my newfound happiness. She was furious. Night after night, backstage at Finocchio's, she launched into the subject of my disloyalty. My old friend never missed an opportunity to question my integrity, intelligence, and maturity. Every queen in town knew Stormy's version of my move from the Victorian on Steiner Street. One night I broke. At exactly the worst possible moment, with a dressing room full of coworkers, I decided to fight back.

"All right, Bitch, you want to know why I moved out?" I braced for the showdown.

"Because you're a self-centered little shit?" she snapped.

"That . . . and because your goddamn husband couldn't keep his hands off my ass!" I spit back.

My training at Finocchio's was complete. I had become as vicious as the rest of the pack.

In retaliation, Stormy began to call our apartment at all hours of the night. She would phone, dub me a thankless whore, and hang up. Hank was drawn into the ongoing charade when an inebriated Stormy called me at four o'clock in the morning, screaming what an ungrateful, snotnose bitch I'd turned out to be. Her call woke me up from my own drunken stupor, and it didn't help my mood to hear Michael egging her on in the background.

"Do you think I can't hear Michael telling you what to say, Miss Thing?" I blasted. Hank grabbed the phone from me.

"Put the bastard on the phone," Hank slurred in his own state of intoxication. "If that son of a bitch wants to say something to Aleshia, tell him to say it to me."

The "son of a bitch" in question got on the phone. It quickly became a match of the Titans. Our boys agreed to meet in Golden Gate Park and finish this conflict man to man.

When Hank started putting bars of soap into a sock for use as a blackjack, I called Stormy. She had been trying to phone me. Michael was coaching their Doberman, Knightmare, to attack and mutilate.

This had suddenly become serious. Our survival training, over a marginalized lifetime, had taught us to dramatize almost every incident and to turn any event into a good story. The men in our lives were attracted to our vulnerability and knew our weakness was generally masked by a flip word and false bravado. It was to these men we turned for guidance and support. We cried in their arms at being forced to live in a twilight world, trapped between being men and being women. Generally, our men, knowing our fears as they did, stayed removed from these minor bitchy freys. Now, Stormy and I decided to call a truce before our men spilled unnecessary blood. In a gush of tears, we forgave each other's stupidity. Hank and Michael were off the hook; Knightmare went back to his tire-iron chew toy; and all was again right with the world.

As ridiculous as the tiff appears, it was a serious situation. For the love of a man, I'd turned on my best friend. Although I regretted hurting Stormy, I'd known no other way. Home had become more than a place of refuge. It was a joyful space, and because of the person with whom I shared it, a place where I wanted to spend every available minute. Nothing was more important than having Hank in my life. He was the only person with whom I'd ever been able to share every emotion. Even as a child with my mother, there had been areas where I dared not go, for fear she'd stop loving me. Now, Hank was my lover and my best friend. Whatever others might think of him, I was deliriously happy. I could never understand that confidants failed to appreciate the depth of my feelings for him. Rather than examine my relationship with Hank more closely, I chose to believe that what we experienced was unique. Maybe other couples did not love with the same passion that consumed us. I had often heard homosexuals express those same sentiments in reference to heterosexual society.

"Honey, they don't get it. For the breeders, matrimony turns out to be a trap. They get married, drop a few kids, stop talking to each other, and start fantasizing about what the queers are doing in their bedrooms. No wonder they hate us." Although I did not think of us as being homosexual, I accepted that the same sort of misunderstanding must be true where Hank and I were concerned. I could only believe that my nonaccepting friends had never needed anyone as completely as I now needed Hank. Maybe my friends had never dreamed impractical dreams.

One night, months into our relationship, I was up late watching television. I was awash in tears when Norma Shearer as Marie Antoinette watched revolutionaries lead her lover to the guillotine. I could stand the anguish no longer. The thought of ever losing the man I worshiped was more than I could suffer. I ran to our bedroom and threw myself, sobbing, onto Hank's sleeping body.

"Please don't die before I do," I sobbed. "Please don't die before I do. I couldn't live without you."

Hank kissed me on the cheek, turned over, and immediately went back to sleep. That did not alter the depth or sincerity of my sentiments.

Not every day was garlanded in hearts and flowers. The emotional upheaval caused by interloping female hormones, exacerbated by my natural mercurial nature, disrupted the rosy days with riotous confrontations. Hank and I lived with emotional candles flaming brightly at both ends. At times our relationship was nothing but a huge ball of tallow.

Even though he worked a regular daytime job, Hank picked me up when the club closed. We'd share a late supper at home and fall into bed. In my early twenties, eating at bedtime was not a figure catastrophe.

One night, we decided to stop and grab a bite at the local drive-in. All evening I had been particularly belligerent and was in the grip of an inexplicable anxiety that sometimes overwhelmed me. I certainly did not want to go home and cook. Had I been a real woman, I would have sworn I had PMS. I was spoiling for a fight.

As we pulled into the all-night diner, a waitress came sashaying over to our car. She was hiding behind huge sunglasses. In my unsettled state, even her glasses were an annoyance to me.

"Do you know who that is?" Hank ventured.

"Anouk Aimee?" I sneered.

I was jealous. Who was this waitress in the shades, and how well did Hank know her?

"You tell me who she is," I said, with as much blistering undercurrent as I could muster. Hank heard none of the warning bells.

"That's the waitress who waited on us the first time we came here," he announced proudly. "Who's Anouk Aimee?"

I had no idea whether it was the same waitress or not. I didn't care. He should not have paid so much attention to her in the first place.

"No, it's not the same waitress," I scoffed.

"Yes, she is!" Hank was starting to stand his ground. I could hear the obstinacy creeping into his voice.

"Is not," I pouted. "You wouldn't recognize your mother at a whore's convention."

Like some lunatic let loose at the Indy 500, Hank pulled the car away from the curb. We swerved out of the drive-in on two wheels, and he sped off as if pursued by a demon. When my initial fear subsided, I spoke.

"Slow down, or at the next red light I'm getting out and walking home!"

Hank slowed down. He never understood me when I was acting like this. Generally, I was more bluster than substance, but when I was crazed he was never sure what I might do. He slowed down. He drove sensibly until we were within a few blocks of our apartment and then he accelerated again. It was a direct challenge. At the red light, I threw open the car door and ran for the apartment.

As I reached the front door, Hank sped into the parking lot. Damn. I couldn't find my keys, and Hank was running down the sidewalk toward the building. Just as I got the entrance door unlocked, Hank caught up with me.

Pulling me behind him, Hank pushed over the large, figured fountain that dominated the lobby. Water went everywhere. Outside our apartment he jammed his fist into the row of mailboxes, then kicked open our apartment door. Still towing me behind him, he dragged me into the bedroom and threw me on the bed.

"Now," he said, towering over me with hands placed firmly on his hips, "is it the same goddamn waitress, or not?"

Hank stood there glowering like a petulant little boy, and I thought he was the most adorable man I had ever seen. My emotional fog lifted. The whole outlandish debacle now struck me as extremely funny. We made love until it was time for Hank to leave for work.

Disjointed, reckless explosion seemed somehow necessary to our relationship. We both reacted strongly to everything around us, but it was Hank's jealousy, coupled with his quick temper, that brought yet another dimension to our domestic life. Shamelessly, I played his possessive nature by bringing attention to any romantic overture that came my way. The fact that one admirer wrote passionate poems and sent them to me, anonymously, at work drove Hank crazy. I loved it. This was the sweet side of jealousy. Evilly, I brought home each love note, propped up in bed, and read the verse aloud to my lover. Hank valiantly tried to maintain a facade of disinterested disdain, but he never succeeded for long. His passionate reaction toward his unknown rival gave me a great sense of security. That this beautiful man found me attractive amazed me; that he was so insanely jealous completely beguiled me. I still failed to understand why he'd chosen to stay with me, after he saw past the illusion. Lee Shaw, my platinum-blonde stage creation, attracted much attention and admiration. I understood that. In my stage persona I owned the universe, but as a male, offstage and out of my follow spot, I was extremely shy and self-effacing. The real person totally lacked any positive sense of self. In my daytime personification, I could not ask a bus driver for directions. I feared that he might poke fun at me in front of other passengers. When viewed by the harsh light of a "normal" world, I was a total wreck.

When I met Hank, I'd been misusing drugs and alcohol for some time. A mixture of uppers, downers, and a pint of liquor to wash them down was a nightly routine. On our way to the club, Stormy and I regularly made a stop at the corner liquor store. With pills in our pockets and booze in hand, we went to work.

Every night at work, I mixed the reds, roses, and White Russians.

"Honey, the car's parked this way," Hank said one evening as I staggered out of the club.

"Then you take it," I snarled. "I'm walking home." I started to weave my way down Broadway. I made it to the corner of Columbus and Broadway—and blacked out. Even in bohemian North Beach, a gay culture icon lying crumpled in the gutter in front of Lawrence Ferlinghetti's City Lights Bookstore was an unusual sight. That evening, in addition to my usual six Seconal capsules, six Dexedrine tablets, and nightly quantity of liquor, I had added marijuana to my program.

The next day, Hank stated his case simply.

"It's either me or the pills," he said.

There was no choice to be made. I stopped.

In the seven months we lived together prior to the Los Angeles surgery, it was Hank who led me into San Francisco's straight, daytime world. My outgoing lover refused to let me hide behind fear or under the cover of darkness. For an effeminate male, daylight dispelled the shadowy protection of Finocchio's and North Beach. Often our daytime outings were nothing more than a trip to an open-air market, but I was learning gradually to be comfortable in the real world. I was discovering myself, yet my sole aspiration remained to be nothing more than an extension of this man.

As Hank and I impatiently waited for my contract at Finocchio's to expire and for the transsexual surgery date in Los Angeles to arrive, our monogamous commitment was seriously challenged.

Before she fell for Michael O'Brian, Stormy had been in a long-term relationship with a gambler named Lucky Hunt. They'd met in New

Orleans, then moved to New York, where Stormy worked Manhattan's famous drag spot, Club 42. When Stormy wrangled an audition at Finocchio's, she and Lucky dropped everything and traveled cross-country to San Francisco. She auditioned three times and was finally given a slot for the summer season.

The night Stormy started her long sought-after job at Finocchio's, her lover shot a man during a card game. Lucky was unceremoniously carted off to prison for this lack of card-room decorum.

After serving his time, the gambler returned to find his woman "married" to another hood. He was determined to get her back, and finally Lucky was able to persuade Stormy to meet him in a posh downtown San Francisco bar. His intention was to convince his lady that he was a changed man. The lady's intention was to convince the gambler that his luck had just run out. Stormy delivered her message first, and Lucky spit in her carefully made-up face.

"Could I please have a napkin?" Stormy asked, motioning the bartender over. She wiped the spittle from her face, got up, and walked out of Lucky's life forever.

Several months had passed since this incident, when the infamous Lucky moved into the Pine Street building where Hank and I were living. I met him in the basement laundry room. As I loaded my washer, Stormy's ex-lover introduced himself. He was, as had been gossiped, a roguish devil. Over the spin cycle, I decided he was also charming. I knew many people who wanted to spit in Stormy's face.

When his romantic poetry started to appear in my mailbox, I was surprised, titillated, and extremely flattered.

"Okay," I reasoned, "Lucky recently got out of the slammer . . . he's merely lonely. If you'd been locked away with antisocial men for a couple of years, you'd be lonely too."

I quickly reconsidered that train of thought.

When Lucky learned that Hank was working out of town, he started to drop by our apartment for coffee. I saw no harm in these casual visits and believed that I could certainly handle Lucky's little crush. When his conversation strayed into personal areas, I simply brought up my lover's name.

"Thank you for the compliment," I'd say. "Hank always says that. . . ."

After weeks of such rebuffs, the real Lucky Hunt finally stood up. He pushed his coffee cup aside, got out of his chair, and ripped the blue velour boat-neck top off my body. Mercy, that brutish display of sweaty, wanton lust got my attention! I could see what Stormy had found so engaging. I, however, slapped Lucky and asked him to leave—momentarily forgetting his history with firearms. Fortunately, he turned, exited, and never came to the apartment again. It was a closed incident, but I decided not to bother Hank with the details.

During the week, Hank was staying about two hours south of San Francisco. His shoe store had opened a branch in San Jose and sent Hank to manage it. It was important that he accept the responsibility of the new position, but I missed him and lived for the weekends when he came home. When a telegram addressed to Hank was delivered to our apartment one day during the week, I accepted it, tipped the messenger, and reluctantly put the yellow envelope aside for my lover's return. All day I kept looking at that damn unopened telegram. "This could be urgent," I told myself. Maybe his estranged father was sick and calling for the son he hadn't seen in over twenty years. This could be a matter of life and death. The Western Union message beckoned me from across the room. Possibly Hank had been in an accident . . . no, that scenario wouldn't work. If he were dead, he wouldn't be notified by telegram. The suspense was driving me crazy. I ripped open the telegram.

DARLING STOP NO MATTER WHAT YOU'VE DONE STOP I FORGIVE YOU STOP JANET

This *was* a matter of life and death. Somebody in San Jose was going to die!

Before Hank's scheduled weekend return, I made some difficult decisions about our relationship. Friday night, I placed the opened telegram in a noticeable spot, locked the door behind me, and left for work. I had cried enough.

If, as an innocent, I'd arrived in San Francisco on the proverbial "truckload of turnips"—I'd fallen off that truck a long time ago. Two different drivers had run their love trucks over me, and there were tire tracks on my back to prove it. This time, thanks to the telegram, I saw the truck coming. I had no intention of being the hit-and-run victim of yet another lover. Like "the brave Jeanette" in *San Francisco,* I was ready to stand there "amid the ruins" and sing.

Hank was asleep on the sofa when I arrived home. Quietly, I put away my coat, went in, and cleaned my face. Then, ready for bed, I gently awakened Mr. Two-Timin' Foyle.

"Welcome home, Darling." I said sweetly. "I see you found your telegram."

My sleepy lover was overjoyed that I was so calm, detached, and rational. I had taken the time to clean my face before waking him, and because of that Hank believed that I was no longer upset about Janet. Men are so naively trusting of a softly spoken word.

According to Hank, Janet was just some unfortunate, misguided girl toward whom he had shown a little kindness. "Girls like that," he shared, "misinterpret the slightest attention for something more."

I could hardly keep from breaking into a rollicking chorus of Handel's *Messiah.* I'd never heard such heavenly bullshit.

It was my desire to keep home fires burning that made me afraid of a showdown. To most men, a female, if "misguided," slattern in San Jose would appear more appealing than a raging, pre-op, transsexual shrew in San Francisco. Afraid to do otherwise, I welcomed my prodigal lover home from the hills. Soon our life appeared to be back to normal. My surgery date was fast approaching, and on the surface Hank and I were closer than ever. I, however, could not forget that I had been betrayed by the only man I'd ever loved.

It was a beautiful spring morning when, having the same day off from work, Hank and I decided to strike out for wine country. As I stood preparing some of our favorite tidbits, Hank announced that he was going downstairs to borrow an ice chest from Lucky Hunt. I could think of no logical excuse to stop him, and less than an hour later, we set off to explore Northern California's scenic countryside.

"It was nice of Lucky to lend you his ice chest," I ventured after we'd crossed the Golden Gate Bridge and headed into Marin County.

"He's a good guy," Hank agreed.

"But . . . " I quickly cut off the sentence.

"But, what?" Hank obliged.

"I'm surprised that he would loan . . . " I broke off the sentence again. "Promise you won't get mad." With Hank's coaxing, I continued.

"I haven't known how to . . . haven't you ever wondered why I never wear that velour, boat-neck top you liked so much?"

"The blue one?" Hank questioned as he swallowed the bait.

My story came spilling out in a well-rehearsed rush. Hank clutched the wheel with white knuckles. He stared straight ahead as I embroidered details onto the Lucky incident. Over and over, I berated myself for having been so trusting of "a man"—any man. There was a righteousness in my delivery.

"I didn't want you to know about this, Hank," I sighed. "But Lucky . . . well . . . it's because of how he has behaved toward me that I can understand about that poor woman in San Jose. You were right, you don't have to do anything to encourage attention from that kind of person."

There was no reason to mention Janet by name. I was sure Hank could remember her without my assistance. I was also certain that he'd equate his sexual infractions to my meeting with Lucky.

Hank suddenly pulled off the highway and got out of the car. I thought maybe he needed to cool off from the news. Instead, he threw Lucky's ice chest into the weeds of California's wine country.

June 1962 ended with a flurry of activity. In two short weeks, Hank and I would be leaving San Francisco. We could not wait to head south to Los Angeles, my surgery, and our future. In the apartment, everything was boxed and ready. Hank had already quit his job. At the club, with only two weeks remaining on my contract, I gave my notice. Mr. Finocchio promptly called a meeting with my union representative. To my amazement, my spokesman firmly sided with my boss. The American Guild of Variety Artists (AGVA) said I had no choice but to renew my contract.

For years I had heard rumors that the Finocchio family did not readily tolerate the loss of their star performers, but this was going too far! The date was set for surgery, and my union contract had run its course. I was scared; if the backstage gossip were true, I was in trouble. Years ago, the first Mrs. Finocchio reputedly had a performer picked up and jailed when he tried to leave the lineup. The Madam had the hapless impersonator held in a cell until he changed his mind about quitting her show. I didn't want to believe the story. I told myself that the rumor was just queenly chitchat. We were, after all, respected impersonators represented by a major entertainment union.

"If you do not sign a new contract with Mr. Finocchio, I'll see to it that you never work again," my AGVA representative threatened. Years of paying union dues were supposed to guarantee that he'd be on my side.

"This is America!" I shrilled. "You can't do this. I'll change my name if I have to."

"You can't change your Social Security number," the AGVA spokesman spit. "You'll never work again if you walk out in the middle of the tourist season. I'll personally check every Social Security number that comes into our office."

Although intimidated, I turned sharply on my spiked heel and stalked imperiously to the office door. I stood there, glaring at my union arbitrator, waiting for the son of a bitch to remember his manners and open the door for a lady's departure. As Finocchio's blonde star, such high-handed audacity came naturally. In my Madam Bertha red crepe gown, with its bejeweled red satin duster, Lee Shaw swished through that opened door and out of impersonation.

Dawn was just beginning to break as Hank and I hurriedly left San Francisco. We made only one detour on our pilgrimage south. I was determined to throw my hated skullcap off the Golden Gate Bridge and let my hair flow free. And I did.

CHAPTER 5

Alfred, Adieu

"Is it all over?" I asked the recovery room nurse.

"You're fine," she answered. The woman was a mistress of under-statement. I was groggy and disjointed, but I recognized this moment as the milestone of my life. My life began at Westlake Clinic on that day in 1962. Gone was my "birth defect." From this day forward I could react to life emotionally, pursue my own feminine dreams of success, and live as an equal partner with the man I loved. I had been reborn woman. I was free.

That I believed to be true.

My idealized existence was based on my skewed perception of a woman's status in America. I trusted that as a female I would be instantly creditable, acceptable, and understood. Automatically, doors would be opened for me, and society would rush forward to reward my feminin-ity with an honored position in heterosexual society. Why not? I was com-plete. At long last, my excessively submissive nature would earn me respect. By being emotionally fragile, I would now be universally desired, and for being a nurturer, I would be cherished. Surgery was behind me, and so were my years of not belonging. I'd been granted a second chance at life—I could now make a life in the social mainstream.

That I also believed.

Presented with a clean slate, I immediately began to mar it. In those first moments of womanhood, all I wanted was Hank. I hadn't been complete for an hour, and already I was attaching my lifeline to a man. I had no notion of my folly, and the women in my world did not see my error. In the early 1960s, the majority of American women were still per-petuating the archaic myth that without a man, a woman is worthless. Few women had found their stronger voice—and so I was striving des-perately to soften mine. I was eager to recline on a chaise and wait for that special man who would peel me a grape. It would be more than ten years before a feminist friend would inform me, "A woman without a man is like a fish without a bicycle." I did not believe her.

Mother was waiting in my room when I returned from surgery. I was blessed by being born to such a strong, nurturing, and loving woman. I don't believe that she ever consciously let me down. If, unwittingly, she at times let me flounder, it was because even she did not realize she had a right to her own power. Mozelle Gillentine Crenshaw had a great zest for life and expressed it freely. She was beautiful and smart. She was also strong—but in spurts. I believe she was very unhappy in her marriage but terrified of living a life on her own. She was, nonetheless, always threatening to leave.

"Leave! If you want out, go!" Daddy would yell. "But don't think you're taking anything with you."

Mother would continue to sputter, rant, and rave, but she always knuckled under to Daddy's intimidation. The threat of being left to her own devices shook my mother. She could not accept the thought of a life without her home, furnishings, or position.

Mother was often peevish and querulous. Daddy was withdrawn from day-to-day family interaction, but you could always sense his overriding disapproval. The threat of his loud and disruptive outbursts bubbled just beneath the surface of our lives. To survive in our household was to tiptoe across a minefield. Fear of a strident male voice and a habit of buckling upon hearing intimidating male tones grew as I matured. I brought that cowering response with me into my new life. I also came to womanhood mimicking my mother's fear of abandonment. I believed I was starting life over with a clean slate. I was not. All the baggage I had previously accumulated was shipped ahead, C.O.D.

When the anesthesia initially wore off, I came back to the immediate moment with a lurch. I was in agony. There was no escaping the pain. Morphine was prescribed every four hours, but it didn't touch the deep, visceral ache. Nevertheless, I quickly became an avid clock watcher. The morphine made me care less that I hurt, but I had not expected such excruciating pain. In my history there was nothing that could have prepared me for the goddamn mind-numbing agony of ripped tissue and muscle as it attempted to heal—only to be ripped open again by the vaginal dilator that I had to wear. Three times daily the vagina had to be enlarged—after first ripping the cotton gauze padding from the vaginal wall. My surgeon's intention was to create vaginal depth; my raw vagina's objective was to snap shut and heal over. As the doctor packed and repacked my new vagina, they crammed enough cotton padding inside me to resurrect the plantation system in at least two Delta states! The Old South might rise again, but I never would.

In creating vaginal depth, Dr. Elmer Belt skinned the penis, took a skin graft from the bottom of each foot, and removed a six-inch square from the back of my left thigh. The sweltering midsummer heat of Los Angeles added to my misery, and open wounds on my feet and thigh oozed onto rumpled hospital sheets. I gave up and surrendered to my agony.

Hank and my mother were always available during my recovery. Their comforting presence made me feel safe and secure. My pride in Hank hit a new high when, soon after my transition, he took a Westlake Clinic nurse to task for repeatedly expressing her moral objection to "that kind of surgery."

"Don't ever let me hear you say 'that kind of surgery' again," he seethed. "This procedure was not a matter of choice, you know. To those of us who love Aleshia, this surgery was no more elective than an emergency appendectomy." Mozelle echoed his sentiments.

That my mother was staunchly on my side was a tremendous relief. I was aware she'd suffered misgivings concerning my gender transformation. Mother was afraid she'd never be able to refer to her son as "she."

"But, James," my mother wailed over and over as she and Daddy crossed the country to lend support for my surgery, "what if I slip and call him—her Buddy?"

She didn't slip. Not once. From the moment she first spotted me, in my skirt and blouse, waiting at the station to greet them, my mother responded as though I'd always been her daughter.

Before surgery, my total focus had been on my emotional turmoil and the impending surgical changes. After the transformation, I still had emotional and psychological work to do. Surgery did not make me a secure woman. It merely opened the door for me to become one.

Not all my concerns, however, were earth shattering. For one thing, I was curious about the appearance of my vagina. I'd never seen one—and now I had my own. In fact, I had a brand-new one! I'd bought the darn thing sight unseen. I wanted to see exactly what it looked like.

The day after surgery, I asked for a hand mirror and tenderly positioned myself for my first peek at a vagina.

"Good God!" I shrieked, "What have they done to me? This looks like something you'd hang in your smokehouse . . . after a hog killing."

I'd never seen anything so gross. It was swollen, red, and *wrinkled.* The wrinkles looked as though they'd been left behind . . . deliberately. This thing needed to be ironed. Over eleven hours of surgery, pure agony as an aftermath, and I had to be left with a wrinkled vagina? Swelling was expected. I might even accept that it would look a bit beat-up and trampled-on—but not like this! *This* was a disaster! This was no little pink rosebud! This was no delicate scalloped shell from the seashore. *This* was a red, wrinkled Venus's-flytrap! I started to cry, which only made matters worse.

Mother rang for the nurse.

"You're perfectly normal," they both assured me. "That's how you're supposed to look."

Who did they think they were fooling? I was having none of it.

"Like *this*?" I keened.

I'd seen my share of nude female statuary. I hadn't been totally lacking in pubescent curiosity. I even had a fair idea of a vagina's function. This wrinkled thing wasn't going to make it on any countenance. I wanted a neat little split. Something that would translate well in Italian marble or, perhaps, alabaster. I wanted something aesthetically pleasing. This thing had folds! I was suddenly reminded of that unattractive rear view as I herded home the cows.

I was truly upset.

"We'll show you," my mother volunteered.

My mother and Westlake Clinic's charge nurse both lifted their skirts, presenting me a view of not one but two naturally born vaginas. By golly, they did have folds. There were four outer labial folds on each vagina. Satisfied that I was normal, I drifted off to sleep.

My mother had made a long, uphill journey to be standing there, displaying her private parts. The trip couldn't have been easy for her. In Mozelle's world, anything smacking of deviant behavior had always been swept under the rug. To digress from the sexually permissible was to be queer. She, like most of the nation, held homosexuals in very low esteem. They were perverts and child molesters. Mother didn't know any homosexuals, but she knew they were repulsive. I'd seen her in action.

At age eleven, I joined Mother on a bus for a shopping spree in Nashville. As we waited for our return bus trip home, we sat on a wooden bench watching people pass through the Greyhound bus terminal. People watching was a favored pastime, and we generally conducted a running dialogue as the world paraded past. One person, a flamboyant black queen, noticeably stood out from this crowd. Flamboyant didn't cover it. This queen didn't pass through a space; he flounced through, making a grotesque statement about his life in transit.

"Would you look at that?" my mother clucked. "He's so sissy, I bet he squats to pee."

I was mortified. I felt as though my protective cover had been ripped to shreds. I couldn't think of anything to say and sat in silent embarrassment, hating that black queen. I reacted at eleven as so many adult closeted homosexuals have since reacted to the transgendered.

"Don't put that spotlight on me!" I screamed inside my head.

I didn't want to believe I was like that outrageous, disgusting person prancing around the bus station, yet I knew there was somehow a link between that "sissy" and me. It felt like a shameful link. That terrible person was in some way distantly related to me, and I knew it. I'd been called a sissy all my life, and now I knew what one looked like. Surely, everyone in the bus station was aware of our relationship. I couldn't believe that my mother, who knew me so well, could not see the sissy in me. If she ever allowed herself really to look at me, could she still love me?

How could anyone love me? There was the basis for the fear. Because I was not like other boys, I felt I must be despicable. Daddy recognized it. I was sure he saw my difference. In response, I consciously tried to create a boy child who might be worthy of love. Painstakingly, I tried to mimic the acceptable traits of other males around me. I knew, and so did my daddy, that the mimicry was a sham. The child of my creation, the boy child, was not real.

All children fear abandonment by their parents. That is one of our fundamental fears. One of the differences for transsexual children is feeling we have already been abandoned. The person we are is not good enough. To be loved, we must create another person, an acceptable substitute. We do not grow up and change into women. We grow up and change back into what we originally started out to be.

People had never heard of a transsexual until the media created a furor over Christine Jorgensen's gender reassignment. Prior to those shocking headlines, everyone different was labeled *queer*. *Queer* meant you were a degenerate. *Queer* meant you were so sissy you squatted to pee.

Mother had indeed come a long way from rural Tennessee.

That summer of 1962, while everyone was dancing the Watusi, I was in Westlake Clinic doing the Transsexual Twist.

After the packing was removed from the vagina, the next step in my recovery process was the insertion of a full-time plastic dilator. The heavy little torture device was approximately seven inches in length and the circumference of a very healthy cucumber. I called my companion Fred. Getting the dilator out at night was no problem. Cape Canaveral missiles have been launched with less velocity. Coaxing Fred back into his dark, dank home was another story. That was an ordeal. Once he was painfully in place, the trick was keeping him there. A dance belt, Kotex pad, plus elasticized panties were poor restraints for an escape artist like my Fred. To sit was excruciating. As scar tissue attempted to form, Fred's job was to rip it apart.

As I improved, Hank took over my mother's all-night vigils. She would slip away to the Hollywood duplex to bathe, rest, and collect herself; Hank would block my hospital-room door and crawl in bed with me. Having lost forty pounds in two weeks, I was an emaciated, unkempt mess, and far from anyone's sexual fantasy. Hank never acted as though he saw a difference. Not once. He would lie down and hold me on those rumpled, sticky, stinking hospital sheets in the sweltering summer heat.

I adored him for the gesture . . . but couldn't wait for him to go home.

Even after Dr. Belt's suggestion that penetration of the vagina would be a good idea, sex was still not a viable consideration. Every time the doctor brought up the subject, I laughed in his face. *He* was outside, looking into my puffy, painful receptacle—*I* knew the feeling from the inside looking out! Even my daily salt-water douches made me think I was being ripped apart. I could imagine nothing worse than intercourse. Even generally randy Hank seemed less than aroused by the prospect.

After almost two grueling weeks in Westlake Clinic, I was discharged. The sweaty little hospital room was behind me, but home was merely a change of scenery. The non-air-conditioned bungalow was just another steam bath. I still sweated, watched the clock, waited for my medication, and squirmed, trying to find a position that would offer a bit of relief. Slowly moving back and forth from bed to living-room couch, I dragged a catheter bag, tubes, and bottles behind me. I was a walking, sweating, smelly zombie.

Physically, my recovery period at home consisted of two daily, excruciating exercises. First was the continuous and careful dilating of the vagina. Second, but of no less importance, were the sessions designed to encourage my newly positioned urethra to void properly. Three times daily I sat in an empty bathtub and turned on the faucet. The sound of running water created an urgency and overcame my involuntary muscle's fear of voiding. What little physical or emotional strength I had was directed daily toward the proper functioning of my new genitalia. Never tell me I don't know the pain of being a woman.

In the past thirty-nine years, reconstructive surgeons have bettered their surgical techniques and have become more mindful of post-operative pain control. Now, when I hear of a relatively painless transition made by a newly born transsexual sister, I cannot help feeling a twinge of jealousy. In today's world, it is common to hear that a sister has experienced only mild physical discomfort. In response, I feel like an antique who suffered for her gender conversion and then trudged thirty miles through the snow to reach a log schoolhouse!

It was a hard summer for goddesses.

While I suffered my postsurgical hell in a small bungalow off Sunset and Western, across town, in Beverly Hills, my idol Marilyn Monroe struggled with and succumbed to her own demons on August 5, 1962. When she died, I felt as though I'd lost a close, personal friend. In my distress, I also managed to convince myself that Hank no longer wanted to be around me. He never left my side except to go to work, but I concluded that his devotion was all an act. Why would he want to be with someone in my lousy condition? I didn't want to be around myself! An odor trailed after me. I could smell it. I couldn't get away from it. I was having a heavy, fetid discharge from the surgery. I felt ugly, and I took my frustration out on the man closest to me.

"Aleshia, don't be so hard on Hank. Are you trying to drive the boy away?" Mother scolded, preaching the standard Appalachian female line. "You have to give a man some breathing space."

My mother the nurse never lost sight of her goal to get me physically and emotionally strong again. She'd always possessed a gentle, magical touch but had waited until my sister and I were grown before pursuing her interest in nursing. Mother was a very focused and persuasive lady. Now, finding herself in the role of both nurse and mother, she convinced me that if I hoped to save my relationship with Hank, I should return with her to Tennessee.

I did go home again, despite Thomas Wolfe's famous admonition that such a trip was an implausible notion. I flew to Tennessee to recuperate and landed in another dimension. No one outside the family was to know I'd returned home, and except for the minister, no one in town was privy to my surgical transition. As far as the town folk were concerned, Buddy Crenshaw was still a sissy chorus boy in San Francisco. We'd keep it that way. Nothing could be worse than the truth. I'd stay sequestered on our farm, recuperate, and return to Hank without anyone being the wiser.

Miss Minnie Lee, my grandmother, squelched that plan. Although she would have welcomed Alfred Brevard home with open arms, Gran was not happy with the return of Aleshia.

"I believe, Mozelle," she confided, "that this is an impostor. This person is trying to pass herself off as Alfred Brevard."

"For what possible reason?" Mother laughed, trying to dispel Gran's notion.

"For the inheritance," Gran whispered.

My mother never spoke to her mother-in-law again. That didn't keep my grandmother from "outing" me at her beauty shop.

"I needed to share this burden with those who care most about me," Gran later grumbled to Daddy.

The story ignited like a barn burning. Our phone would ring at all hours, and an unidentified voice would ask, "Is Buddy there?" Our seldom-traveled country road became a curiosity seeker's thoroughfare. Cars would idle by, toot, and speed off. The more brazen country sightseers parked by the side of the road, waiting for a glimpse of the home-grown oddity. I could have sold picnic lunches—the rednecks would have eaten that up. The insensitive invasion was hard on the entire family.

Mama and Granddaddy Gillentine, Mother's parents, drove three hundred miles from East Tennessee just to lend their support. By the time they arrived, my nerves were frayed. When my grandparents pulled into the curved driveway at Twin Elm Place, I was in the upstairs bathroom, nervously applying layer after layer of mascara to false eyelashes. I was scared witless.

"Where's Rosy?" Granddaddy's voice boomed as he came through the front door. "Where's Rosy?"

"Rosy" was upstairs pearling her lashes.

I'd earned the nickname when I was about three years of age. My mother had again run home to her parents, and the grandparents were playing baby-sitters while my feuding parents slipped away to a movie. All went well until Baby Buddy woke up. When I found my parents gone, nothing would quiet me. I was inconsolable. I squalled until Grandaddy dressed me in Aunt Bobby Jean's skirt, put a red hair ribbon in my curls, and called me Rosy. When my parents returned from the movie, they found their three-year-old "Rosy" dancing up and down the stairs. I was entertaining the entire family.

"Where's Rosy?" Granddaddy now boomed as he came through the door. I don't know that I ever properly thanked him for that kindness.

While madness reigned in Hartsville, Hank was in Hollowood working at a gas station on Sunset Boulevard. To finance coming to me in Tennessee, he had a second job painting houses. Unfortunately, most of what he earned was spent on AT&T—predivestiture. I waited greedily for his calls. I missed Hank desperately. I missed him so much that I possibly ached—in my condition, who could tell!

Although he assured me he was earning money and we'd soon be together, I knew Hank. This was the same man who'd pawned our blender in order to send a beautiful Bird of Paradise arrangement to me in the hospital. Hank would never change.

When we'd arrived in Hollywood for my surgery date, finding work was difficult for Hank. Rather than upset me, he lied and said he'd found a job. Every morning I proudly saw my man off to work. Once out of my sight, Hank spent his day looking for a job or sitting on a bench in the park. Unfortunately, Hank's misplaced sensitivity did not pay our bills. There was a decided downside to the man I loved. His way was to delay facing the truth until he could postpone it no longer. He knew his half-truths would boomerang, but he always attempted to paint a brighter picture.

By the time he finally found a job pumping gas on Sunset Boulevard, we'd eaten up almost everything we'd saved toward surgery. I had to beg money from my parents.

Now, with surgery behind me and my lover alone in California, there was only one thing to do: go *shopping*! My after-five glitz did not wear well in Tennessee—and I was determined never again to don boys' clothing.

Physically, I was incapable of much walking, but Mother and I slipped away to Nashville for a short shopping spree. Even there I was spotted by a Hartsvillian. She was the daughter of my grandmother's beautician.

"I knew it was Buddy," she reported. "I only saw him from behind, but I could tell. He was with Mozelle, and I recognized the walk. You know, that sorta sway Buddy has to his hips? Oh, I knew right away."

Bitch! For all those years, I had thought my James Dean saunter was successfully camouflaging my telltale swish.

That shopping spree again confined me to the farm. Mother and I did make one side trip. We went to see Edith, the wonderful black woman who had practically raised me. When I was a child, Edith and her husband, Alex, lived on the farm in a tenant cabin. Edith was my second mother. It was to "Ed-ee" I'd take my Santa Claus list, so she could fly it up her chimney. Once she accidentally burned the list, but I totally believed her explanation that elves hiding in the flue had read the list before it burst into flame. Ed-ee was quick on her feet. Most of all, it was the fanciful stories of her youth that captivated me. I would listen with my mouth hanging open while Edith told tall tales of the Deep South.

"One afternoon, Baby, I was a-sleepin' on the Arkansas side of the Mississippi River . . . when a big ol' tornado come down. It picked Ed-ee up, Child, and deposited me, plum smack-dab on the other side of Ol' Muddy. Laid me down, gentle as you please, in Tennessee."

That, as she told it, was where her troubles began. Edith met Alex in Tennessee.

By the 1960s, Edith and Alex had left the farm for the "colored section" of town. In a still strongly segregated South, they'd built a home on "the hill." For over a century, the precarious economic and cultural framework of small agricultural towns in the South had dictated strict racial and social boundaries. Despite Supreme Court rulings, nothing had really changed.

Until leaving home, I hadn't understood that another way of life existed. Where I grew up, children from "the better families" did not associate with poor white children or with those from other races. That was the strongly restricted world into which I'd been born. I'd never questioned it, even though Edith, when she first moved to the farm, tried to help me understand.

"Child, you can call me colored," she said shaking her finger in my face, "you can call me a Negro, but don't you *ever* call me a nigger!"

I had no idea what Ed-ee was talking about. For me, there was no difference in the words. I was strongly aware, however, that my new friend heard an important distinction. My love for Edith was enough to make me careful of the words I chose.

Mother and I went to "the hill" thinking we could be of help to Edith, who was recuperating from her second heart attack. As usual, it was Ed-ee who took care of us. Seeing me in a size twelve gray wool sheath did not phase Edith, but the cruel reaction of my hometown did disturb her. I was still "Ed-ee's honey-child."

"Oh, Baby," Edith whispered. "Your ol' Ed-ee sure wishes she could get up out of this bed. Child, I'd take your hand and we'd go down that hill to town. We'd show that white trash what a real lady looks like."

I turned to my mother. "Are you ready to go to town?" I asked.

"Anytime you are," Mother said.

Edith smiled up at us proudly from her goose-down pillows.

"You know," she said, "you've always been my favorite white folks."

Mother and I drove off the hill and headed for town. It was a short distance in miles, but it was a tremendous journey for me.

Mother parked in front of the courthouse square; I squared my shoulders, and marched into Vaught's drugstore to buy a wand of mascara. Mother, as always, was right behind me.

With my significant purchase accomplished, we left the drugstore. I should have taken time to thank the proprietress. As my drag ex-coworkers would have expressed it, "Honey, that woman didn't drop a stitch." Miss Patsy treated me like any other welcome customer. Outside the drugstore, however, the sidewalks were filling with curious onlookers. No one said anything, not that I remember, but by the time we left the store I had emotionally removed myself from reality. In a daze I walked, toe-heel, down that small-town sidewalk, never looking right or left. I didn't see one face. Everyone was a blur, but still it seemed we'd never reach the end of that block. It was like leading a parade. People kept coming out of the stores behind us as we made that long, long walk. The townspeople filled the sidewalk behind us and unabashedly gawked.

Just before we reached our car, someone approached and hugged me. It was the preacher from the family church. His name was Brother Doaks. In the Church of Christ, the ministers are called "Brother"—for some fundamental reason I've forgotten.

"I think you're very brave," he said as he hugged me. We talked briefly about my well-being.

"If you don't feel up to coming back to church quite yet," he soothed, "I'm sure the good Lord will understand."

I went to church because of my respect for the preacher. A few members of the little congregation went out of their way to make me feel welcome—I fondly remember Miss Hale, who never failed to compliment my appearance. This compassionate lady would chase me down the broken sidewalk in order to say a few kind words. Otherwise, Sunday-go-to-meeting was a nightmare. I can still see a distant cousin peering through a crack between the church doors. That Sunday he was acting as usher and voyeur. The Peeping Tom was in his fifties, old enough to know better, but he wasn't alone in his unbridled curiosity. An old schoolmate came perilously close to toppling backward into the churchyard while trying to navigate the church steps, handle her newborn, and catch a glimpse of the town's first transsexual. Getting close to the Lord, for those who differ, can be a nerve-wracking ordeal.

Shortly before our birthdays, solace finally arrived on a bitterly cold December night. I'd been by the window all day, impatiently waiting for Hank. I wanted him safely home before the predicted blizzard. When I saw the headlights of our old 1937 Cadillac sweep over the hill, I let out a yelp and bolted through the door. Mother was right behind me.

Snowflakes were swirling around us as we stood there clutching each other, but Hank and I were oblivious to the cold. Tears streamed down our faces.

"You two can cry in the house," Mother scolded through her own tears. "Get inside. You'll catch your death out here. Aleshia, you're in your house slippers, for goodness sake. Hank, make her come inside. Come on. Let's get inside to the fire. I'm freezing if you're not."

That year we had a jubilant country Christmas—Mother and Daddy, my sister and her husband, and Hank finally home with me. That holiday season everyone got along beautifully. This was the family unity I'd always wanted.

Hank's presence stemmed much of the community's negativity toward me. It was the same story all over again. Hank was a handsome, brown-eyed, strapping six-three figure of a man. Because Hank was seen as a man, I was allowed to be a woman.

"This glorious male specimen is sticking around," the townspeople seemed to say, "so perhaps Buddy isn't a boy after all."

With Hank Foyle in it, my life was easier on all fronts. People were less obtrusive—and in some cases exceptionally accepting. On one Sunday's trip to church, Hank and I stopped at a gas station operated by the parents of the currently reigning Miss Trousdale County. Hank got his gas, went inside to pay, and returned to the car beaming his lopsided grin.

"I just want you to know," the beauty queen's mother had said, "that you're with the prettiest girl this county ever produced."

What a kindness that thoughtful lady offered Hank! I have no doubt this proud mother considered her daughter the most deserving beauty queen Trousdale County ever crowned, yet she was generous with her praise at a time when Hank and I both needed it. Would that all people could be so kind. Issues of clouded gender often frighten and challenge the uninitiated, yet there are always those who go to great lengths to be accepting.

Life was becoming tolerable. Now, when I walked down the town's main sidewalk, Hank was beside me.

"Hold up your head, Baby. Be proud," he'd say. "You're the prettiest thing this town's ever goin' to see." Hank gave me courage. His presence also gave me great pride.

Edith had been moved from her home into the local clinic. Her condition was worsening. Hank and I often stopped by to see her, and Edith was always her delightful, up-tempo self. She'd taken to "that handsome gentleman," as she called Hank, immediately. When, after our first visit, it was time to go, he bent down and kissed Edith on her cheek.

On our next visit, Edith was all aglow with the news.

"Lord, Child, you'll never believe what happened after you two left," she chuckled. Several of the nurses had rushed into Edith's room to kiss her cheek.

"I just want to put my lips where that handsome man put his," one nurse had giggled.

Hank beamed; I fumed.

Around the farm, Hank continued to display the qualities I found so beguiling. When, one frosty morning, a gaggle of tenant farm children came to the well to fetch water, Hank was appalled that they had no jackets. They were a regular ragtag group of poor kids. Hank, hit hard by the reality of their poverty, went to his closet and brought each child a cardigan sweater. Hank prided his cardigan collection and had gone to great lengths to find just the right colors and fabrics. Now, he gave them away.

"If I ever see you kids here and you're not wearing one of these sweaters," Hank bullied the runny-nosed kids, "I'm goin' to kick your butts."

The kids were impressed almost as much as I.

His heart was in the right place, but still Hank didn't cut it as a farm-hand. As long as I had known him, he'd bragged about his ability to drive in the snow. With our first snow, Hank promptly drove the old Cadillac into a ditch. The farmhands brought a mule to pull the stuck vehicle from the ditch, but again, Hank's big heart got the best of him. As the mule strained and pulled, the animal began to perspire. In the cold morning air the perspiration froze, and icicles started to form on the mule. Hank could tolerate no more.

"Put the goddamn horse back in the barn where it's warm," he blurted.

"This city boy don't know the difference between a mule and a horse," the tenant farmers laughed. "This city boy would let his car stay in a ditch rather than discomfort a dumb-ass mule."

For a short time Hank remained the brunt of the neighborhood joke, but his charisma and affability eventually won everyone over. Every-one was charmed—except my father. As a result of Daddy's religious training, he saw everything in very definite terms. His Bible spoke in absolutes. Everything was good or bad, black or white. Unfortunately, I had been decidedly gray for a long time. Now, with Hank, Daddy had two gray beings on his hands. Daddy thought us "crazy as hell."

The return of my health caused another problem. Hank and I had been a couple since first sleeping together, had shared an extremely physical relationship, and now wanted again to share a bed. Daddy could not permit it. If we closed the door to Hank's room, one of my par-ents was likely to walk in without knocking. We had no time alone. The time had come for us to return to our way of life. Unfortunately, we had no money. Since coming to Tennessee, Hank had worked on the farm doing whatever there was to be done, but no money was ever involved.

"To be around Aleshia, that boy will work for a roof over his head and a few packs of cigarettes," Daddy joked to my mother. To my parents, this was not a favorable trait.

Then, to make a bad situation worse, Hank proceeded to blow the job my mother had found him in a posh Nashville shoe store.

"It's an eighty-mile drive every day, Aleshia!" he complained. "Besides, I don't have the right clothes to work in a store like that."

I understood exactly what he was feeling but was alone in my empathy. My parents had no tolerance for such behavior. In my family there were no excuses; one merely did what has to be done. That I also understood. That's how I'd been raised. Mother set the example by doing whatever was necessary for our survival, and that was how things remained. Daddy, with his lack of ambition, always had trouble measuring up to his wife's resolve. In this case, however, Daddy was Hank's greatest detractor.

So Hank, not having whatever it took to face me or my family and tough it out, pretended that he had taken the shoe-store job. Hank, too, was following his habitual inclination. The ax fell when Mother and I dropped by to see him at work. He wasn't there, nor had he ever been. That was that! Hank was ordered to leave Twin Elm Place.

I was shattered.

Hank had arrived in Tennessee bearing a treasure that he shared freely. It was his acceptance of others. He loved people for what they were rather than what he assumed they were supposed to be. My entire family, each member in his or her own way, was a recipient of Hank's gift. He perceived and loved me as the woman I needed to be. My sister, Jeanne, remembers Hank making her feel good about herself when she was pregnant, feeling awkward and unattractive. Hank also made no judgments about Jeanne's husband, although a negative stance would have found much favor with my parents. To Hank, my father was master of his home, and as such, his beliefs were respected; to my mother he accorded the affection and love she deserved. The unquestioning acceptance that Hank brought into our home was a gift the Crenshaw household desperately needed.

We let him down. Instead of loving Hank for what he brought to us, he was judged for what he did not have to offer. He was a joyful, loving man, but that was not enough; he also had to be a stable provider. As a man, he was supposed to stand his ground and make things happen. To earn my family's approval, any man must be the whole traditional package—and that Hank was not capable of being. Recognition of my own failures only caused me to love the imperfect Hank more.

I begged, I pleaded, but the pronouncement was final. Hank had to leave. He would return to Asheville, North Carolina, the place of his birth—without me! He couldn't take the old Cadillac; the tires were ruined and we had no money to replace them. Most of his clothes he left behind. Nothing, none of it, made any sense. On the day of his departure, I drove Hank to the crossroads that would take him away from me. The cursed junction was located at Paine's General Store.

My life was ending, and I could feel nothing. Perhaps if I beat my hands against my own head, this lunacy would suddenly make some sense. I wanted to strike out, but nothing in my universe was solid enough to hit. Nothing would solidify. I prayed to find some new argument, some way of coping with this insanity. I couldn't think. I couldn't feel. I was numb. The essence of my being was being taken away, and I was totally helpless to stop his going. Nothing stuck together. It seemed as though I was moving in slow motion—as though I were living in a trance induced by very high fever.

As Hank and I approached Paine's Store and the crossroads, I searched for an answer.

"I'll leave the car here. I'll hitchhike to Asheville with you," I blurted out. "We'll leave together. We'll just leave Mother's car and go."

Hank would not even consider my last desperate option.

"You're not strong enough, Baby," he said. "Besides, it's too dangerous. Having you with me on the road hitching would cause the wrong people to stop. I can't protect us both. It's too dangerous."

Bless his beautiful blind spot. Hank believed what he was saying. He'd always believed it. The image he'd formed of me that first night at

Finocchio's, as he sat watching me remove my red knit sweater, still remained intact. That enticing image was what Hank still saw in me. Sometimes, out driving, he would pull off the road, take my face in his hands, and just look at me. To Hank Foyle, I was the most desirable of beings. Basking in his loving appraisal, I could almost believe I was the woman he saw.

"Do me one favor," Hank asked as we approached the intersection. "Let me out, drive off, and don't look back. Please. Don't look back, Aleshia. I don't think I could stand that."

I let Hank step from my mother's car and out of my life. He stood there at the side of the road, both of us unabashedly sobbing. He turned and motioned me away. As directed, I turned the car around and drove away. My heart was breaking; I could hardly see to drive; but I did not turn to look back. I did not know if I would ever see him again, but I did know that he loved me. I drove toward home, watching in the rearview mirror as Hank Foyle faded away.

CHAPTER 6

The Coed

THAT A love cannot exist makes it no less a love.

After leaving Hank hitchhiking on the side of the road at Paine's Store, I rushed home to beg Mother for enough money to follow him. "Just let me be with him," I implored. "That's all I want. Please!"

In retrospect, I'm sure my mother shared my desperation. I must have hurt her deeply with my willingness to forsake her, the family, and life as I'd always known it for a man. I could only see that Mother was deserting me. I believed her oblivious to my pain. On my knees, I begged Mozelle to help me go to the person I loved most in the world. She would not relent.

Hank had left Twin Elm Place, but he called every night from North Carolina. It distressed my parents that he remained in my life. Their plan to separate us was not working. It only made me want him more. We were Romeo and Juliet, victimized by society and family. My gallant was staying with a friend, saving money so we could get married, and I applauded his every move. To my parents, my lover was the worse kind of blackguard, and their excessively emotional child was totally under his spell. Daddy decided to find out more about Hank Foyle.

"And the son of a bitch is living with a woman in Asheville," Daddy finally announced, "His *friend*, Aleshia, is some woman who lives in a house trailer. I guess she's the one keeping him up now."

I could find no more words for Hank's defense.

This man for whom I was willing to sacrifice my family, the man I could not live without, had put me in an indefensible position. His infidelity left me speechless, yet I was not totally surprised. I knew Hank. Without me to pull in his reins, my man was definitely capable of acting rashly. He'd proven that with Janet in San Jose.

"I never want to see him again," I blurted. It was a lie, but I couldn't think of anything else to say.

They were the very words my family was waiting to hear. They quickly dispatched me to my grandparents in Erwin, Tennessee, before I changed my mind—or before Hank could change it for me. I went gladly. My only choice was to save face, put on a convincing show, and wait until Hank came to rescue me. Now, when it was too late, I realized that I was a fool for not getting Hank's phone number or address in North Carolina. My parents had forbidden my contacting him, and as always, I'd respected their wishes. My romantic union was not unconquerable after all, but I would be more careful in the future—if we had a future. Sometimes love alone is not enough to keep a coupling intact.

In the following weeks, my lover called, sent telegrams, and wrote letters to me at Twin Elm Place—and I was three hundred miles away.

"Aleshia's not here," my parents said to Hank when he called. "She never wants to see you again." When I called Mother to see if Hank had called, my mother said she'd heard nothing. To my parents, Hank Foyle was a closed chapter.

I unraveled.

My obsession was too much for my mother's family. They thought I was crazy. In the South, good families do not lock away their mentally deranged—they display us in the parlor for all to see. Every family needs its resident loony—I was it. I longed for Hank so hard that I began seeing him. I'd glance out a window and see him quickly slip behind a tree. He'd come to get me. He was never there.

When I'd made my transition into womanhood less than a year before, Hank and I had shared such high hopes. Everything was going to be perfect. Now, I was a woman alone. I was again in the town of my birth, and more disjointed than when I'd lived there as a boy. Each new day brought a heightened state of desperation. Had I never known the joy of being with him, I could have stood his absence. Life without him was now intolerable.

When my deteriorating emotional state was reported to my parents, they rushed to Erwin, bringing Hank's telegrams and letters with them. They did not know what else to do.

Hanks first letters were mailed from Asheville, North Carolina, and in them he proclaimed his innocence. The woman with whom he'd been accused of sleeping was merely a friend—someone willing to help him save enough money to marry me. I didn't know who to believe. At this point it didn't matter. I would have forgiven him anything.

His second batch of letters came from Atlanta, Georgia. Their message was much the same. The last batch of letters Hank mailed from New Orleans, Louisiana. Hank Foyle was moving farther and farther away from me.

"Darling, Hank," I wrote, as soon as I'd finished reading his last letter, "this has gone far enough. Please come get me."

My short, desperate plea was returned unread. On the envelope, the United States Postal Service had stamped, "Moved/no forwarding address."

Something shriveled inside me. I needed advice. If any member of my family could understand my panic, surely it would be my uncle Jack. With his extraordinary good looks and mischievous sense of the absurd, he'd long been the Gillentine family's favorite black sheep. By our mountain community's definition, Uncle Jack put Clark Gable to shame. In everyone's estimation, my uncle was a gorgeous rake. Surely, my mother's youngest brother would understand the intensity of my feelings. Jack could empathize.

"If you cared anything about this family," Jack scoffed when I approached him, "you'd have killed yourself before bringing this mess home."

Damn! Black sheep are romantic only if they're brown-eyed handsome men.

In 1963, the State of Tennessee altered my birth certificate to officially list Aleshia Brevard Crenshaw a naturally born female. Legally, I could get on with my life. Unfortunately, I'd never planned further than becoming Mrs. Hank Foyle.

Not knowing what else to do, I enrolled as an art major at East Tennessee State University. That fall semester also marked the transition of East Tennessee State College to university status. It was a new beginning for us both. For my first day as a coed, I dressed carefully in a striking knit dress and, of course, spike heels. For good measure, I snuggled into one of my stage corselets. Even without the corselet, I proudly maintained more than a ten-inch differentiation between my waist and ample, forty-two-inch hips. The Finocchio's stage corselet, however, could whittle a girl's waistline down to nothing. I wanted a waspish silhouette.

As a teenage boy, full hips had proven an embarrassment; now I worked diligently to keep that waist/hip differentiation. I had yet to develop the proud bustline to which I aspired. In the meantime, there was always Frederick's of Hollywood. My brassiere featured a compartment that could be inflated to the appropriate size. If your contouring left something to be desired—huff, puff, and blow up your chest.

That first day, as I toe-stiletto-heeled it into the new university's student center, pandemonium broke out. There were wolf whistles, and a few guys even crawled on their tables for a better look. Was I expected to take an encore or run from the room in tears? I had no idea what real college girls did when boys got rowdy. The attention was embarrassing—but very exciting. Wolf whistles are not something a proper young lady would encourage. I loved them! I was going to enjoy higher education.

"May I join you?" A rather collegiate-looking kid asked as he approached my table. Bill was president of the student body. He'd come to apologize for the unruly welcome I'd received.

"When did y'all arrive?" he drawled politely.

"Y'all?" I questioned.

"Aren't you with the orchestra?"

Because I didn't look like East Tennessee coeds, the rowdy boys jumped to the conclusion that I was on campus for the new university's celebration dance. They thought I was a big-band singer! The corselet might have been overkill.

"Would you like to come to the dance with me?" Bill asked. "I will be greeting people and playing host, so I hadn't intended to take a date. But if . . . "

I jumped at his offer.

"Hey, folks! Look what I snagged," I'd yell as I came through the front door. "I'm off to the university prom with the president of the student body." My family would then see that this was no Hank Foyle without two cents in his pocket. They'd be impressed. They might even foolishly believe that I was over Hank.

The family reacted the way I'd expected. The lesson was clear. If I intended to be a real girl, I was expected to hook an enterprising mate.

It wasn't a bad ball, as college dances go, but I'd never seen so much white tulle in my life. I thought I was dazzling in my strapless black sheath with its over-one-shoulder, floor-length panel. The gown had seen its share of Finocchio's production numbers, but who was going to know that? I wore black full-length opera gloves, and onyx earrings rested on my exposed shoulders. Everywhere I looked I was surrounded by would-be-virgin white. I stood out like a black widow spider on a bouquet of white carnations.

"Oh, you can't believe this girl who's going to State," one coed told my uncle Jack after the dance. "She's a true whore. They say that's how she makes her living."

"Really?" Jack mused.

"Yes. Everybody knows it," she giggled. "Can you stand it? She's dating the student body president! It's a scandal."

"I believe it," Jack wagged. "She's my favorite niece." My uncle was finally on my side.

Even Jack's approval did not save me from having to leave my grandparents' home. Accidentally, I broke another rule.

The young man who sold tickets at Erwin's Trailways bus station was reputedly queer. The boy might have merely been effeminate, but it was his difference that branded him. He did not fit the Appalachian male norm. I knew the boy only from purchasing tickets for bus rides to the university, but I found him a breath of fresh air. He was sweet and soft-spoken. In a provincial mountain community, those qualities were damning for a boy.

One afternoon, sitting on the steps of my grandparents' home, I called out a greeting as the young ticket salesman walked past. He seemed surprised by my acknowledgment but stopped to chat. The meeting was less than sinister. Such easy neighborliness, in fact, was one of the attractions the mountain community held for me. I adored the pine-covered highlands, but I truly loved the down-home friendliness of the mountain people. Their warmth was not, however, extended to the effeminate young man. He was being effectively shunned.

"Everyone in town knows him for what he is," my generally warm-hearted grandfather said. "You can't be seen talking to him."

"Rosy's" grandfather saw no irony in his pronouncement, and I could not let the matter drop. Even though the soft local boy was merely a passing acquaintance, I refused to be part of his ostracism. I was not being courageous, nor was I a crusader; it was simply impossible for me to pretend alliance with the homophobic community. The issue was far too personal. I left my grandparents' home and found a room a few blocks from East Tennessee State University, fourteen miles away in Johnson City.

Heterosexual womanhood was not the bliss I'd anticipated. In only twenty-three months, I'd lost my lover, offended my family, and left behind a California community where I'd found comfort. Alone in my new room, I cried every day.

Thirty-eight years later, I no longer accept the emotional upheaval of those first female years as being totally of my own design. I blame instead the large doses of hormones I'd ingested by 1963. The mood swings had become almost predictable. If not cyclical, they were monthly mood swings that, from great peaks of joy, slid into deep valleys of despair. I'd always been excitable, but I'd now lost all control over my behavior. There were too many things about my transgendered body that I did not understand. I even feared I might differ internally from genetically born women and was afraid an X ray might expose my dark gender secret. Was it true that women had one more rib than their male counterparts? Sunday school had insisted it was true. I didn't think that possible but wouldn't chance being wrong. My past at all cost must be kept secret. In the hands of a small-town, gossipy doctor, my transgendered past might make me more an outcast than the unfortunate ticket-sales boy in Erwin. Medical questionnaires filled me with dread. An incorrect response concerning the date of my last period might cause a doctor to look at me negatively or to ask more embarrassing questions. I no longer had doctors to whom I could turn for help. Drs. Belt and Benjamin had been left behind in California. Few physicians in the country had any sound medical understanding of my uniqueness, and fear of discovery overrode my desire for clinical help. Finding a doctor I would trust with my secret was an ongoing issue for the remainder of my closeted female life.

It was Thanksgiving, and I was in one of my depressed states, when I read an article stating that Blue Bell morning glory seeds were hallucinogenic.

"What a trip," I thought. I bought a packet of morning glory seeds and went to a holiday party. Hank was no longer around to curb my self-destructive tendencies. Near the end of the Thanksgiving bash, my gullet filled with seeds and stoned out of my gourd, I collapsed in the lap of a stranger. In my morning glory glow, nestling in his lap, I accepted the newcomer as totally trustworthy. My eyes brimmed to overflowing; mascara dripped off my chin; and I spilled my entire gender history. Maybe this stranger could make my pain go away.

Rather than a soul mate, my stranger turned out to be a felon on furlough for Thanksgiving holiday.

"This can be our little secret," he told me later in his bed. "I don't say nothin', you don't say nothin', who's the wiser?" Now that I was no longer hallucinating, I winced as I realized that he did not bear the slightest resemblance to Hank Foyle.

"This ain't nobody's business, Sweetheart. Believe me, I know how to keep a secret. I don't want nobody to know, neither. However—so you don't 'forget' me, you understand . . . " He paused for effect. "When I want you, Bitch, you better be here. Got me?"

Post-op transsexuals generally go through a compulsive gender exposé period. After transformation, many of us tend to seek the validation that we are complete, desirable, and lovable. My "tell-all" stage lasted until I decided that if genetic women see no reason to discuss what makes them female—then neither did I.

My escape from the felon was plotted by my longtime friend Joyce Nordquist. She'd been my friend since I first hitchhiked to California and taught at Arthur Murray's Dance Studio. Early in my Murray's training period, the dance studio's door opened and in walked a statuesque blonde goddess with the most perfectly shaped head I'd ever seen.

"My God, Kim Novak lives," I gasped.

On the basis of our mutual narcissism, we became fast friends. Joyce and I were also marvelous dance partners—she had a strong lead and I followed divinely!

In spite of my lifestyle change, the bond with Joyce Nordquist remained as strong as ever. Now, while vacationing east, my dear friend was stopping to visit me in East Tennessee. From the moment her plane began circling the Tri-Cities Airport, she was appalled by my Appalachian highlands.

"I had no idea I'd be landing in a cow pasture," she announced in the airport waiting room. "Did they wave the plane in with a coal-oil lantern?"

Granted, Joyce had missed the glory of the rhododendron that blooms, pink and white, in the spring. She had never witnessed the magical moment in October when an entire mountain chain bursts into orange flame. My friend was willing to take my word for the grandeur. If it meant sticking around Appalachia, she wasn't interested in seeing the mountain magnificence for herself. The natives made her nervous.

One afternoon, as we trudged the cracked sidewalks of the college town, Joyce announced she'd be much happier sipping a cocktail. Stylish in her Los Angeles attire, with her hair in a French twist, and appearing the personification of every Hitchcockian heroine of the 1960s, she was anticipating a posh little watering hole. There was none in Johnson City. We ended up at the Trailways bus station, where we ordered two fountain sodas and lapsed into deep discussion—totally unaware that Joyce had caught the eye of an East Tennessee bus-station swain. Joyce was strikingly beautiful, blonde, and sophisticated, yet the rube felt he was the manly answer to her prayers. Wanting to get her attention, he hitched his shabby trousers up around his waist and slyly placed a praying mantis on my friend's arm.

He got her attention.

The mountain man grinned his snaggletooth grin, giggled, and sidled out of the bus station. He was as pleased with himself as if he'd stolen his first kiss. The hillbilly meant no harm. Possibly, in his mountain "holler" back behind Possum Ridge, such an antic had once won him a sweetheart. A mountain lass of twelve or thirteen might well have been delighted by his manly attentions. Joyce was horrified. The charm of our more bemused mountain folk totally evaded her.

The misty mountains of Tennessee and the sun-washed shores of California are separated by more than miles of desert and cactus. I wanted my fundamentalist family to hear that, beyond our limestone ridges, few people actually believed their original grandparents had lived in a lush garden, produced two sons, and damned the world to torment. I thought my family would be fascinated by the news.

"Joyce, why don't you share your religious views with my folks?" I suggested, trying to get a meaningful dialogue started.

"Well, being an atheist . . . ," Joyce began.

The room fell silent.

Grandmother Gillentine rose deliberately from her chair and sought the safety of her kitchen.

With one godless word, my friend had established herself as a heathen. My family shut down. A ghoul had come to Tennessee to prey upon Aleshia, their perennial innocent. Joyce was their worse nightmare. No one understood that I had, quite literally, placed my own ass in the hands of an unscrupulous felon. To their way of thinking, the worst thing that could happen to me was to lose my faith.

It was Joyce who came to my rescue. She would not leave me to wither in a backwater abyss.

"But what about college?" I lamented. My fear of leaving home sent me scurrying for any excuse.

"There are some pretty good universities in the West, you know."

Joyce, in addition to being the smartest person I knew, was also the nicest. Promptly, she traded in her remaining vacation airfare for two tickets to California. Aside from facing my irate mother, the only remaining obstacle was that our California flight left from Chicago's O'Hare Airport. We didn't have enough money to get to Chicago.

Accepting that one man's intentions are much like those of another, I aimed my developing charms at a door-to-door salesman. He was overjoyed to drive me away from the protective eye of my family. Joyce and I had a ride to Chicago.

Until the very end, my mother tried to keep me safely by her side. She fervently believed I could be happy there. I wished that were possible; I knew it was not. I'd tried pretending that transsexual surgery had not changed my life. My self-imposed amnesia was a miserable failure. Living among the people with whom I'd spent my early life made it impossible for me to be myself. My family was more comfortable with my true history buried. No one wanted to say the wrong thing, so they said nothing. It was an extremely trying time for everyone. Only in my heart and at Finocchio's had I been a girl. Buddy, the external boy, was the only me the Tennessee relatives had ever known—until I quite suddenly came home a female. Everyone now struggled to understand and accept Aleshia. The resulting tension made my transition all the more difficult. Yet they united to form a protective fortress around me. I sensed that my gender transition was a family embarrassment, but my loyal relatives were unconditionally loving and supportive.

Rather than some misguided felon intent on blackmailing me, I was fleeing my mother and her family's protection. Because of my desire for their acceptance, I couldn't tell them I still needed to learn what it meant to be a woman. I was desperate for those I loved to accept my gender choice as the right one for me. It was important that my loved ones be proud of me. My mother had always been the most important person in my life, but now my survival depended on our separation.

Mother stood on the curb waving goodbye until our car was out of sight. I was headed for Chicago and points west. I was leaving my mountain home to find myself.

CHAPTER 7

Burlesque Queen

I WAS back in California, with no male attachments—not even my own. Now, far away from family scrutiny, I was spreading my fledgling female wings. I wasn't flying high and free.

Since returning to California, I'd been staying with Joyce in her small apartment in Pasadena-Home-of-the-Rose-Bowl, California. I slept on her sofa. I'd even found a particularly unrewarding sales position at the Broadway department store. If this was a normal existence, I wasn't thrilled at the prospect of long life. Give me my gold-plated watch, let me die, and the Broadway could continue on its profit-driven way.

In-house personnel were my problem. If my Broadway superiors represented capitalism at work, where were those dreaded communists we kept hearing about? It was 1964, I was in a cold war with bureaucracy, and, personally, I hoped that the Russians were coming. The Broadway's bourgeoisie were too self-important for my taste. My immediate supervisor in particular needed to get over her shopkeeper mentality and give me a rest. The woman had no idea of the difficulty involved in my getting to the job. I wasn't a woman who could roll out of bed, run a comb through her hair, and head for work. An ex–drag queen needs a lot of preparation to face the day.

Finding my place in society was important, but my immediate goal was to escape haberdashery. Mercantilism was simply not that important in the overall scheme of things. Young men were dying in Vietnam, the world was falling apart, and yet the Broadway insisted that I kowtow to in-house hierarchy. Life as a shop girl is a far cry from that of a drag diva.

Although male-to-female transsexuals should never attempt to drag male privilege into their new lives, it comes as a shock to discover that you have been socially demoted. Before surgery, I'd been so overwhelmed by my unhappiness that I'd failed to notice I was not alone in my fight for acceptance. The fact that women were treated as second-

109

drunk as a loon and pinned against his car door, I still thought it important that he not think ill of me.

"It's not you," I assured him as again I removed his hand from my breast. "It's my fault. I'm afraid of sexual intimacy. It's me, don't you see? I don't want you to think that you've done anything wrong."

With that, I proceeded to explain the reason I was afraid of fornication. I still had a compulsive urge to purge myself.

I had found the key that unlocked the door to his car.

Safely inside the apartment, and tucked in for what remained of a misspent evening, I was awakened by a loud pounding on the door.

"Oh, hell!" I thought. "He's come back." I decided not to answer the door.

"Shoot," I moaned as I pulled the pillow from over my head, "I've got to stop that racket. Joyce is sleeping in the next room."

I left my bed, stumbled to the front door, and found Pasadena's finest standing on my doorstep. It was early for the boys in blue to be selling tickets to the Policemen's Ball.

It was not a philanthropic call.

The disillusioned gentleman had filed a complaint saying a "man in women's clothing" had tried to seduce him. I couldn't believe it. Even after my heartfelt explanation, the guy had gotten the punch line wrong.

Neither my word, my Social Security card, nor my driver's license would suffice as proof of my identity. The police wanted more. They had a hot tip. I might be of questionable gender, and these boys wanted to see irrefutable proof.

A policewoman was called to the scene of the crime. She, at least, apologized for what she was about to do.

In tears, I submitted to a strip search.

I passed her inspection with high marks. Without a word, the disgruntled policemen stomped off in search of other desperadoes.

Joyce slept through it all.

For many years I did not tell my friend about the humiliating invasion. I was embarrassed. Joyce had little tolerance for social injustice: she'd grown up female in a straight culture. She had a very different view of her position in the social pecking order. I did not believe I had a right to protest such treatment. I'd come from a gay subculture, where humiliation at the hands of the police was expected.

After my brush with the gender patrol, I quickly left Pasadena and the Broadway.

In Inglewood, on the southern side of Los Angeles, I found a job in a beauty salon. I became a receptionist. This job I liked. In the beauty business, unlike the Broadway, they encouraged me to be outrageous . . . then gave me perks for succeeding. Not a bad gig for a proselyte woman. I even got free hair styling and beauty tips. No longer did I have to pretend to be an in-house mannequin; in the beauty shop I really was one.

"Aleshia, darling, with your coloring you really should have been born a redhead," my favorite stylist cooed. Since I'd been born with auburn wisps, I agreed that the beautician could return me to my natural look. I was shocked at what he created. Go-Go Red was far from natural—but everyone agreed it *was* me. My hair would stay that brilliant shade of blue-red for the next thirty years.

My plumage may have been colorful, but as a fledgling chick, I still hadn't learned to fly as a woman. I was more the bird in a gilded cage. Who would ever have thought that a girl might need to protect herself from men? Not me. I thought a man was a gadget you screwed on your bed to protect you from intruders.

I even looked men in the eye as I passed them on the street. I looked everybody in the eye. No one had ever told me that a woman needs to demurely drop her eyes. Maybe that knowledge comes only with experience. A woman learns she must drop her gaze or run the risk of being perceived as sexually interested in the male she's passing. Heavens! As a woman, everything seemed to revolve around whether or not I was sexually aroused. I'd always heard the phrase "It's a man's world," but I never believed it until I was no longer male. What I needed was a guidebook to the heterosexual world. Many biologically born females could have used such a book. It was an awkward time for all women.

Women in the early 1960s seemed to take one of two primary approaches toward survival: there was the religiously sanctioned "good girls don't" path—then there was the "bad girls do" superhighway that I was traveling. Many of those "bad girls" were shopping at Saks.

We weren't strumpets. We weren't even without morals. We were searching for something more tangible than what life allowed us on our own. Some of us were merely looking for someone to believe in. It took me many years to discover that *I* was that special someone.

For centuries, women had been trying to work their way, blindfolded, through a patriarchal maze. In 1960, "good girls" and their more rambunctious sisters were still trying to find their way out of the damn thing. There were even a few women who, finding the societal female role oppressive, were beginning to seek their own power. In a society where females wield little power, women have to fight for their security. I was, unfortunately, still trying to hold a man with my knees. You fight with what you have at your disposal. I had great knees.

Although chronologically beyond the age of consent, as a woman I was an infant. I wasn't interested in changing the world or becoming a warrior in the battle between the sexes. I wasn't secure enough for such a fight. I would accept any gender bias that society directed toward me—as long as men considered me womanly. More than anything else, I wanted to be loved. So if men—the wielders of power—were primarily interested in sex, the rules seemed fairly obvious to me. I fed the male appetite and ate the scraps that fell from his plate. I did not have enough confidence or experience to know there might be a better way.

In this free-wheeling state, I went to see a stand-up bass-playing girlfriend at her new gig. After a lot of booze and very little encouragement, I joined the trio in a song or two. I was lousy.

"You, Sweetheart, could be the next Peggy Lee," a neon-lit-suit type drawled from far back in the smoky recesses of the club. I tried to believe him.

With this relationship, I kept my mouth shut about surgery. Had he mentioned the removal of an ingrown toenail, I would have sworn no such procedure existed. I'd have taken an oath that such surgery was not possible in this country. I was taking no chances. I now knew better than to share the story of my transsexual past with any man. I shouldn't have shared my body.

I was safe on the issue of surgery. He didn't waste time talking.

Georgio was a good-looking *guido* with a certain expatriate-type charisma. He supposedly worked in a garage somewhere—doing something, in some nebulous capacity, in which I had no interest whatsoever. My lack of interest in his profession was fine with him. He didn't like talking about his job. Instead, he took me to the races, clubbing, and to all the fashionable spots around Los Angeles. If we weren't living in the fast lane, we were running close to the inside track. The man was a high roller, and I was enjoying every roll.

"We need to have a talk," Georgio called to say one October afternoon. I agreed to meet him in an hour.

"This will be the night," I said hugging myself. "I'll definitely say yes if he pops the right question." I had already said yes to the wrong question. Sex was merely something that one did.

I settled deep into his leather couch as he poured himself a drink at his mahogany bar.

"I don't work at a garage like I told you, Kid," Georgio confessed.

I had, in my day, heard worse news.

"That's just a cover," he continued. "It's in case I need to prove employment."

"Uh-huh," I thought. "So?" I wanted him to skip to the good stuff, get down on his knee, and ask me to be his bride.

"I'm a runner for the syndicate," he said.

He poured another double shot from a crystal decanter. Why had it never dawned on me that this man was no grease monkey?

"I might have to leave town quickly. You know, on a moment's notice," he explained. "I don't want you thinking I've skipped out on you."

That should have been my line.

"If you ever really need me and I'm not around, you can call this number and leave a message," he purred. He handed me a printed phone number for Trenton, New Jersey.

"Oh, God," I sighed to myself. "La Cosa Nostra." Worse yet, he was not even *capo di tutti capi*. "Well," I thought, "not everyone can be chief. There's got to be a few *goombata*—Indians." We made love on the floor.

"Girl, this is not a good sign," I thought as my lover snored beside me. "At this rate, you are never going to get married." After humming a few bars of "O Sole Mio," I woke my dozing lover.

I should have let the bastard sleep. Georgio continued drinking, but he was no longer being kind and considerate. The evening was not heading toward a proposal; it was leading to a brouhaha.

"You're nothing but a good piece of ass," he slurred.

In other circumstances I would have been delighted with such news. Now, I was alarmed.

"I was a fool to trust you, Bitch!" he yelled. Suddenly, in a fit of rage, he lunged at me and knocked me across the room. He repeatedly pummeled me in my side and on my back, then grabbed my throat and shook me hard. I passed out.

I woke to find Georgio kissing my welts. "I love you, Baby," he soothed. "I lost control because I love you so much. I don't want to lose you."

I was in no position to argue. I hurt.

Later, home and safely locked in my apartment, I had a surprise visitor. Stormy stood, leaning against my door frame, with one hand perched on her hip. My fairy godmother had arrived, recently returned from Morocco, where she'd had transsexual surgery. I had not seen her since her return. She'd been busy. Stormy had come back and promptly married Michael O'Brian. As with me, wedlock had always been her number-one objective in life. Our role in life, as we saw it, was to be supportive of our man and to bring comfort to him. His role was to have a career and make all final decisions. It was because we shared this feeling about marriage, hearth and home, that the male doctors of our day thought us unbelievably womanly.

Stormy had waited a long time to make her union legal. To make sure the marriage vows "took"—she married the man twice. They had both a civil and a Catholic wedding and then set off to Mexico for an Acapulco honeymoon. Now the former Stormy Lee, Finocchio's stellar stripper, was standing in my doorway as the respectable Mrs. Katherine O'Brian, of San Francisco, California.

"Get something together," she said in her same old take-charge fashion. "Mike and I are on our way to Vegas, and you're coming with us."

She had no idea how badly I wanted to get out of town.

"What happened to you?!" She blanched as I quickly changed clothes. My neck and back had turned a piteous purple, mottled with yellow.

"I'll get Mike," my old friend said immediately on hearing the story. "You're moving in with us."

San Francisco worked for me. She always had. This was the only city where I'd ever felt at home. Now, with Kathy and Mike, I also felt safe.

In the following months, I slowly regained my confidence, found a job, and started to date again. Life might knock me down, might even bloody my nose, but living means you get up and move forward. Soon I was seeing someone on a steady basis. I knew no other way to continue. I found a man who would make an Appalachian mama proud.

His name was "StevedeTinoAttorneyatLaw." He said his name and title as though they were one word.

Pow! Upside my head. Steve was prone to slapping me in order to get my attention.

"When I tell you 'Look, Aleshia,' I have my reason for telling you, 'Look, Aleshia.' *Capisce?*"

Although I was very fond of Italian men, I was beginning to duck when I saw one coming.

In no time at all, Steve got me a better job. I went to work as a cocktail waitress just around the corner from Finocchio's in North Beach. I'd come back to my old stomping ground. My old friends were headlining drag queens, but Aleshia, the real girl, was slinging drinks in a neo–National Socialist Workers' Party barroom. Every night as the German national anthem blared over the sound system, patrons rose from their tables and offered a hearty straight-arm salute. Boys will be boys; Nazis will be Nazis. I made no judgments. As a big, buxom, practicing fraulein, I was making many a deutschemark. Easy street lasted until, one evening, a trench-coated patron goose-stepped out of the bar and shot someone with his German Luger. The city closed down my place of employment. I was out on my not-so-Teutonic ass.

Young men from all over our country were being shipped out of San Francisco's port, headed for Vietnam. At the time of President John F. Kennedy's 1963 assassination, only sixteen thousand American "military advisers" were in Nam; then the newly appointed president, Lyndon Baines Johnson, pronounced that more aggressive action was needed. American troops were soon headed into the fray. Our boys were looking to have one last stateside fling before shipping out, and North Beach mobilized to rake in their dollars. Adult entertainment was booming on Broadway.

As young men sailed off to put their lives on the line, I worked to entertain the troops. I'd become a stand-up comic in a Broadway strip house. I sang a little. I danced a little. It was the same old act with a new musical arrangement, plus I'd added every dirty joke that Rusty Warren, Belle Barth, or Redd Foxx had ever delivered. This time, the city of San Francisco closed *me* down.

"Customers are leaving the club and telling those filthy stories out on the street," the sheriff said. It was true. The fresh-faced servicemen did not bother to clean up their language. I, on the other hand, was fantastic at finding euphemisms for the word *penis.*

"Have you heard the story about the hunter who shot eighteen gaping holes in his piatra? That's Italian for cucumber. . . . "

Somehow the Goddess always provides. Who knows? Maybe She was tired of my euphemisms. Whatever her reasoning, I ended up in Reno as a stripper. Those gods and goddesses sure work in mysterious ways!

By the mid-1960s, burlesque was sighing a death rattle, and it needed more than my reconstructed body to save it. The sultry art of disrobing without exposing in the days of Vietnam was far too tame to be lucrative. Yet no sooner did my gig end in San Francisco than a red velvet burlesque curtain was opening for me in Reno. I sang a little. I danced a little. I joked a lot. I'd glide around the floor, dropping a garment here and a garment there. I never went too far before interrupting the seductive routine to tell a story.

"People always ask me what I think while I work," I'd muse. "Well, I was thinking about the hunter who blew eighteen gaping holes . . . " The music blared on. I didn't dare let anyone think I was serious about disrobing. I was quick to laugh at myself before anyone else had a chance. It was the same technique for survival I'd learned as a boy on the grammar school playground.

After my opening, I got a wonderful blurb in Art Long's *Reno Entertainment Section*, "Night Notes."

"Aleshia Brevard, new addition to the Club Basin Street exotics lineup, has a pair of stems that are among the most lovely seen hereabouts as of recent. For a dancer she uses a different approach. Mixes the terp with storytelling that gets the laughs, albeit mucho indigo."

The good press notice possibly saved my job. I certainly did not know what I was doing.

My first night on the job, I stripped down to my tried-and-true red merry widow from "My Heart Belongs to Daddy" days, bowed quickly, and stepped behind the red velvet drapes, pulling them securely closed behind me.

There was applause! There was a lot of applause. The club's strapping little female manager was waiting for me behind the curtain.

"They want more," she said. With one quick move she ripped my merry widow open with one hand while pushing me through the curtains with the other.

"My God, you have virgin nipples!" she exclaimed as I went toppling forward to take a topless bow.

I soon had more than baby nipples to worry about.

Our master of ceremonies, an old queen, was positive that he recognized me from my presurgery days in San Francisco. Incensed that an impersonator would dare to strip, he took the story to my fellow artistes. The strippers did not believe him, and that drove the master of ceremonies into a snit. He alone would uphold the prestige of burlesque—where only born vaginas were allowed to wear the sacred G-string.

I was on my way home after work one crisp Nevada night when someone called out: "Hey, Lee! Lee Shaw!"

I turned around. Ooops!

The master of ceremonies had invited one of Finocchio's waiters to fly to Reno, all expenses paid, to identify me. The next day my detractor presented the waiter as proof to management.

When I arrived for work, my boss called me into her office. She explained that she was having a problem with "one of the employees." Someone, she said, was questioning my gender.

"I'm going to have to have a look-see."

"Oh God, why me?" I asked as I dropped my drawers. "What the hell," I told myself. "You've passed far closer inspection than this. Don't make a big deal of it." I stood there, exposed, for management's perusal.

Club Basin Street's tough little manager took her time browsing and then walked to the office door.

"Looks like a *twat* to me," she yelled out to no one in particular, "and I've seen a million of 'em!"

That was the end of that. I should have offered her a cigar.

Gradually, I met other performers around town and began to feel at home with my new profession. I especially liked Candy Cane, a go-go dancer working the Mapes Showroom with Jim Burgett. I was fond of all the girls from that Swimmers Review. After work, we would all gather at Harrah's lounge for the last show. We loved it when Louie Prima was in town. The dancers and I were there almost every night and felt a personal rapport with the onstage personalities. We thought ourselves special because we personally knew the guys in Louie's backup band, Sam Butera and the Witnesses. We weren't simply civilians; we were enter-tainers in our own right. That was one of the perks of being "in the biz."

One evening, Sam Butera, bored, invited Candy onstage to dance with the band. She was marvelous and enthusiastically received by the small audience. Aware of a good thing, Sam next invited the dancer sit-ting across from Candy to come up onstage. We were suddenly in the midst of a dance-off. Because I was seated at the end of the table, it was clear that I would be the last one asked to dance. I didn't care for my placement on the impromptu bill. I would never be able to top what the professional go-go dancers had already done before me. The girls had well-rehearsed routines, and since I did not, I would look ridiculous. I was from a different type of show entirely . . . and *there was the solution to my problem.*

As predicted, the twins were invited onstage together. They stepped on the ringside table, onto the stage, and with a perfectly coordinated terpsichorean display, wowed the audience. The size of the audience had grown. It was my turn in what had become an undulating battle of the chorines.

Sam invited me to the stage. I took a deep breath, stepped on the table, and reached for the zipper of my one-piece mini dress. The dress fell perfectly as I stepped onto the stage. I did a pivot, caught the dress on my toe and sent it arching into the audience.

"Help! The big broad's taking her clothes off!" Sam let out a whoop and made a mad dash for the stage curtains behind him. The band leader was saving himself.

There was no need for alarm. Under my mini dress I was wearing a black merry widow and matching tights.

I got my long string of beads rotating, and, with Rolly Dee blowing mean accompaniment on saxophone, unleashed a move or two of my own. I could bump with the best of 'em. Management sent champagne to our table.

Reno was nonstop innocent fun. We were a bunch of overgrown kids out on a lark. Entertainers would often gather on a sidewalk and wait impatiently for an unsuspecting tourist.

"Here comes a group, make it look good," someone would whisper. As the tourist approached, all the girls would toss their room keys on the sidewalk and squeal excitedly as the guys scrambled for a key.

"I got Candy's," one guy would whoop.

"Aleshia, you're mine tonight!" someone else would crow.

The properly scandalized tourist would pass with a righteous display of indignation, and we'd fall over each other laughing. We would then retrieve our keys and wait for the next gullible group to come our way.

In the midst of all this frolic, I met Tommy Leonetti. He was the lounge singer's lounge singer, but to me he was the embodiment of Michelangelo's *David*. I had a major crush and caught every Leonetti show I could at Harold's second-floor Silver Dollar Club.

He finally noticed me. My drool on the bar gave me away.

Our first date was at a little after-hours club. On the dance floor, after one particularly energetic move, the zipper in my dress completely gave way. Not knowing what a long-time woman would do in such a situation, I stepped out of the disreputable garment and kept on dancing.

The Fates refused to be foiled that easily.

Back at the bar, after hearing an amusing anecdote, I lustily threw back my head to laugh. My wig fell on the floor. I sat there, with a stocking cap tied in a knot atop my head. No one laughed. They just stared at me. I bent back, picked up the offending hairpiece, shook it out and deposited it back on my head. Then they laughed. I think that episode is what won Tommy over. I adored the singer until the moment he casually tried to pass me on to his friend, Jack Jones.

Jack was opening the next night in Lake Tahoe, and I was introduced to the talented Mr. Jones during Tommy's set break. During their conversation, Tommy casually suggested that Jack give me a ride back to my place. It wasn't the suggestion, exactly, that upset me; it was Tommy's delivery.

"From me to you, you know what I mean, pal?" That was the innuendo I heard in Tommy's suggestion. I was crushed. I thought Tommy really cared about me.

I could have graciously declined the ride or even stomped off into the night, but I had to be Olivia de Havilland ascending those steps in *The Heiress*. I wanted to make a statement. I smiled and accepted Mr. Jones's kind invitation for a ride home.

Jack was charming. He even wanted me to attend his opening-night party the next evening. I was complimented. I was, in fact, flabbergasted.

Could I have misconstrued Tommy's offer? Naaah!

Little me, who had learned so much in a short period of time, fell for the ploy. The singer was so sincere, and I desperately wanted to believe him. Mr. Jones said he would send a car for me so that I could attend his opening.

The next day I bought a dress especially for the occasion and went to work dressed in my go-to-the-Jack-Jones-opening outfit.

There was no car waiting at the stage door after work. There was no car waiting around the corner—either corner. I looked. This stripper would be staying home.

Why did I have such a big mouth? I had told every exotic dancer at the club that I was going to the Jack Jones opening-night party. Now there would be egg all over my carefully made-up puss. I would become the laughingstock of Club Basin Street.

The next night on my dressing table there was a lavish orchid display with a card from Jack Jones himself.

"Aleshia—sorry we missed each other. I gave the driver the wrong address. Forgive me. Jack."

It took a major part of my next paycheck to pay for "Jack's" apology. I have not liked orchids since that day.

I did not get over the Jones fiasco until something much more depressing obliterated that memory.

On a weeknight after my second show at Club Basin Street, a well-appointed gentleman approached and offered me his card. It merely stated his name. That didn't matter. The gentleman wanted to discuss my future and proposed that we meet the following week. I was ecstatic. My talents had been recognized, and I was going to be offered a position worthy of my theatrical gift. I could sense it. I wouldn't remain a stripper until I was saggy and past my prime. No. I was cut out for bigger things, and now a professional agent finally realized this.

I was determined to set just the right tone for my Svengali when our appointed hour arrived the following Wednesday. Everyone in the boardinghouse was pulling for my success. My colorful thatch was neatly coiffured, and I was bedecked in borrowed finery as I demurely descended the stairs to the parlor. This moment would become legend to all those who came after. I, like Lana Turner at Schwabb's Soda Fountain, was about to be discovered.

The gentleman did not rise as I entered the parlor. I thought that odd. Perhaps he hoped to catch me off guard and sign me to a contract at a rock-bottom price. I was prepared for that.

"I've been watching you," the entrepreneur began without so much as a "How do you do?"

I deduced that he was a very busy person and that I should be direct and to the point. I didn't know what the point was.

He told me.

"I'm here to offer you a job at Mustang."

"Where is Mustang?" I queried politely.

"Mustang Ranch is outside of town," he countered.

"Mustang Ranch? That sounds very . . . !" I was suddenly speechless.

Without preamble or ceremony, I had been offered a job in a whore-house.

I started to cry. The gentleman who was to launch my career got up and stalked out. I didn't even get the chance to explain that what I aspired to was stardom . . . not whoredom.

With my career at a standstill, I turned my attention toward romance. Where else?!

We met between shows at Club Basin Street. Looking very spiffy in his uniform, the cocksure lieutenant approached the table where I sat, like a forlorn Cheré in *Bus Stop,* drinking with a customer. I was drinking tea, but the customer believed he was buying me alcohol. The subterfuge was part of my job.

When Harve La Liberte sauntered up to my table, I was awed by his audacity. He didn't even offer to buy me a drink. I liked his moxie, as well as the fit of his uniform. What he wanted—I already knew.

Harve was in Reno to take part in United States Air Force winter wilderness survival training. The completion of the course was an actual weeklong trek through the mountains. According to the young navigator, he would even have to trap his own food. It was a rigorous ordeal, but the survivors were rewarded by a lavish, Uncle Sam–funded dinner and dance afterward. Not only would he survive, Harve boasted, but he would attend the celebration with me on his arm. I uttered a silent prayer that God would send a jackrabbit or two Harve's way. The expensive Jack Jones opening-night outfit was still hanging in my closet, waiting for somewhere to go.

When Harve left Club Basin Street, he had both me and my San Francisco address in his hip pocket. If I stood him up, the brash lieutenant threatened, he'd come looking for me. I had no intention of standing him up.

The morning after meeting the handsome young lieutenant, I was awakened by a frantic call from my mother.

"Are you all right?" Mother anxiously asked. "I keep having the worst dream!"

When my mother had a dream, everyone in our family took notice. She had an uncanny way of "knowing" when something was about to happen with members of her family. In the mountains I called home, it was not uncommon to hear that an intuitive person had been born with "the sight." Some folks were said to "j'st know things." It was part of our Scots heritage—or perhaps it came from the Cherokee ancestors.

"I'm fine," I cautiously replied.

I was very guarded during our conversation. I was afraid Mother's call stemmed from her displeasure at my having left home. She'd certainly be displeased if she knew I was working in a burlesque house. I was a featured act, but Mozelle would detest that her daughter had become a stripper.

"Are you sure you're okay?" she pushed. "This dream just won't let me rest, Aleshia. Are you positive you're in no danger?"

Mother was having trouble putting her nightmare to rest.

"In the dream," she stammered, "you've been shot in the stomach. It's a shotgun wound. We take you to a hospital, but they refuse to help you. I keep begging them to do something," she started to weep. "Finally a nurse gives you Empirin #3. Are you sure you're all right? The dream keeps coming back night after night."

I scoffed at my mother's fear. Nothing was wrong with my stomach, and it was highly unlikely that I would ever be blasted with a shotgun. I was in twentieth-century Reno, for heaven's sake. It wasn't exactly the wild and woolly West. Trying to change the subject, I launched into my excitement over attending a huge party hosted by the United States military. We gossiped casually until Mother reluctantly hung up the telephone.

The next evening, I was delighted to see a large audience for my second show. Downstage right, a group of businessmen were getting a little rowdy, but I was still glad to see them. Stripping for empty chairs was worse than being forced to drink with the customers.

"I didn't bring my friends to hear some broad sing," I heard from down right. "Hey, baby, take it off."

For a stripper who does comedy as part of her routine, hecklers are par for the course. I gave the loudmouth a few verbal jabs.

"Take it off? Already? But I just put it on! You wouldn't want me to catch cold, would you?" I was trying to tease the guy out of disrupting my act. With most boisterous customers, you could give them a little attention, make them feel special, and they would become your greatest fans. Charm did not work on this bozo.

"Would somebody put a saddle on this jackass and ride him out of here?" I quipped. "Mister, we ought to do an act together. I'll ask for toilet paper, and you come rolling in."

That got a good laugh. The dupe was, in fact, making my act more interesting. The audience was loving it, and I, too, was having fun until the clod lapsed into profanity. I then shot him down with my tried-and-true one-liner.

"Mister, I'd tell you to shut your mouth, but I wouldn't want to ruin your sex life," I purred.

The men at his table went wild with glee. It was obvious that the offensive customer was furious with me, but he sat down and shut up. I finished my act to much applause, particularly from the downright table.

As I entered the lounge, I was approached by the heckling leader of the group. He was quite pleasant. I assumed that he had seen the harmless humor in my jibe and had forgiven me my impertinence.

"Won't you join us at our table?" he offered. "My employees would like to meet you."

I had to drink with the customers somewhere, so I agreed. As we reached the table, he pushed me roughly into a chair. Once I was pinned between him and the table, he started a stream of foul and abusive language. I tried to get up. He pushed me back down and grabbed my breast. I kicked him. Hard. He backed away. Now, with just enough room to get out of the chair, I sprang to my feet and followed through with a solid, resounding wallop across his face.

Bouncers materialized from every section of the club. There was no danger of his physical retaliation. There was no need for it. The obnoxious businessman wielded a more potent power.

I was fired on the spot. Having passed the manager's vaginal inspection, she expected a woman to know better than to cold-cock a paying customer.

*A curly-headed "Buddy"
Crenshaw at age three.*

*With my sister, Jeanne,
and sporting my favorite
shirt at about age nine. I
couldn't wear ribbons
and lace, so I settled for a
little color with pictures
of ice cream sundaes.*

This 1958 photograph was a Christmas gift to my priest partner, taken at the same session as my female likeness head shot for Finocchio's. They were both an act. I was never this "butch" in all my life.

With Mother and Daddy on my last trip home before surgery. I don't know who I thought I was fooling.

Publicity shots taken by Romaine's Studio, San Francisco, 1961, prior to surgery.

With Mrs. Eve
Finocchio.

Actress Nancy Kwan backstage with the Finocchio's cast. I am the blonde behind
Nancy, on her left.

The red merry widow and sweater from the "My Heart Belongs to Daddy" number at Finocchio's. Photo by Romaine's Studios, San Francisco.

My mother, Mozelle. The apple doesn't fall far from the tree.

Mrs. Aleshia Lee graduates from Middle Tennessee State University, 1967.

My first professional head shot after the 1962 transsexual surgery.

Promotional shot for Universal Studios' The Love God. *Photo copyright © 2001 by Universal City Studios, Inc. Courtesy of Universal Studios Publishing Rights, a Division of Universal Studios Licensing Inc. All rights reserved.*

With Don Knotts and the
Pussycats in The Love God.

Publicity photograph used for
The Love God *billboard on
Sunset Boulevard, across from
the Playboy Club.*

Publicity photograph used for **The Owl and the Pussycat** *tour in the early 1980s.*

I sent my mother, the nurse, a photograph saying, "I can be a nurse, too!" "Not with those nails," she wrote back.

At the end of my career, an aging Aleshia goes blonde.

CHAPTER 8

Miss Congeniality

IT WAS almost three years since surgery, but the quest for a cottage, backyard, and apple tree, with a darling little picket fence surrounding a picture-perfect existence, remained the focus of my life. Searching for perfection is a strain. Unfortunately, my life resembled more that of a quick-change artist than it did the stable, secure woman I'd set out to become. In January 1965, I was in Reno headlining as a stripper. By February, I was in San Francisco putting on coveralls rather than taking off chiffon. The paint I now smeared on my face came from a Kwikset bucket rather than from a Revlon tube, and I'd traded in my G-string for a tool belt. I was helping Kathy and Mike O'Brian prepare their second beauty salon for its grand opening.

Kathy and I worked from sunup well into the night, readying the new salon on Chestnut Street. The business represented much more than financial security. Kathy, Mike, and I had escaped San Francisco's Tenderloin District and were determined never again to return to that gay ghetto.

Caught in a half-world between male and female, Stormy and I had found ourselves captive to the street existence reserved for the city's misfits. As transitioning transsexuals, we were more secure among the dope dealers, gigolos, ex-cons, addicts, bamboozlers, pimps, and whores of Turk and Levenworth Streets than we were braving the numbing disapproval of our city's less notorious areas. It was in the Tenderloin that we polished our female presentation while developing an instinct for survival that becomes second nature to those who live in the ghetto. Living on the fringe of society demands constant vigilance. If you are gender imperfect, it is always to your advantage to know who's on your blind side. Keeping one's back against the wall becomes a survival instinct. On the streets, awareness can save your life when violence suddenly erupts around you—or is directed at you. Lessons learned in the Tenderloin would remain with us for the rest of our lives, but by the mid-1960s, we'd made our bid for uptown acceptability.

Shortly before Kathy and Mike's Chestnut Street salon opened, Mother's dream, the recurring nightmare she'd had when I was in Reno, made another bid for center stage.

Generally, at lunchtime I would scamper off to a nearby pizzeria, pick up our order, and rush back to the unfinished beauty shop. Everyone would take a break, hunker down around the cardboard box, and wolf down huge, greasy slices of pepperoni and double cheese.

On this, another perfect San Francisco day, I was in especially high spirits. The day was more glorious because I'd met the darling pizza-shop owner. I couldn't eat for describing the Italian "restaurateur." As my friends stuffed themselves, I entertained them with my girlish enthusiasm. Every new man I met, after all, presented me with another chance at my picket fence, backyard, and apple tree. My picture-perfect fantasy could never be complete without the perfect man.

"No matter what you think of his pizza, the man is decidedly a piece of Italy's finest," I teased.

Suddenly, I was very ill. One minute I was giggling and stuffing my face . . . the next minute I was clammy and nauseous.

"Girl, it's either paint fumes or a bad piece of pepperoni," Kathy quipped. "Ain't no way you're pregnant."

That night Kathy and Mike rushed me, screaming in agony, to the emergency room. Once the hospital's admission office discovered I had no insurance, I was ignored until I passed out in the waiting room. After I crumpled and lost consciousness, I was lifted to a gurney in a hallway. I lay there until I awakened in excruciating pain. I pleaded for relief—but never saw a doctor. Occasionally, an intern would mosey down the hall, poke on my stomach, and take a long look at the transsexual with a bellyache. Under normal circumstances, I would never have shared my carefully protected gender secret, but I was afraid that my trans-sexual past had somehow caused my abdominal agony. Having no insurance was damning enough; I should never have added the element of gender dysphoria. I lay there, begging for mercy, until the pain subsided and I was discharged.

Back in our Steiner Street Victorian, I collapsed across the first bed I saw and fell into a deep sleep. Adhesions had tightly wrapped around my intestines, and subsequently, the intestines had ruptured. Body waste was spewing into my abdominal cavity, and peritonitis was weaving its deadly spell. I was being poisoned by my own waste. Whether it was the outcome of my mother's recurring dream, bad karma, or my lack of insurance that kept me from receiving medical attention, the result was the same—I *was* dying.

Kathy, not knowing the problem but fearing the worst, called from hospital to hospital, just as my mother's disturbing dream had predicted. Her frantic calls reached a surgeon who instantly recognized my symptoms. I had by this time turned a bright yellow.

"I'll meet you as quickly as you can get her to the hospital," he said.

Upon my arrival, the surgeon immediately slit my protruding belly, reached into the abdominal cavity, and spread my entrails across my chest. After removing a tattered six feet of intestine, he patiently removed the chewing gum-like adhesions that stuck to my organs, then unceremoniously dumped my guts back into the cavity. The waiting began. If the intestines sorted themselves out, I would live. If they refused to cooperate, my run had been canceled.

The doctor said my parents should be prepared for the worst.

After receiving the alarming call, my mother booked the next flight from Nashville. When she landed in San Francisco, Kathy was there waving a sign. With lipstick she'd printed MOZELLE in huge red letters. My mother was told to conserve her energy and concentrate on getting me well. If she wanted to go somewhere, Kathy would drive her. Gratefully, Mozelle did as she was told and stayed in my room on Steiner.

Before making up their mind to cooperate, my butchered intestines rolled around in my body. When it finally appeared I would survive, I was moved to a private room.

"What are you giving her?" Mother asked the medication nurse who, in a flurry of efficiency, had breezed into my hospital room.

"What's ordered," the nurse briskly replied, indicating that I was to swallow the pill.

I meekly downed my capsule while Mother tried to engage the nurse by recounting the prophetic nightmare.

"Aleshia *wasn't attended at the first hospital*; and her friend Kathy called *from hospital to hospital looking for a doctor*," Mother repeated. It was true. They later told us there had been riots in South San Francisco that evening. The emergency room had been overwhelmed with *shot-gun* wounds.

"At the end of the dream," Mother explained to the nurse, "Aleshia was given Empirin #3."

"You can put your dream to rest," the nurse said, looking slightly shaken. "This is Empirin #3."

As the people of Appalachia have always known, some people are born with the gift of sight.

During my prolonged hospital stay, two very gratifying things happened to me— three, if one counts the fact that I did not die. First, a large bouquet of flowers arrived from the Italian pizza man. With pure bravado, I now told everyone he was responsible for "tying my guts in a knot." It was an attempt at being my old, irreverent self. I was not. I was more scared and vulnerable than I'd ever been in my life. With the bouquet came hope that I might still be desirable. I'd barely outdistanced death, but still I failed to realize that a woman could have a goal in life other than finding a man. Now, over thirty years later, I'm convinced that my mother and Kathy sent those flowers and signed the pizza maker's name. It only magnifies the significance of that bouquet.

The second surprise was a letter from the brash young lieutenant I'd left behind in Reno. Harve La Liberte had called, as threatened, to see "why in the hell" I'd stood him up. Kathy found his cheeky nerve refreshing and told him to contact me.

"Well," he wrote, "it seems you cannot take care of yourself. I guess I'd better stick around and protect you."

Those words rang every southern belle in my addled brain.

Today, for many men and women who have come of age in a post-feminist America, such marriage-minded tunnel vision seems ludicrous. To some it is even offensive. "How did you feel being nothing but a sex object?" those people ask. The term *sex object* had little relevance for most women in the 1960s. Finding a good man, one who could protect and provide, was a way of life. I was doing nothing that was not being done by the vast majority of my heterosexual female friends. We often went out together, scouting for promising, available males. It was a different romantic world—men still picked up the checks! What perhaps makes me a throwback is the fact that I enjoyed the power. I enjoyed being a delectable specimen. Rita Hayworth said it in *Gilda*: "If I were a ranch, they'd call me the Bar Nothing." Her seductive performance caught Rita a prince, Ali Kahn.

As soon as I was discharged from the hospital, I returned to Tennessee for my recuperation. I immediately started compiling a cookbook labeled *Harve's Soon to Be Favorites*. I'd only seen Lieutenant La Liberte for a small portion of an evening in a Reno strip club, but that did nothing to blur the romantic picture. I lived between the covers of *Better Homes and Gardens*, my favorite tune was "The Wedding March," and I was in love with delusion. I was even planning a trousseau for my wedding—to which I had not been officially invited. That was when Kathy stepped forward with her own agenda.

"Girl, hurry up and get well," Kathy ordered over the phone from San Francisco. "You've got a job in Honolulu waiting on your tired, sick ass!"

Without consulting me, the former queen of burlesque had assured her agent that in less than two months I would report for work at The Dunes in Honolulu, Hawaii.

"There is one 'little' drawback," Kathy added. "We're booked as America's Leading Transsexuals. I'm the featured act and you are co-feature."

Harve's cookbook went back on the shelf.

Without thinking to ask who'd voted Kathy America's Leading Transsexual and me Miss Congeniality, I rushed back to San Francisco. I did the costume sketches while Kathy bitched and complained about every detail. Finally, we agreed on a look, bought the required material, and ran to our dressmaker. The night before our departure, America's Leading Transsexuals were stitching sequins and beads on their gowns. We couldn't show up without glitz—people might think we were impostors!

Because Turner and Smith, our Las Vegas producers, said we would be met by the Honolulu press corps, we made the flight in Kimberly knit suits. On the Hawaiian tarmac, waiting for the press, we sweltered as we posed in our fashionable knits with their boxy little jackets. The photographers did not arrive. America's Leading Transsexuals and their complete sets of matching Samsonite luggage were picked up in an open jeep and carted off to rehearsal. It was a breezy, bouncy ride out Nimitz Highway, past Pearl Harbor, to The Dunes. We arrived a wind-blown, disheveled mess, but we didn't complain. The lush beauty of The Dunes made up for any discomfort.

"Las Vegas Nights," with America's Leading Transsexuals, was the swank nightclub's premiere show, and our eight-week run was to be followed by the legendary Sarah Vaughan. We were quite impressed with ourselves. We even loved that we were housed, along with the show's showgirls, at an apartment complex owned by The Dunes Cor-poration. Two doors down from our apartment lived singer Geraldine Jones. Formerly with the Clara Ward Singers, Geraldine was headlining at the company-owned Forbidden City. Ms. Jones was a show-stopping blues and gospel singer with a delightful take on life. Later she would serve as the inspiration for Flip Wilson's wonderfully hip Geraldine character. We arrived that first day to discover that Geraldine also had a fabulous recipe for barbecued ribs.

Not everyone in the complex was so welcoming. A few military fam-ilies lived at Barritania Apartments, and they were, unfortunately, not on The Dunes' payroll. Transsexuals, Vegas showgirls, and army wives are oil and water. It didn't take long for our lifestyles to clash.

Our first day on the island featured a particularly grueling day of rehearsal, and it was well past midnight when we returned home. Every-one was exhausted The balmy night and the shimmering water made the apartment's pool irresistible—in unison, we stripped off our sweaty rehearsal clothes and plunged into the welcoming water. We didn't think twice; nudity was our profession. We were splashing in Hawaiian heaven when the car pulled into the parking lot beside the pool.

"Probably time for the bars to be closing," Joanne, our English ex–Blue Belle dancer, commented. Before anyone had a chance to disagree, the gate opened and four uniformed policemen paraded into the enclosed pool area.

I pinched my nose and headed for the bottom. "If they want me, they're coming in after me," I bubbled to no one in particular on my way down. I was tired of vaginal inspections.

The officers, seemingly enjoying their patrol, understood our need to cool off but suggested we call it a night. They'd received a complaint from a resident on the second floor. Soothing her colicky baby by taking a midnight stroll, a military wife had managed to stretch over the balcony railing far enough to peer down on the naked civilian harlots in the pool. Incensed by what she'd strained so hard to see, she'd called the cops.

No real harm was done. The policemen laughed and joked with the pool full of naked women and then went on their way. When "questionable gender" is not an issue, nudity can be a very minor offense.

That evening I was reminded of exactly how far I'd come in seven short years. Buddy Crenshaw had needed a string of gorgeous showgirls when, at eighteen, he reported to the Los Angeles draft board.

As Kathy and I prepared for bed, I launched into the story of my draft notice fiasco.

"I was living with a priest," I began.

"I remember," she smirked.

"Anyway, when my draft notice arrived, I freaked out." I stopped talking for a moment as I pulled off my false top and bottom eyelashes. "John tried to convince me there was nothing to worry about. He'd coach me through it."

"He coached you through a lot of things, I'd say!" Kathy stopped dabbing eye-makeup remover around her eyes and held my gaze in the mirror.

She was right. John had orchestrated my life, so when the draft notice arrived, I'd naturally expected him to save me. He told me to mark a huge X where the questionnaire asked "Are you a homosexual?" If that didn't work, I was to tell the person in charge that I "performed wifely duties" for an older gentleman.

"That'll work," Kathy roared.

I did mark the big X as John had directed me to do, but claiming the homosexual exemption was terribly embarrassing. I felt I was lying. My real problem, however, came after I took the aptitude test and filled out all the papers. I was ordered to "strip to my skivvies." John hadn't mentioned a physical examination. If he had, I wouldn't have worn my black stretch-lace bikinis. To maintain some composure, when I was ordered to strip down, I stood there humming "A Pretty Girl Is Like a Melody"—with one knee forward and slightly bent. Before and behind me stood young men in boxers, jockey shorts, and every male under-dressing known to Fruit of the Loom. I was the only draftee in black lace. Individuality does not garner praise in the army.

I was well into the third chorus of my song when I was finally jerked from line and sent to the office of a governmental psychiatrist. Oh, hell. Now, to escape wearing khaki fatigues, I had to prove I was not only queer but crazy.

"If there exists a loving God," I thought, "please let this army psychiatrist have a smidgen of color sense. I simply cannot do two years in olive drab."

The shrink's questions were tasteless and a waste of taxpayers' money. Any self-respecting doctor would have known that the army did not want me in a barracks full of men on the night of a romantic harvest moon. Still, instead of kicking me out of his office, the military therapist asked a bunch of impertinent, pointed questions. Because of all his sexually explicit interest, I began to believe he was "cruising" me. That was a war game I knew how to play. I relaxed, peeked from beneath my lashes, and demurely explained a femme's role in bed.

With no further ado, the psychiatrist wrote "Assertion undeniably true!" in big, bold, official strokes across my file and sent me home to my priest. The United States Army did not want me in their mess tents, their latrines, or their wars. Thanks to the military psychiatrist, I would never receive a dishonorable discharge, stand before a military firing squad, or receive a Veterans Administration Housing Loan.

That experience with the United States' war machine had done nothing to soften my vendetta against the military. In the 1960s I was not alone in my anti-armed forces stance. Many Americans were protesting the fiasco in the jungles of Vietnam. Our cast was more enraged by the senselessness of the war than we were by some stupid military wife who'd called police to stop our pool party. We couldn't fight the government, however, so the military couple upstairs would have to do.

Harassment of the couple started almost immediately. Kathy and I started it. We were the ones living in the apartment beneath the targeted party. As a fiery redhead, I was designated "Agent Orange."

After attending our opening-night party, Kathy and I arrived back at our apartment feeling on top of the world. The "Las Vegas Nights" opening had gone well, but the party afterward was a major victory. We staggered onto our lanai and promptly decided to have another Mai Tai, whether we needed it or not. A drunken plan of revenge soon evolved.

"Oooh, yes!!" we moaned. "Please!! There. There! Please touch me there . . . no, not there, fool, *here*. Please!! Touch me *here*!!" Then we moaned some more for good measure. We were pretending to be Vegas harlots entertaining gentlemen callers. Now let the sanctimonious wife upstairs call the police and report fornication at Barritania Apartments—if she dared. The police wouldn't waste any time running to check out that call! Occasionally, we were forced to stop moaning so we could run inside and stifle our laughter.

"Well, that should give 'em a shock," Kathy laughed.

"Good," I added as I followed her into the apartment. "If we woke up the husband, he'll be chasing that woman around their bedroom the rest of the night."

Kathy smiled as she locked our patio door. "Bet she'll tend to her own business from now on."

Our attempt at sexual harassment backfired.

We'd gotten the husband's attention, all right, but he'd decided to come to the source. Every night as Kathy and I left for work, he was on his balcony watching us. America's Leading Transsexuals both understood that look.

The Dunes' publicity for our act had also backfired. The servicemen stationed in Honolulu liked our show and refused to believe that two of the girls had formerly been male.

"Why do you let them say that about you?" concerned young servicemen would often ask.

"A girl has to earn a living, Sweetheart" was my standard reply.

We'd been hired to entertain the troops, and that's exactly what we did. Neither Panama Hattie, Shanghai Lil, nor Miss Suzy Wong had anything on America's Leading Transsexuals. We weren't selling our wares, but we were doing a magnificent job of touting them. Our neighbors upstairs might have believed an orgy was always in full swing, but the imagination is generally capable of conjuring up something much worse than the truth—and generally does. The parties weren't overtly sexual in nature, but there was always a party going on in our Honolulu apartment. Kathy and I always managed to have an escort, courtesy of Uncle Sam and the war in Southeast Asia.

GI Joe upstairs became more and more fascinated. His was a penis with a man attached.

Late one evening, Kathy and I came straggling home to find our upstairs neighbor waiting at our front door. He'd brought his next-door buddy along for amoral support. They were both drunk. It was like a scene from Rita Hayworth's *Fire Down Below*. We might be novice females, but we'd been on the streets long enough to know better than to allow two drunks inside our apartment. A stoned, sexually aroused male reacts the same whether you're a real girl or merely look like one. The next morning, both husbands were found sleeping it off outside our door.

That afternoon, two wives, both carrying babies, flew back to the mainland.

Finding oneself hotly pursued around a tropical island is heady stuff, but Kathy and I had gone too far. As women, we needed to learn the rules of our gender. Number one: drunk or sober, husbands are off limits.

Just as the run at The Dunes' ended, Kathy and I were presented with an opportunity to stay in Hawaii and work at the Forbidden City. The Dunes Corporation wanted us to work for them as strippers, with no further mention of anything transsexual. Kathy and I tripped over each other jumping at the chance. Surgery had opened vistas I'd only dreamed about. This was the sort of romance and intrigue that filled the films I'd grown up loving. This was Marlene Dietrich in *The Devil Is a Woman* and Dorothy Lamour in *The Jungle Princess*, all rolled into one. In short order, we were living off the entertainment value of our positions. Drinks were always available, and some man or another was always good for a free dinner. In Hawaii, life as a woman was a prepaid luau, and we were eating high on the Hawaiian hog. Apart from intangible things like love, respect, and self-esteem, my life was everything I wanted it to be.

We saved every cent we made in burlesque. Kathy's money went home to Michael. I didn't have a husband, so I banked mine. Six months later I left Hawaii with an admirable bank account, a suitcase filled with floor-length muumuus, and far more confidence than I'd brought to the Pacific Paradise.

From the moment I returned stateside, Harve La Liberte, the Air Force lieutenant, and I were inseparable. Emotionally, we were not close; physically, we were dynamite. My desire for a wedding ring made for a hot relationship. This had to be what it felt like to be born female; every woman I knew was stitching on the same domestic Home-Sweet-Home sampler. Despite the implied freedom of the sexual revolution, it was still the sanctity of marriage that earned a girl respectability.

Out of the blue, Harve called me from Travis Air Force Base, about forty miles across the Bay, where he was stationed. His squadron was on alert.

"Go get your blood test," he said, taking immediate control of the conversation. "I'm restricted to base for the week, but I'll get my test done here. When the alert is over, I'm coming to San Francisco and we're getting married."

Grass did not grow under my feet. I got a blood test, bought a white chiffon mini dress for the ceremony, and started bidding farewell to my city. My girlfriends were thrilled by my good fortune—one tearfully expressing her envy that I was beating her to the altar. She would have had apoplexy had she known a transsexual was winning the race. It was a wonderful whirlwind week, even if I was leaving San Francisco to become a lowly officer's wife at Travis Air Force Base. The military had finally managed to get me in their damn system.

Around Harve, I studiously avoided any mention of transsexuality. He wouldn't understand—we couldn't even agree on Vietnam. My fiancé was a stickler for the macho company line. So, to my list of argument-provoking topics such as napalm, genocide, and the communist threat, I silently added the subject of gender alteration. I didn't feel the least bit deceitful. Harve never discussed his circumcision, toilet training, or first sexual experience, so I believed the same guidelines should apply to my original gender. It wasn't, after all, as though I had a penis that needed to be explained away.

Rather than fret about the past, I concentrated on the future—but even that presented problems.

"Say you're in line at the PX with a loaf of bread in your hand, and a senior officer's wife approaches with a fully loaded cart. What would you do?" Military protocol ranked high on Harve's list.

"Smile at her?" I suggested.

"No, Aleshia. You'd step back and let her go first," he explained patiently.

"You didn't tell me that she had a gun!" I snorted. The fact that I considered his chosen career a joking matter did not sit well with Harve. He did not forgive me until bedtime.

After that, I tried to clean up my act. I desperately wanted to be a military matron, complete with adorable husband and government housing.

When Harve arrived in San Francisco on the weekend of our wedding, it was obvious that something was wrong. He wouldn't break his silence until we were alone at the wharf restaurant.

"We can't get married," Harve stated flatly. "I'm being shipped out."

I screamed.

"I've been thinking this over all week," he continued. "I can't marry you and then leave you behind."

"Yes, you can," I squealed.

"Promise me you'll wait for me," he said, taking my hand.

At that moment I would gladly have rescinded my 4-F draft classification and gone to war in my lover's place. Was he kidding? Of course I'd wait for him! I would wait the rest of my life, if necessary.

I'd grown up on goodbye scenes like this in World War II movies. I understood my role. This was Greer Garson sending Walter Pidgeon off to Dunkirk in *Mrs. Miniver*.

"We'll meet here at this restaurant when I come home," he said. His sentiments only hurt me more. "I'll bring my parents and you'll bring yours. Aleshia, we'll spend the rest of our lives together."

How could I have labeled what we had together "merely physical"? How could I have been so unfeeling? This beautiful man was going off to war, and I was the one person he was worried about. I didn't deserve a man like this.

We spent the rest of Harve's weekend leave in bed, and I catered to his every whim. He had several. Like Ingrid Bergman in *For Whom the Bell Tolls*, I would keep the home fires burning and my man alive in my heart.

When my phone finally rang, the call was from the wife of Harve's best friend. "This is none of my business," she started, "but I have to tell you something."

"What's happened to Harve?" I gasped.

"Nothing, unfortunately," she said. "I just thought you should know that Harve is not being shipped overseas. He's staying right here. He simply decided that he doesn't want to get married."

Right along with my buttered popcorn, World War II romance movies had sold me a bill of goods.

I'd lived two lifetimes since surgery. Two years and one month after my sexual reassignment, I registered again for college. I was twenty-five. With the money saved in Hawaii, I'd returned to Tennessee in pursuit of a bachelor of arts degree. Perhaps this would prove a less elusive bachelor.

Before I had a chance to begin my fall semester at Middle Tennessee State University (MTSU), my mother found employment with Murfreesboro's Veterans Administration hospital. We moved in together. My father was left minding the farm and relegated to weekend visits. I felt sorry for him. His wife was deserting him, and even if Mother insisted she was making a business decision to secure a nursing position with the government, I knew she was escaping the farm. Unfortunately, in families such as ours, there had to be a loser before someone could win.

Nevertheless, the two years spent with my mother in that off-campus attic apartment were extraordinary. Mozelle and I were on a wonderful adventure. We'd always spoken a language of emotion that Daddy resented and had never understood; now Mother and I were free to enjoy each other's eccentricities. We found humor in everything. My mother proved to be the perfect roommate, and school was an entirely new and rewarding encounter.

Somewhere along the line, while searching for myself, I'd blossomed. Suddenly, I was outgoing and popular. Yet, when my drama club nominated me to run for the Miss MTSU title, I declined. I could imagine little more exciting than being in a beauty pageant, especially one leading toward Atlantic City—but I was afraid I might win. Too much attention could ruin my life. Anyway, our nation was not ready to crown a transsexual Miss America.

Later, I declined an offer to run for student body president, but that was another matter entirely. I'd returned from Honolulu wearing short, short miniskirts, mesh stockings, and spike heels. The miniskirt craze had yet to reach Central Tennessee, so my inventive addition of spike heels and mesh hose pushed my image right over the top. My image presented the MTSU administration with a bit of a problem. I was carrying a 3.8 scholastic average, had been named their theater's "Best Actress of the Year," and was well thought of by my professors—my personal presentation, however, was an embarrassment to the school. The dean of women summoned me to her office.

"I'm worried about you," she confided. "I know you're a nice girl, but I'm worried about what the merchants downtown might think of you."

She paused dramatically and leaned toward me across her desk. She looked me straight in the eye.

"Aleshia, we're a conservative campus here, and . . . well, you're just not . . . "

I waited for some follow-up to this revelation. There was none. It was my turn to comment on the obvious.

"Thank you, Dean," I smiled sweetly. "I certainly have not intended to cause you concern, but . . . as far as the dirty-minded merchants downtown go, I could care less what they think. They'll answer to their own maker." With that bit of sanctimonious rhetoric, I excused myself and left her office. She was still leaning forward on her desk.

Somehow, news of our exchange spread across campus. Being a do-right, all-night woman was paying off; I was an overnight sensation. I didn't think it was enough, however, to propel me into campus politics.

My years at Middle Tennessee State University were a wonderful respite. I felt normal, secure, and accepted. I found a career direction and, in Mrs. Dorothe Tucker, found the best director I could possibly have had at that stage of my theatrical development. She was my first real role model. Articulate, talented, and with a zest for life that I'd never before seen in any married woman, "Dot" Tucker was the self-fulfilled human being that I hoped to become. Here was the woman I wanted to emulate. It was Dot Tucker who helped me believe that there were indeed possibilities ahead for me. In theater I found another side of myself and discovered that life choices do exist. I didn't have to be a stripper or a showgirl—I was a talented actress. I could even teach. A better life was possible for me. As I moved toward my late twenties, I decided it was time to mellow into old age. I expected to be dead before forty.

In two years at MTSU, I starred in five stage productions, was twice named "Best Actress of the Year," received the highest praise for practice teaching in Nashville, maintained my grade average, and still managed an active social life. I was extremely pleased with myself. For once in my life I wasn't looking for a husband. I'd discovered that there can be emotional pitfalls along the marital path.

That's when I met Kelly Pitt.

I was sitting in the upper branches of a friendly art professor's apple tree when I saw the spiffy little sports car speeding up the dirt road toward the house. I sat, straddling a branch, and watched as the blonde, crew-cut driver was warmly greeted by the professor and his wife. Soon, the visitor was mobbed by female apple pickers. From my lofty perch, it seemed every woman in the world was preoccupied with finding a mate. For once I kept my seat.

"So you're Aleshia," I heard from far below me. "I've been hearing about you, Lady."

"Good or bad?" I retorted, dropping an apple into his upturned hands.

"I've liked what I heard," he smiled, "but I like what I see a whole lot better."

I laughed to myself. I'd spent my life being a sucker for smooth talkers, but Nordic blondes had never been my downfall. He didn't bear the slightest resemblance to Hank Foyle.

Kelly Pitt was an industrious young artist who had won regional acclaim for his painting skills. After our initial introduction, I'd found that I liked him very much. He was an immensely talented artist, and the only black mark against him was that he taught school at Castle Heights Military Academy in Lebanon, Tennessee. The war in Vietnam was rapidly escalating. In April 1965 there were 25,000 troops stationed in Southeast Asia; by the end of that year, the number would reach 184,000. Across the nation, students, faculty factions, and many grassroots organizations were raising united voices to protest the war. Although Middle Tennessee State University was far from being an antiwar campus like Berkeley, Jackson State, or Michigan State, I still had misgivings about dating a man who worked for the army's fodder machine. Otherwise, Kelly Pitt fit my new life scenario to a tee. He looked right, he was creditable, and he was acceptable in the world I now wanted as mine. I spent most of my weekends bumming around with Kelly in his MG convertible. I served as his artist's model or sat quietly as he threw his pots. I slept with him and, since my artistic lover was far from loquacious, waited for him to share his thoughts. I was learning the secrets of respectability.

There were times when I would have a relapse. Those were the nights when I'd put on my false eyelashes and drive out to Seward Air Force Base. On those excursions, my disgust with the war was conveniently set aside.

"I'm to meet Major Green at the officers' club," I'd brazenly lie to the sentry at the guard post.

I was never denied admittance to the base. I loved the officers' club. So, I might add, did my less worldly girlfriends from school. Sometimes I'd go alone to meet the fictitious Major Green; sometimes I'd take a carload of friends. Once inside the officers' club we'd announce that we were there to meet the fictitious Major Green. With each influx of Royal Air Force (RAF) officers over from Britain, there must have been three dozen Major Greens. What a gallant bunch of men. Hail, Britannia!

Yet I always came home to Kelly.

"What actress do I most remind you of?" I once asked.

"Anna Magnani," he replied.

"What?!" I shrieked. I'd expected to be told about my striking resemblance to Kim Novak or Arlene Dahl. I was seeking reassurance. "What do you mean, Anna Magnani?" I spit.

I was aware of that she was one of the best actresses in the world and had won an American Academy Award for *The Rose Tattoo* in 1955. Everybody knew that. Everyone also knew that she was no world-class beauty. How dare he?

"Would you say that again?" I gasped.

"Anna Magnani," Kelly repeated. "I think you're womanly and earthy like Anna Magnani."

I calmed down and took him to his rumpled bed.

"There can be no true beauty without a slight imperfection," Kelly whispered. He then tenderly kissed my abdominal scar and traced it with his tongue. "You are perfection because of your imperfections," he murmured. Kelly was very good with words when he put his mind to it. My exposure to Kelly Pitt and the positive environment of the small university gave me confidence that I'd never before experienced.

Everything was going perfectly until six months prior to graduation, when the Fates delivered a one-two punch to my solar plexus.

His name was Martin Gene Lee but he called himself Lee Martin. He was an arrogant pup, six years my junior, and I met him at an off-campus, predominantly gay theater party.

"Oh, you've met Lee," someone said as I stood happily trading insults with the devastatingly handsome youth.

"Yes," I replied. "It's a shame he isn't straight."

"Oh, he is straight all right!" a rather fey young man said disappointedly.

"Darling, there's the difference between us," I smiled. "I don't care."

After the party thinned out, Lee picked up his guitar and started to sing. The evening ended with me sitting, hopelessly infatuated, at the pretty boy's feet. Lee took me home from the party. At my front door he kissed me briefly, got in his car, and drove back to Alabama.

The next morning my mother walked into my room and found me in tears.

"What on earth's the matter, Aleshia?" Mother asked, alarmed.

"I met this man last night," I sobbed, "and I know what's going to happen." I did know. I also knew that Kelly was the man I needed. He'd teach, I'd teach, and together we'd attend faculty teas. I did not want Lee Martin disrupting all my respectable plans for the future.

The Fates who control human destiny heard that and smiled knowingly.

The Fates—Clotho, Lachesis, and Atropos—were quietly slipping up on my blind side. I continued to study; Kelly Pitt continued to paint; and Lee Martin continued to drive up to see me from Alabama. Then Clotho, the spinner of circumstance, knelt on all fours behind me. Lachesis, the measurer of kismet, gaily pushed me backward over the crouching Fate. When I fell, Atropos, the cutter of the thread of destiny, put her foot across my windpipe.

The Fates then hit me with their coup de grâce.

Kelly Pitt was awarded a two-year art scholarship for study in New York City, with a third, fully subsidized year to follow in Paris. I was thrilled for us both.

"I have to go alone," Kelly said.

I blanched.

"You're still in school, Aleshia," Kelly faltered.

"I'll quit!" My solution was simple.

He sighed. I heard what my tongue-tied lover was unable to verbalize. He was leaving Murfreesboro without me. Kelly Pitt had a marvelous opportunity and could abide no distractions.

Two months later I married Martin Gene Lee. Clotho, Lachesis, and Atropos were my bridesmaids. The Goddess gave me away.

CHAPTER 9

Call Me Mrs.

"MARTIN GENE LEE married Aleshia Brevard Crenshaw in a Murfreesboro, Tennessee civil ceremony. The love knot was securely tied around Aleshia's neck by a local justice of the peace." That's how my wedding announcement should have read when I married, on the rebound, early in July 1966.

It was four years since my rebirth at Westlake Clinic, but I was finally fulfilling my lifelong dream of becoming somebody's wife. Unfortunately, it was the wrong somebody! Even the old country gentleman who read our vows realized that Lee and I were not destined for a lifetime together.

"Y'all come back, now, ya hear?" the justice of the peace droned as we left his office. The official knew a doomed union when he saw one.

As we exited the courthouse, my groom mumbled something in my direction. I didn't understand him. I took Lee's arm, leaned toward him, and looked up quizzically.

"You realize this doesn't mean a hell of a lot to me, don't you?" he snapped again.

My heart sank. For all my bravado, marriage did mean something to me. It meant everything. It had taken a lifetime and several engagements to get this wedding ring on my finger. I'd plotted my destiny as artfully as Frank Lloyd Wright had designed his houses, and this day was the culmination of my every romantic dream. I knew exactly why I'd taken my wedding vows. No woman, except a lesbian, could live a complete, fulfilling life without a man by her side. Certainly none that I knew! In fact, at that time I'd never heard of a transgendered person who was lesbian identified. Finding a man to love us was the major thrust of a male-to-female transsexual's life.

How could my husband say "I do," kiss his bride, then five minutes later consign his marriage to hell by announcing it meant nothing? Especially after I'd tried so hard to make this moment special for him, too. Hadn't I forgone most of my long-cherished plans for a large wedding and settled on a justice of the peace? Lee didn't want family members in attendance; I respected his wishes. Lee didn't want any folderol; I cut out the fun. Our marriage ceremony was less emotionally moving than the blood test.

The mere fact that Lee Martin was the groom had been a major concession. He was not my first, second, or third choice.

Still, I was married. I had a husband of my own. My boyhood dream was a reality. Not everyone, however, was happy for me. My mother was as crushed by my marriage as she had been by my sister's elopement. Jeanne devastated our mother by choosing a husband who did not like Mozelle very much. Mother hated him. Now, I'd saddled Mozelle with a second unresponsive son-in-law. My sister and I had both managed to find husbands who were controlling, condescending, and determined to be the undisputed heads of their own households.

"Why did you have to settle for that guitar-playing bastard?" Mother moaned. She was still sulking, months after my marriage. Mozelle never quite grasped her children's desire to star in their own history.

Even before my honeymoon ended, however, I grasped the error of my ways. After our wedding, Lee and I had gone to his apartment in Huntsville, Alabama. It wasn't Niagara Falls, but it would serve my purpose. My husband was going to eat his hurtful words about our marriage meaning nothing to him. Eve accomplished a lot with one apple, but with the tricks I'd mastered over the years—I had an orchard at my disposal.

Lee outflanked me. En route to our nuptial bed, he stopped to visit his former girlfriend. My husband was already taking control of our marriage. Lee's unpardonable behavior so closely resembled lifelong patterns of authority established by my father that I found it strangely comforting. Graciously, I sat through a long afternoon of inside jokes and tasteless sexual allusions. I was trying to convince my husband that I would make him a good wife, so I sat with a smile plastered firmly across my face. I could gleefully have shot them both, chopped their remains into tiny bits, and spread the severed scraps along Alabama roadways to be buried by creeping kudzu. That lurid fantasy saw me through the day.

"Come, husband number one, we're going home," I snapped when I could stand no more. Lee fell in line behind me.

At last I was alone with my husband. As I took down my hair and prepared to consummate our union, I replayed the disastrous afternoon. Perhaps I'd overreacted. Underneath his posturing, Lee was an extremely sensitive young man. When he chose, he could be surprisingly sweet. I hadn't married *totally* to spite Kelly Pitt—not entirely. Mr. and Mrs. Martin Gene Lee were *simpatico*. True, Lee could be thoughtless at times, no doubt about that, but he wouldn't deliberately spoil our wedding night. Why would he? I felt guilty for doubting him. The smoldering youth who waited expectantly in our marriage bed loved me. Had not this professionally hip young man gone against type and insisted on waiting until we were married before having sex? Beneath his macho image, Lee was a traditional southern gentleman. He neither fondled, touched, nor caressed. I was ashamed of myself for doubting him. I was the one who'd kept deep, dark secrets. Someday, I'd tell my husband that he'd married a transsexual, but before sharing that secret, I wanted him to know he'd married a woman. Quietly and tenderly, I went to our wedding bed.

Martin Gene Lee was asleep.

I pushed, pulled, and finally kicked my sleeping husband. There was no rousing him. My bridegroom wasn't to be aroused for many nights to come. The issue of sex suddenly became very important to me. I was getting no affection, no tenderness, and no nooky! I demanded to know the reason.

According to Lee, the problem was with my breasts. They weren't large enough. His German hausfrau, Helga, had been blessed with giant, Teutonic ta-tas. He also assured me that he had not been able to keep his hands off Helga-of-the-mammoth-German-breasts.

The truth was clear: I was not worthy of love.

I turned on myself with a vengeance. All personal accomplishments were forgotten. My new husband saw the real me—the worthless human being. My father, my husband, and I knew that I was not worthy of affection. In the 1960s I could have flown in and out of every airport in the world and still not have lost all the emotional baggage I was lugging around with me.

Because I could never please him, Lee Martin was exactly the man I wanted. I'd chosen my perfect mate. I'd grown up, moved away from Daddy's negative judgments of my worth, only to marry a man who would consistently reinforce my own low opinion of myself.

When the day for my graduation from college arrived, it was a May scorcher—hot, humid, and muggy. The heat was not all that was making me miserable. From this terrible day forward, until the end of my life, I would be living full time with my husband. This was a dreadful day in every respect.

Mother, Daddy, and Lee dutifully sat together in the open-air stadium, waiting to see me receive my diploma. Sweat dripped from their chins, but they struggled to remain cordial. Guests from all over the country crowded into the bleachers to watch their loved ones graduate. The Middle Tennessee State University campus was overflowing with well-wishers. From New York City, my ex-lover, Kelly Pitt, was part of the congratulatory throng.

As one of the graduating students, I was lined alphabetically on the east side of the football stadium. I stood daydreaming and trying to ignore the heat. Lazily turning like a weather vane following a slight breeze, I saw Kelly standing at the north end of the field. He was standing outside the chain-link fence, his fingers linked through the barrier.

Like Katharine Ross in *The Graduate*, I grabbed freedom. I ran to Kelly and stood kissing him through the chain-link fence.

"I hear you're married," Kelly finally said.

"It doesn't mean a thing," I sobbed.

As I sprinted back across the fifty-yard line in time to receive my diploma, Kelly called after me, "I'll call you tonight at eight."

I returned home with diploma in hand; Lee furiously sped back to Alabama; and my mother exploded in my face.

"You're a married woman!" she ranted. "What could you have been thinking? Sometimes I just don't understand you, Aleshia."

"It's my life," I sulked.

I couldn't bring myself to share that my husband found me undesirable. That would mean admitting my marriage was a sham. Worse yet, it would say my reconstructed life was not perfect. I feared my parents would feel transsexual surgery had been a huge mistake.

"Kelly's calling at eight o'clock, and I'm taking his call" was all I could say.

Eight o'clock came and passed. The phone did not ring. By eight-fifteen, Mother's moral high road, Daddy's disdain, and my overwhelming fear of desertion became more than I could stand. I slammed out of the apartment. Shortly after I left, the phone rang.

"Aleshia is not available to you, Kelly," my mother stated flatly.

Kelly Pitt returned to New York. I settled into an uneasy feud with my parents, my husband, and life in general.

Kathy, never able to pass up a good showdown, flew in from San Francisco. She absolutely refused to stand idly by while I married, graduated, and went to war with my parents. Calling on her past stripper expertise, the former Stormy Lee wrangled a headlining position at Skull's Rainbow Room in Nashville's Printers Alley. My new husband and I picked her up at the airport.

"Oh, Girl," she bubbled on our drive back to Murfreesboro, "you'll never believe how lucky Mike and I have been. You know I've always wanted a little leather dress shop?"

"Uh-huh," I responded, keeping my eyes on Lee's car speedometer.

"Well, last year on a San Francisco flight from L.A., I sat next to this hippie. We ended up talking, naturally, and I told him about my dream for a leather shop," she beamed. "This hippie, a real character named Charles Manson, says 'I've got some girls who sew leather,' so I told Mike about him, and now we've got our shop. We're calling it North Beach Leather."

After dropping us off, Lee returned to his home in Huntsville. Kathy pleaded exhaustion, said goodnight to my mother, and we retired for the evening. As soon as we closed the bedroom door, Kathy grabbed my arm.

"Where'd you find her?" Kathy laughed.

"Who?" I asked, amused by her wide-eyed exuberance.

"Your cute little husband!" she chuckled. "The minute I stepped off the plane, I said to myself, 'Oh, God! Now, she's gone and married a queen!'"

I was dumbstruck. Kathy thought Lee was gay! I wanted to slap her.

"You're joking," I blanched.

"Don't tell me you didn't know!" she squealed. "Where'd he find those plaid pants he spray-painted on? He's queer as a three-dollar bill."

I was very angry, but she kept insisting that it was obvious to everyone. It wasn't obvious to me. It wasn't obvious to my family, and it wasn't *obvious* to any of my friends. Lee couldn't be gay, or someone would have noticed before now. Anyway, gay men were not attracted to me. Uhhh-oh!

Silver Fire, a.k.a. Kathy, a.k.a. Stormy Lee, enjoyed her stint in Printers Alley almost as much she enjoyed watching me squirm. Even with Daddy around on weekends, our small apartment was festive, upbeat, and filled with laughter. It was like living in a dormitory. Mother loved having "her girls" around and always introduced Kathy as her "adopted" daughter.

"Please, come to the Alley with us, James," Mother teased. She was trying to cajole Daddy into seeing Kathy's burlesque act.

"Why should I?" Daddy retorted gruffly. "I've already seen everything she's got to show."

My father was not a patron of the arts.

In spite of Daddy's disapproval, Mother fell in love with burlesque.

"There's not one thing dirty about that show," she mused. "I'm sorry I didn't see a strip show a long time ago. I bet I'd have been pretty good at that myself."

Gypsy's Mama Rose was alive, well, and riding in the front seat of my husband's car. In the back seat with Kathy, I was trying to find a comfortable position.

My back had been bothering me lately.

Near the end of Kathy's visit with us, while doing a leisurely bathtub soak, I discovered a vaginal lump. I was soaping and out popped a knot. One minute all was well with my labia; the next there was a knot in the right outer fold. I screamed bloody murder for Mozelle, the nurse.

"Let's not jump to conclusions," Mother soothed, "but just to be on the safe side, I'll get some recommendations for a good gynecologist." Kathy was hardly on her plane for San Francisco before Mother had me in a doctor's office in Nashville's North End.

"*North* End does not quite seem appropriate for this particular problem," I quipped as we sat in the waiting room.

"You must tell the doctor about your surgery," Mother continued, ignoring my joke. Since she'd made the appointment, we'd had an ongoing debate. I was totally opposed to mentioning my transgendered past; Mother demanded I tell. I argued that if a gynecologist didn't know the difference, I needed to find another doctor. The truth was that I hated admitting my male past. Our debate was a waste of energy. The moment my feet were in the stirrups, I blew my cover.

"Doctor, could this possibly be because I did my own castration?" My embarrassment hung in the air as my "gyno" sent for his colleague.

"Do you know what you're seeing here?" my physician asked, testing his partner. The confrere launched into his diagnosis of my problem.

"No, no," my gynecologist corrected him, "did you realize that you're examining a transsexual patient?"

The air that supported my composure was sucked from the room, and my embarrassment came crashing down around me. I was back in my freshman biology lab—I knew exactly how a guinea pig felt.

I had a tumor. It extended from the protruding knot on the labia back to my spine. The doctor wanted to operate immediately and cautioned that the growth was possibly malignant. For perhaps the first time in my life, my gender issue was secondary. If I were going to die, I'd die on my own terms and do exactly what I chose to do for my final days. What I chose was to open my college production of *Light Up the Sky*. I was playing, Irene, the lead.

With the news of his wife's impending death, Lee became gentle, reassuring, and understanding. His tenderness surprised everyone— especially me. The tumor was removed early on a Wednesday morning, but there was no information immediately forthcoming.

"I have to know about my wife," Lee demanded as he marched up to my surgeon on a Nashville golf course, at the tenth green. "I've got to know how she is."

As he'd promised my impatient husband, the doctor brought news as soon as he had the biopsy report back from the laboratory. The tumor was benign.

"Your husband loves you very much," the doctor said as he squeezed my shoulder. With the news that I'd live came an overwhelming sense of gratitude and warmth for my concerned husband. For better or worse, Lee and I were together.

The Martin Lees should have settled for being great friends. He couldn't get past being a husband with a sexual role to fulfill; I couldn't allow him to forget it. The relationship floundered as we fixated on playing husband and wife. We were also reeling from financial stress.

The Red Carpet Lounge wasn't show business as I knew it, but when I answered an ad for "evening work," I came home a go-go dancer. My job was to dance in a cage for the entertainment of beer-swilling Bubbas. The burly lads were perfectly harmless—as long as you stayed in your cage. In an Alabama roadhouse, the rules are simple: don't mention Martin Luther King, don't defend Darwinism, and never genuflect before you take off your clothes.

Early in my new career, I was visited by a couple of female customers. The two women came to my dressing room between shows. I was only guessing that they were female. Two things I knew for sure—(1) they were carrying purses, and (2) drag queens would never leave home looking like these two.

"We came to warn you, Missy," the more hulking of the two sneered. "We'd better never find our husbands in this here bar lookin' at you without us bein' with 'em." Her cohort chimed in, "Hussy, we know your type can be had for fifty cents. You get what we're telling you?" I understood—(3) they were women, with husbands to prove it.

Not all people strive to be the best that they can be. I know that. What I still fail to grasp, however, is why women so gross, uncouth, and menacing—even though genetically female—would ever be considered more womanly than a well-behaved transsexual. From conception I was more ladylike than those two women. Since my gender reassignment, and after five years of female living, I was now more confused than ever by what it truly meant to be a woman. As a transwoman, I recognized my obligation to be the most deserving female I could be. I was, after all, pledging the Sorority of Womankind. As with any sorority pledge, my sisterhood depended on my acceptance by the founding group. Yet what had those two offensive, unsightly women done to earn their sisterhood? If a choice must be made, I failed to understand why their womanhood was more valid than mine.

I was twenty-nine years old, educated, married, and in a go-go cage at the Red Carpet Lounge—doing "the Mashed Potato." Whistles and catcalls were not the acceptance I'd longed for as a woman. Get real!

My husband, for his part, was happy working for IBM forty hours a week and singing with a band on the weekends. My wifely duty, as he saw it, was to cheerfully support his endeavors. Life in the South is different for a man than it is for a woman. Each weekend, my starstruck husband would seat me at a ringside table and join his band on stage. During the musical breaks he would table-hop, flirt, and preen. As the lead singer's wife, I was expected to stay in my place. I was off limits. No one spoke to me, asked me to dance, or joined my table.

One Sunday, I called the band's drummer to my table during a break. That was the extent of my disruptive behavior. I didn't screw a bootlegger in the back of a van; I talked to a member of the band for approximately fifteen minutes. My husband was livid. I'd embarrassed him in public.

After the last set, Lee stormed off the stage and headed for the exit. Grabbing my purse on the run, I managed to catch him as he gunned his Mustang out of the parking lot. He saw me, screeched to a stop, and, making sure everyone heard his verbal tirade, ordered me into the car. I got in. We rode in total silence, speeding down the Alabama highway. Afraid to cause a scene and knowing better than to comment on our speed, I braced as we approached each new curve. Lee sped to the home of two male friends, slammed the car door, and started for the house. I heaved a deep sigh and followed.

"You're not welcome here," he snapped, turning on me.

"Why not?" I pleaded.

"Because my friends can't stand you." My husband turned and walked into the home of his allies.

Mother was talking to my husband on the phone when I walked in her front door.

"Yes, I'm in Tennessee," I shrieked at Lee. "Stay in Alabama with your boyfriends. I'm going to England."

"England?!" he yelped.

Good. I had his attention. All I needed now was to finish him off with a noteworthy coup de grâce.

"Yes, England," I parried before delivering my finishing thrust. "Great Britain, where men are men and *I* love it."

I proceeded to weave a total fabrication about a raffish RAF officer, Major Green. The fictitious flyboy wanted me to divorce my husband, marry him, and jet away to the British Isles.

"I might as well marry him," I concluded. "He's not afraid to sleep with your wife." I slammed down the phone.

Mother was speechless. She stood in the kitchen staring at me. She had no way of knowing that I was lying, or that my difficult husband had called at the worst possible moment. On my retreat home to Tennessee, I'd been stopped by a Alabama highway patrolman.

"I'll calm you down, honey," the patrolman leered when he saw that I was weeping and upset. "You just pull your sweet self up that side road over there, and I'll take care of you."

The thought of unsolicited physical consolation from the buck-toothed, public servant pushed me totally over the edge. My tears dried up. Rage at Lee, marriage, and all of life's little inequities was unleashed on that grinning buffoon. I took his badge issue, demanded his name, and wrote down his license plate number. Righteous indignation surrounded me like a choir robe. This Alabama Bubba had two choices— shoot me or send me across the state line. Perhaps because I was an educated, married white woman, he kept his weapon holstered and sent me home to mama.

After the night I'd had, I was in no mood to take more crap from Martin Gene Lee. I took the phone off the hook and went to bed.

The next morning, when Mother replaced the receiver, the telephone began to ring. My husband was in the psychiatric ward of a Huntsville hospital. After our telephone conversation, Lee had slit his wrist and, with his blood, written my name on his friend's wall. Being a perfectionist, he chose to make a particularly deep gash on his left, guitar-chording wrist. He severed the tendons. Lee would live, but the doctors said he might never play guitar again.

My plans for divorce were forgotten.

Lee was the one who wanted out now. His therapist believed the pressure of marriage was killing my husband.

"Who ever heard of such bunkum?" I wailed to Mother. "I might be killing Lee, but the marriage is good for him."

As soon as Lee was released from psychiatric care, he came to see me in Murfreesboro.

"I can't stay married any longer," Lee began. "I've been fighting homosexual tendencies all my life, and I thought you could save me. You can't. I can't take the pressure of being married to a woman."

I couldn't believe my ears. Except for the fact that he found me physically repulsive, Lee seemed like any other extremely handsome, sensitive, talented young man. He wore lumberjack shirts and work boots, for God's sake! Gay men didn't dress like that—not in 1967. What kind of crazy karmic backlash was this, anyway? My marriage was a disaster because I *was* a woman?

"If that's all that's bothering you, forget it," I blurted. "I'm a transsexual."

Lee fled for Huntsville and safety. He hated me for deceiving him. It took him four months to understand that by rejecting my gender history, he was also rejecting my essence. He softened. For better or worse, we were connected. There was no workable label for our marriage; we didn't know what to call ourselves, but we agreed that together we shared something we did not have separately. That "something" we called love.

Somewhere in the background, there were three Fates dancing a jig.

CHAPTER 10

Teacher! Teacher!

SID GRAUMAN'S famous theater was the first place my husband wanted to visit when we moved to Hollywood in 1967. How could Grauman's Chinese Theater look so radiant after forty years in the glare of klieg lights and California sunshine? Surely, the grand old dame had had a face-lift—or two. She'd been around since 1927. Gosh, it was good to be back in Tinsel Town—where looks still counted for everything.

In the golden land of fruits and nuts, my husband valiantly tried to pretend we were like any other newly married couple. Apart from the fact that we'd been married for over a year and had yet to successfully consummate our marriage, we were exactly like other West Coast couples. He looked like a stud; I acted like an addle-brained bride. Who'd know the difference?

With the luxury of hindsight, I see what connected me to Lee for so many years. He was handsome, bright, filled with energy—and every bit as confused as his wife.

The phrase "Keep the good and dump that which weakens or oppresses us" had yet to cross my lips. I was too busy collecting feminist cast-off disabilities in the name of femininity. I wore their discards like a charm bracelet. Yet for some American women "the times, they were a' changing." Activists, led by Betty Friedan, author of *The Feminine Mystique,* had recently formed NOW, the National Organization for Women. Ms. Friedan was telling American women that they could do *anything*— and more than a few were believing it. A mere five years after the painfully introspective writings of Sylvia Plath, American women were aggressively marching toward liberation. In living rooms across the nation, women were practicing assertiveness training and holding consciousness-raising sessions. In the tradition of Susan B. Anthony and Elizabeth Cady Stanton's woman's movement of the 1800s, a new generation of women began throwing off the shackles of assigned gender roles and societal expectations for women. Because of women supporting one another, the seedling of change soon burst into full flower. As the new women's movement surged ahead, I lagged behind, still trying to comprehend the traditional female role. Not having been raised female, I lacked a socialized foundation to support my feminine predisposition.

While the world wrestled with changes in traditional male/female roles, Lee and I struggled along as husband and wife. We found an affordable, bougainvillea-covered white stucco apartment in Playa del Rey. The apartment, with its great view of the harbor, was an easy drive to Lee's new management job in air freight. His "old ball 'n' chain," the family member with a college degree, could walk to her waitressing job at a nearby Mexican restaurant. I resented my subordinate position, both as wife and as waitress, but jokingly told everyone I was "paying my dues."

"When I become a star, this waitressing experience will make a great story for the *Merv Griffin Show*," I laughed. Actually, I'd had difficulty finding any job. I didn't type sixty words per minute—and no employer wanted a career woman who lacked that necessary skill. Five years previously, when I was an uneducated boy, employment agencies had shown a great deal more interest in me.

In the food-service industry I was a disaster. My service was extremely slow, I spoke no Spanish, and I didn't know a taco from an enchilada, but I still made more tip money than the other waitresses. The gratuities were because I entertained my customers. The kitchen staff was not amused.

"Is this my enchilada platter?" I'd ask, standing in the center of the kitchen, pointing at steaming plates. The cooks spoke no English and ignored my sign language. Their kitchen was no place for some *"estupida gringa."* The restaurant business swirled around me until I was fired on Halloween day.

"I might have known," Lee sneered when I came home in tears. If he had hit me, it would have hurt less. I'd failed him again.

A bust at slinging rice and beans, I decided to take a civil-service exam. Social workers don't have to know anything. I'd witnessed their ineptitude firsthand, the year President John F. Kennedy was assassinated and a nation's hope for Camelot died with him. In 1963, I was sharing an apartment with a girlfriend, her twin sons, and two daughters in Inglewood, California. Money was very tight. At night, while I worked as a cocktail waitress, Bonnie was with her children. During the day I played surrogate mama. My friend couldn't afford child care.

Naturally, a man was at the root of my girlfriend's financial predicament. He was a divorced father who couldn't support two families. He chose Bonnie's, his wife brought charges, and being a deadbeat dad landed him in jail. Both families ended up on government support. Enter a social worker—in red, white, and blue patent-leather three-inch spikes.

I sat in awe, mesmerized by the symbolism of those stilettos. I was less impressed by the civil servant's surly manner.

"Have you had your hair done?" she interrogated.

"I had it cut," Bonnie meekly explained.

"Uh-huh. I see," smirked the government twit. She was jotting down everything that could possibly be construed as an infraction.

"I have to maintain my appearance," Bonnie protested. "I have to keep my job."

In my estimation, the humiliating incident was a mockery of public assistance. It was four years, however, before I decided to become a *respectful* civil servant. The moment I passed the written civil-service examination, I went shopping for patriotic shoes. I would make a difference in the system—and I desperately needed the job. A personal interview was all that stood between a new career and me.

"No sweat," I told everyone. "We'll talk, they'll realize I'm a nice person, and I'll be assigned my first case. How hard can it be? Dealing with people is my forte!" Besides, I only knew of one person who'd ever failed a personal interview—and that fool admitted to smoking marijuana!

"Mrs. Lee," the interviewer warbled, "if you suspect a male is living on the premises with a welfare mother and her children, what action would you take?"

"Probably none," I quickly replied. I sat forward, on the edge of my chair, with my legs neatly crossed at the ankles, my hands comfortably resting in my lap. I was looking the interviewer squarely in his eyes. I knew how to present myself when on an interview. "I don't believe children should suffer for the sins of their parents," I concluded.

My interviewer twitched, shifted his gaze, and did some scratching in my file.

"Looking as you do, how do you feel you could possibly be effective working in underprivileged areas?" he asked, looking at me over his glasses. I was prepared for this one.

"Because I care, I'll be extremely effective," I smiled, nailing the answer squarely. "I often receive more respect from those less fortunate than I do from peers. Beauty can be a curse for a woman, you see."

I was thanked, sent home, and flunked.

Crushed, I decided that perhaps a party would take my mind off my failures. Bobby Blackburn and Harry Worth, two old friends, were invited to Playa del Rey for dinner.

My friendship with Bobby had developed at Memphis State University, where, as flighty college roommates, we'd danced the Charleston atop our dormitory beds. We were addicted to music from *The Boyfriend*. Since college, we'd stayed in touch. Bobby had even met his life partner, Harry, while on a trip west to visit me at Finocchio's. I loved them both and wanted my life with Lee to include Bobby and Harry—as my life with Hank had.

"Love-of-my-lifetime," I cooed to Lee, "if you don't get out of this house, I'll never be ready for guests." I enjoyed playing my wifely role to the hilt.

"I'll go shoot a game of pool," he mumbled, ambling for the door.

"They'll be here about eightish, so use your own judgment about getting home." I was glad to have Lee out from underfoot.

Our guests arrived on time, bringing with them a lovely bottle of wine. My husband was not home to drink it. Dinner would have been at nine, but Lee wasn't there to eat it. It was past ten when my husband leisurely strolled into the apartment. Dinner was ruined, and so was my mood. Bobby and Harry beat a hasty retreat.

I threw away the dinner and went to bed. There were no words to express my anger. The next morning I found them.

"Where were you, you no-good son of a bitch?"

"I went to play a game or two of pool" was his exasperating reply.

I lost my composure, yelling, screaming, and cursing Lee for his thoughtlessness. "Oh, you're such a *man*," I sneered.

Lee just looked at me.

"My mother was right," I fired over my shoulder as I stalked into the bedroom.

Mimicking me, he followed, asking, "And what did *Mommy* say?"

I turned, cocked, lowered both barrels to groin level, and fired. "She said you swish more than she does!"

I hit the floor so hard that, for a few moments, I forgot what had caused it. Lee's punch knocked me across the bedroom and into the closet. I landed on my shoes. I could either take a spike heel and kill the bastard—or put on my shoes and hit the pavement.

I dressed and left the apartment.

That evening, at Donkin's in the Marina, I met six feet and eight gorgeous inches of well-toned flesh. Bob Grant was awe-inspiring, but this was not an evening for romance. I was bent on revenge.

"You're wonderful, Bob," I purred as the bartender gave last call. "I really want you to come home with me tonight." My plan was brilliantly simple. I'd arrive home with eighty inches of magnificent prime beef, introduce my husband as my brother, and wait for Lee to explode in a jealous rage. Bob Grant would then mop up the floor with my husband's lying, cheating, and violent ass.

Unfortunately, I had not married a fool. My husband looked Bob Grant up and down, sat in a chair, and pretended to be my brother. It was time for my first divorce.

After leaving Lee, for the first time in my life there was no gender confusion, homophobic discrimination, or overpowering husband convincing me I was worthless. The world becomes a brighter place once the wrong man is out of it. For the first time since surgery, I knew what it meant to be free. From this point forward, my life would change. From this time on, my transsexuality would be less intrusive in my life. As if it were an omen, I immediately found work as a substitute teacher for the Los Angeles City school system.

When the full-time history teacher from Venice High was injured in a horrific skiing accident, my substitute position turned into a long-term assignment. The broken and battered teacher requested that I, specifically, be assigned to his classroom. History was not my chosen field, but he asked for me. I was a miniskirted, flaming-haired liberal, who drove the front office personnel to distraction, and that was exactly why the teacher asked for me. The important thing was that, as his choice, there was nothing the conservative school staff could do about it. Mrs. Lee would teach history.

I cherished the time spent with my students, even though there were extreme differences in their academic status. On one end of the scholastic scale perched my accelerated class of top-notch students; the other end was weighed down by a remedial class that despised both school and history. The accelerated group pushed hard for magnificent SAT scores; the rebellious remedial group merely pushed.

"What's all that dead stuff got to do with me?" a fifteen-year-old cried. Taking me to task and challenging the importance of history, she punctuated her point by banging her fist on the desk—repeatedly. Angrily spitting out the facts of her life, she silenced me with her descriptions of the birthing process. The unwed teenage mother had a legitimate, if violent, objection to our educational system. The young woman needed a kind of help that did not exist in her textbooks. Practice teaching had not prepared me for this teenager's reality, and her situation unsettled me.

There are no accidents. These insurgents were the reason the incapacitated teacher needed me in his classroom. My responsibility was now to make history real for these students.

Unless education can be geared toward the needs, interests, and enrichment of the student, the rote memorization of dates and locations is a meaningless exercise. This group of insubordinate teens taught me how to teach. We hashed, rehashed, haggled, and debated history's relationship to the rough-and-tumble existence of life as they knew it. Generally, the classroom was a volatile free-for-all, triggered by discussions of current events. The learning experience was a noisy, theatrical happening. By tying the personal events of their teenage lives with historical sum and substance, both the students and I came to understand the importance of history. My greatest coup, however, was in bringing a record player and chart-topping 78 to class. I boldly announced that I wanted to learn the Pearl, the current dance craze. Naturally, I chose the most assertive, disruptive member in the group as my tutor. Acceptance by this antihero gave me immediate hip status. Soon I was being hailed with a new affectionate title. As I crossed campus, students would call out, "Hey, Big Red, how's it goin'?"

It was "goin' fine" until I was called to the principal's office. "Mrs. Lee," he began from behind his massive oak desk, "I'm concerned by the overly familiar manner by which your students address you."

What was this man talking about? I'd expected a pat on the back. He should be overjoyed with my progress. Grades were up, absenteeism was down—more important, my students were learning that they create their own history.

"This 'Big Red' nonsense," he continued. "Your students aren't showing you the proper respect."

"I disagree," I countered. "I believe they are showing me the utmost respect and callin' 'em as they see 'em. In my stocking feet, sir, I'm almost six feet tall; my hair is indeed Go-Go Red; and my students are free to call me anything they please—as long as they come to class to do it."

Timid Buddy Crenshaw would never have found the mettle to stand his ground against a bureaucratic minion. Buddy feared hearing, "What would a sissy know about it?" My shame at being "different" would have silenced me. Most of those fears were behind me. This altercation was light years away from my childhood experiences in Tennessee.

The matter was dropped. The issue of what to do with "Big Red" paled by comparison to the other problems faced by academia in the late 1960s. Student unrest and vandalism in Los Angeles' schools was a public matter of concern. Soon, Venice High exploded in riot. Youngsters spilled out of classroom doors and windows, streaming into California streets, vandalizing cars, and destroying property. My rowdy, street-smart urchins stayed with Big Red. They knew I was on their side.

By the late 1960s, I'd met a mere handful of pre-op and post-op transsexuals. There weren't many of us around. We came from different areas of the country, of the world; had varying degrees of education, social position, and family acceptance; but we were united by our desire to find a place in mainstream society. Becoming a heterosexual woman was the only goal I knew existed for transsexuals. I did not meet a female-to-male transsexual until the late 1990s, nor did I realize that transsexual women could be lesbian identified. The transwomen I knew were willing to risk everything in order to live their lives in sync with the American standard of womanhood. That was our American Dream. I thought I'd arrived. After six years as a post-op transsexual, I felt at home in mainstream community.

Seemingly, everyone in greater Los Angeles shared a dream of film stardom. David Silver was the only person I knew who was doing something about it. Like me, he'd come to Venice High as a substitute teacher, but his goal was to act. David was even taking acting lessons. He wasn't cast in the glorious physical mold of a Bob Grant, but he might be much smarter than my strapping Adonis. Bob was *waiting* to be discovered.

Until I found out which man was on the right professional track, I'd run with both.

David introduced me to John Heath, his acting coach—Bob arranged for me to meet the cast of *The Beverly Hillbillies.*

Max Baer, Jr., who played Jethro Bodine on the popular show, was my escort's roommate. Bob Grant's approach to obtaining star status, although not based on study and dedication, was certainly exciting. On the Desilu lot, I was like a precocious child at Disneyland. Bob introduced me to the entire Clampett clan: Buddy Ebsen as Jed; Irene Ryan as Granny; Donna Douglas as Elly Mae; and of course, his roommate, the strapping Max.

More than anything, I was captivated by the make-up technique used on Donna Douglas. She had white lines drawn all over her face. I didn't want to embarrass her by staring, but I was dying to know the reason for the strange white streaks. I suspected the actress was a wee bit older than the fresh-faced Elly Mae she portrayed onscreen. If caulking one's face could fool the camera, I needed that information. Miss Douglas was named Miss New Orleans in 1957, so we were more than likely the same age. I was past thirty! Silently, I thanked God that I'd always looked at least ten years younger than my actual age. I didn't believe God had made a mistake fashioning me; I accepted that my transgendered life had a purpose; but much of my theatrical life span had certainly been wasted correcting His botched half-assed assignment. I'd have a few questions come Judgment Day.

Bob Grant's theatrical connections got me onto the set of every show that was filming on Desilu's Gower Street lot that afternoon. The popular *Petticoat Junction* was interesting, but the real excitement lay around the corner on the set of *Green Acres*. I was enchanted by the relaxed mastery of the stars, Eddie Albert and Eva Gabor. The crew hummed like a well-oiled machine. The energy was high, the scenes flowed effortlessly, and the set appeared to be totally free of stress. "What a nice way to work," I whispered to Bob as a scene ended.

There was only one major disappointment at Desilu—I was not discovered.

As we departed the studio through its arched gates, my escort took my arm. "It's a myth that Lana Turner was discovered while sitting on a stool at Schwabb's drugstore, you know," he slyly whispered. If Bob Grant could identify my bid for attention, my drag queen-inspired eagerness needed toning down.

One of the difficulties I'd encountered since transitional surgery was finding a presentational level that was not "over the top." Onstage, as Lee Shaw, my acceptance had come because I was a diva. Onstage, however, everything is bigger than life and projected to the back row of the theatre. Now, although I wanted to be colorful, I didn't want to be a cartoon. Even my family and first husband warned me against being "too much."

"You should wear more subdued clothing," Lee often said during our marriage. "You overwhelm your natural beauty by being too outrageous." His criticism hurt, but I felt drab and uninteresting in conservative togs.

Meeting John Heath, David Silver's acting coach, was a major step toward modifying my . . . excesses. I started studying film technique under John's expert tutelage.

"Oh, my dear, if you do not learn to hold back some of your, uh, exuberance," John would scold, "you will be laughed off every drive-in movie screen in this country."

John believed in my innate ability but felt I displayed a serious defect in harnessing it. "Darling Child," he'd say, holding up his hand to stop an acting exercise in progress, "why do you refuse to trust your own charisma? Don't work so hard! Let it flow. You don't have to act the part, relax and let the part become you. You're naturally quite charming, you know."

John supplied me with clothing, confidence, and an occasional meal. He also became my personal manager yet refused to take a salary for his representation. "We'll talk about that when I've made you a star," he'd say.

Having the support of John Heath was not my only cause for celebration in 1968. That year I also obtained an annulment from my first marriage.

The Martin Gene Lees parted ways in Playa del Rey, but nothing had been done to alter our legal status. I was teaching, studying, and dating both David Silver and Bob Grant. I had my hands full. There was no time to worry about being legally tied to Lee. David disagreed.

David Silver was born into a family of doctors and lawyers—and then there was David. He was an on-again, off-again teacher, would-be Hell's Angel, actor wanna-be, and music publishing disaster. I adored David's steady, secure parents and, like them, hoped their son would eventually follow in their prosperous footsteps. I suspect that's why the Silvers willingly accepted a tall, married heathen into their inner circle. It was David's brother, a promising attorney, who was chosen to represent me in my divorce proceedings. It was his idea that I get an annulment rather than a divorce. If I were to become a Silver, it was better I not be a divorcée. Being Gentile was bad enough.

Going to court was a mere formality, or so I was told. My plea for an uncontested annulment on the grounds of an unconsummated union would be presented to the courts, and that would be that.

It wasn't.

"Mr. Silver," barked the judge, "would you please approach the bench?"

"Oh, my God!" I whimpered to David, "They're going to send me up the river for this."

The judge didn't buy our claim of nonconsummation of my marriage vows.

"Why not, your honor?" pursued my young, green attorney.

"My God!" hissed the judge. "Take a look at her."

Before dissolving my marriage, the magistrate wanted to have a word with me. I had to testify. "This will get me fifteen to life," I sighed. As I took a seat at the bench, I noted the superficial resemblance the judge bore to my father.

"All right, young woman," he began, "why is it that you never consummated your marriage?"

As with all great stage moments, inspiration was instantaneous. I stared "my father" in his wrinkled, old face, held his gaze a moment too long, then turned away. When I looked back at the judge, my eyes were misty with unshed tears.

"I guess he just didn't like me, Your Honor." I walked out of the courtroom a single individual.

"Now, let's go get married," David suggested as we strolled toward the car.

"You've got to be kidding," I laughed.

My personal manager, John, decided it was time to find me an agent. He selected a stunning black sheath, had me stitched into the garment, then took the dress and his protégée to see Mitzi McGreggor. John chatted away as he drove me across the hill to see the Universal City–based film and television agent. He was trying to take my mind off the upcoming audition. I'd always assumed that the San Fernando Valley community was named for the famous movie studio, Universal, and was fascinated to hear the true story. Early filmmaker Carl Laemmle chose the name Universal City for his 230-acre chicken ranch in 1914. Big changes had certainly taken place in film and chicken ranching—now, it was my time to crow.

Based on my rehearsed scene, my tight dress, and John's glowing recommendation, Ms. McGreggor signed me as a client.

My phone was ringing by the time I got home.

"You have a casting director's audition tomorrow at Universal Studios!" John shouted. If possible, my manager was more excited than his fledgling actress. That evening, he showed up with a gift. The beat-up pink bunny rabbit had only one button eye, but John insisted that I carry the dilapidated creature on all future auditions.

"He's flipped," I fumed, after closing the door after my manager. "I bet Sarah Bernhardt didn't have to carry a dumb March hare on her audition for *La Dame aux Camelias*. How am I supposed to look sexy while I'm carrying a damn rabbit? It's crazy, and I won't do it."

The next morning, at the appointed hour, Aleshia and her unkempt bunny were in the office of Universal's casting director, Joe Rich.

"Well," said Mr. Rich after listening to my audition piece, "you're too tall to ever be a leading lady. Your makeup is all wrong, and although you have an interesting voice, about halfway through your monologue I started hoping your dress would fall off." So much for one-eyed rabbits.

I listened politely, plastered a smile on my face, and thanked the casting guru for his helpful critique. Then I lugged the bunny back to my car, sat in the parking lot, and cried for thirty minutes. Various men had hit, defiled, and abandoned me, but nothing had ever hurt as much as Joe Rich's words. He was a respected casting director, and I'd hoped to enter Universal Studios professionally through Mr. Rich's door. Unfortunately, he hated me. Worse than that, Joe Rich didn't respect my talent.

There was a message from my agent waiting when I returned home. Joe Rich, the casting director who thought I was a loser, had scheduled me an interview with the producers of Universal Pictures' *The Love God*. I dropped the phone, ran to my car, and rescued the tattered hare.

By recommending that the film's producers see me, Joe Rich, with his withering casting director's eye, made my first film possible. Perhaps his negative assessment had been Joe's way of testing a neophyte. Whatever his reasoning, I would forever be grateful to him. Universal Studios signed me to my first film contract. I was Sherri, the red-haired "Pussycat" in *The Love God*, starring Don Knotts. The role offered little dialogue, but I was making my motion-picture debut in a major Universal Pictures film. Equally exciting was discovering that I had eight luxurious costume changes and time on film in which to wear them. Don's character, Abner Peacock, would be surrounded at all times by four tall, voluptuous women called "the Pussycats." Skinny, sissy little Buddy Crenshaw from Hartsville, Tennessee, had burst into bloom.

My film career began on a Universal Studios soundstage. Despite 6 A.M. calls, the tedium of waiting for a specific shot to be set up, and the strain of trying always to appear up-tempo and energized, I was having the time of my life. It was ecstasy merely to be on a studio lot.

I shot myself in my untrained theatrical foot during my first few hours on the set. After my makeup session, I returned to my soundstage trailer to await my call. There was nothing for me to do, so I sat and studied my face in the mirror. I didn't like what I saw. The studio's makeup artist had obviously made a terrible mistake. He'd downplayed my character. Sherri needed *oomph*! I opened my own makeup case and went to work. Soon I was called to the set.

"Do you have on eyeliner?" questioned the on-set makeup artist before the scene started.

"Yes," I replied, honestly. I was proud of my improvements. The professional makeup artist stared at me, with his mouth hanging open, as I explained what was wrong with the original artist's endeavors.

"Uh-huh," he laughed. "Well, Sweetheart, just keep your eyes open, and don't even think about blinking on camera. Stage makeup doesn't work on film." I blanched. "Don't worry," he said patting my exposed knee, "you'll be fine today, just keep your eyes opened wide. At all cost, do not blink on camera, or they'll fire us both."

At least six takes were filmed of that first scene—I didn't blink in one of them.

To my surprise, I was assigned a new makeup artist. I'd reacted thoughtlessly by changing my makeup, and yet I was being rewarded for it. This new cosmetologist was brilliant. He even asked me how I saw my character, Sherri. I could have kissed him. He carefully listened to what I had to say and then set about visually creating a stunning showgirl. Patiently, he individually applied both top and bottom false lashes. His patience achieved what I'd attempted to create with the cursed eyeliner. I looked better than I'd ever looked in my life. This time, I kept my mouth shut and took notes.

Our film was guided by Nat Hiken, the celebrated director of the television series *Sergeant Bilko*, featuring Phil Silvers. Mr. Hiken was recognized as a master of the comic genre. I idolized him. More than anything, I desperately wanted to please my director and worked very hard to develop quickly some mastery of the craft.

Early in the filming, we shot a montage that involved the Pussycats in various wardrobe changes. We were supposedly in different locales, walking seductively behind Don. The effect was actually achieved by walking in place on a conveyer belt while location shots were projected on a screen behind us. Rather than relaxing while the cameramen checked their angles and prepared for the filming, I was in position on the conveyer, learning to walk with grace and confidence on the moving belt.

When the camera crew was technically ready, the assistant director called for the Pussycats. His job was to instruct us as to the proper attitude and feel for the upcoming shot.

"Leave Aleshia alone," Mr. Hiken called out. "She knows what she's doing." I was stunned. The famous director had taken notice of my extra effort. More important, Nat Hiken knew my name! His approval was more important to me than my salary—almost.

Not long after the conveyer belt achievement, my agent called in an early-morning frenzy. "You'll never work again," she ranted. I'd overslept and missed my 6 A.M. makeup call. Not that it mattered, but I did have a good excuse. During the night I'd been awakened by a persistent ringing. In my stupor, believing the ruckus was my wake-up alarm, I reached over and turned off the clock. The noise continued. My telephone was ringing.

"I'm exhausted," I snapped, hung up, and went back to sleep. I failed to reset my alarm for four o'clock.

By the time my agent called, it was three hours past my scheduled call. According to Mitzi, the entire company was waiting. I had to be there before they could shoot a ten o'clock scene in front of Universal's Black Tower. By oversleeping, I'd held up an entire production crew and my incompetence was costing Universal a fortune. I jumped into the first garment I saw and ran out the door. I didn't even brush my teeth. In abject terror, I sped over the hill toward Universal. When I raced into the studio, the makeup crew was waiting for me. Three artists, in concert, worked their magic, and in short order, I was sped by car to the set location.

"We haven't notified anyone that you weren't here," whispered my favorite makeup artist. "Perhaps they're behind schedule."

My late arrival went unnoticed by everyone—save for those wonderful souls intent on keeping the neophyte's tardiness hush-hush.

By the time of my third screw-up, I'd learned enough to keep my mouth shut. This little foible, however, was immortalized on "celluloid."

We were shooting a scene where Don Knotts exits an elevator with his quartet of Pussycats, eight abreast, behind him. My costume for that particular scene included a huge lime-green marabou hat, which I adored. It was smashing with my red hair. I was in my usual place, on the right side of the line, when the director called, "Action!" I cleared the side of the elevator door, but my beautiful marabou chapeau did not. I could feel the feathered bonnet wobbling on my head.

"Oh, shit!" I muttered.

"Cut and print," called Nat Hiken. I didn't mention my filmed vulgarity. Time is money in the movie business.

CHAPTER 11

A Playboy Bunny

THE BUNNY was again in my arms; I was in my snug black sheath and on my way to Paramount Studios. John drove me to the famed studio for my appointment. *Paint Your Wagon* would soon begin filming in the Northwest, and my manager had wrangled me an audition. With the prospect of new film work ahead, all was right in my world—until John parked in a back lot, far from the executive offices. I'd pointed out several parking spaces along the way, but John had ignored my suggestions. What could he be thinking? John might force me to trudge across Paramount's back lot in a tight dress and stiletto heels, but I'd bitch and moan every painful step of the way. Next time, maybe he'd remember to treat Aleshia Brevard like a lady.

As we made our way toward the executive offices, male heads started appearing at the windows of the design shops lining our path. The boys in construction were spreading the word. Our walk was soon accompanied by whistles and catcalls. My brilliant manager, by forcing me to promenade through the studio's set building area, was guaranteeing an "announced" entrance at the executive offices. I stopped whining, jauntily positioned the rascally rabbit on a hip, and with black patent pumps clicking a happy tune, sashayed toward my audition.

By the following week, my triumphant Paramount parade had totally slipped my mind. I'd been sidelined by a heavy-lidded, smooth-talking saxophone player. The musician blew a few bars of "Come Fly with Me," and like Marilyn Monroe's Sugar Kane in *Some Like It Hot*, I went.

Paramount Pictures picked that particular amoral week to offer me a contract for *Paint Your Wagon*, starring Lee Marvin and Clint Eastwood. I was incommunicado in San Francisco, shacked up with a jazz musician. My beleaguered manager had no idea where I was or how to contact me—no one knew where I was. I lost the film.

John did not have to lecture me on my stupidity; I was already heartsick. Professionally, my life dried up after the Paramount fiasco. I didn't go on one audition for the next three months. With nothing in my life to boost my sagging morale, I succumbed to the 1969 Hong Kong flu epidemic. Illness came calling between Christmas and New Year's Day. Being bedridden was my feeble excuse for having no holiday, no career, and no future.

When my annulled ex-husband, Lee, showed up at my door laden with soups, juices, medication, and Kleenex, I was never so glad to see anyone in my life. He'd come to help. Every man I'd been dating had taken my confinement to bed as a golden opportunity, but here was a man who didn't expect anything sexual in return. Why hadn't I appreciated that quality when I was married to it? Within two months, Lee and I were again living together. Our relationship picked up exactly where we'd left it.

"Aleshia," Lee would say, harping on his favorite free-love theme, "the world is chucking puritanical hang-ups. People are sleeping around. You're the only namby-pamby person I know who clings to the worn-out, romantic fairy tale. Grow up."

Why is it that homosexuality makes a man appear more handsome than when you think he's straight? It seems to work that way. Lee's homosexuality was no longer a taboo subject, and suddenly he was gorgeous. He was in the midst of testing for the Marlboro Man advertising campaign when a physician friend introduced Lee to Rock Hudson, the closeted film star.

"I hope you told them about your actress friend and ex-wife," I fumed. Lee had just returned from a bash at Rock's estate in the Hollywood Hills and was giving a vivid account of the evening.

"Carol Burnett was there," he continued. "And, when Rock introduced me to Julie Andrews, I . . ."

"Did you mention that your wife is an actress?" I again asked, a little louder this time. "You never know, someone important might remember my name on a casting call."

"Why in hell would I mention a wife?" was his deflating reply.

My career needed a nudge, and Universal Studios obliged with televised talk shows, radio spots, and newspaper interviews. *The Love God* was due for release, and I was offered a promotional tour of the southern states. I couldn't pack fast enough. The tour offered an escape from my failed relationship and a boost for my stagnating film career.

Lee didn't want me to do *The Love God* tour, and for the next few weeks, home-churned butter would not have melted in his mouth. He called three or four times a day from work; at home he was the essence of hovering attentiveness. On the weekends he was never far from my side. The charm lasted until I made my position clear.

"Are you out of your fruity gourd?" I scoffed. "If I have to crawl every step of the way, I'm going home to Tara."

Universal knows how to host a tour. Limousines whisked me from one press party to the next, and at each exciting stop I held court as the honored guest. My only task was to pout, dimple prettily, and be as printable as possible. Traveling with a studio publicist who takes care of every last technical detail leaves a starlet free to cleverly simper and preen. "You need something, you buy it" were the publicist's explicit instructions. I was born equal to that task! Hungry at the end of a day, I called room service. When dining out, I ate at four-star restaurants and drank their best wines. The studio publicist, when we arrived in Nashville for a round of talk shows, tracked down my former hairdresser and paid him handsomely for a private appointment in my hotel room. I loved being treated like a celebrity. Perhaps a paid publicist is the only man a woman really needs in her life.

Before I could get too comfortable with my self-importance, it was time for the grand opening of *The Love God.* I joined Don Knotts in Atlanta for our final publicity push, and my parents came down for the film's premiere.

Don left for Los Angeles before the film's opening, and plans for a grand premiere at the historic Fox Theater went with him. The debut flopped. No longer did I have a limousine, champagne, or klieg lights with which to impress my parents.

Originally, my intention had been to hang around, basking in my parent's excitement over their daughter's film success, but my shining star had fizzled. Neither the lavish attention of my studio, my hometown newspaper treating me as a returning celebrity, nor the money I saved from the film experience impressed my father. Daddy saw my life as a self-centered exercise in hedonism. Nothing had changed a great deal since I'd left home. My father still resented me, and his indifference still hurt.

It never dawned on me that perhaps Daddy was a man, doing his male-identified best. I hated my father for believing, thinking, and acting as he'd been conditioned to react. Daddy was doing what males of his era did. In years to come, I'd eventually conclude that being lover, father, and provider must be a chore for all men. In 1969, I wanted only my father's approval. I still felt a need to prove my worth.

Before leaving on the Universal tour, I'd auditioned for Bob Slatzer, the producer of an upcoming independent film called *Bigfoot*, but I'd dismissed the frustrating audition from my mind. Most of my audition time had been wasted by Slatzer's bragging about his marriage to Marilyn Monroe.

"Joe DiMaggio, maybe; Bob Slatzer, never," I thought. My Marilyn, I believed, would never have married the man I personally regarded as a blustering, rotund, B-grade movie maker. I didn't believe a word he said.

Back in Tennessee, my agent called to say I was immediately needed in Hollywood. I was cast in *Bigfoot*. The bad news was that I'd been cast as a female Sasquatch.

"Let me get this straight, you want me to rush back to California in order to play a seven-foot mother ape?" I gulped.

It was true. Aleshia Lee (Brevard), the ex–Monroe impressionist, had been cast by Robert Slatzer, a man professing to be Marilyn's last husband. He wanted me to play a mama yeti. A munchkin from *The Wizard of Oz* would play my Sasquatch child. There would be no Academy Award for this acting stint. In film history, no Sasquatch has ever received the coveted statuette. The only appeal to the potboiler was its cast. John and Chris Mitchum, brother and son of screen luminary Robert Mitchum, were in the debacle. I was more thrilled to be working with the magnificent screen legend John Carradine. I could learn something from an actor of his stature.

John Carradine taught me to play poker—and I paid dearly for the privilege.

Each morning, bright and early, Wally Westmore cemented coarse hair to my face. I spent each day sweltering in a hair suit, waiting to be called before the camera. Many days I never filmed a scene. I spent twelve- and fourteen-hour days inactive, in full gorilla makeup. When I could stand no more, I contacted my agent. Screen Actors Guild intervened, forcing the producer to show more concern for my creature comforts. My success with my union did not endear me to Bob Slatzer.

The only actress having a good experience on this turkey shoot was Judy Jordon, a down-to-earth beauty, fresh from the "Jackie Gleason Show" in Florida. I was jealous of our star. Judy got to speak human lines and appeared in a bikini. I was in an itchy hair suit. Miss Jordan was fairing better than I.

While filming this anthropomorphic epic, Judy Jordan met Sonny West, pal to Elvis Presley and member of the King's notorious "Memphis Mafia." Shortly after the film wrapped, Judy and Sonny were married. They lived on the Presley Hollywood estate. Judy Jordan West had faired *far* better than I!

One *Bigfoot* experience stands out as more than annoyance. Our cast and crew generally lunched together as a group, and since the head grip and I enjoyed discussing theater, we often sat at the same table. I admired him. Poetry was his passion, and his stage-technician work financed his more aesthetic interests.

"My car is in the shop, Aleshia," my grip friend explained on my last day of shooting. "I'm just off Sunset, down on Gower, could you give me a ride?"

The grip's apartment was on my way home, only a short drive from the small Sunset Boulevard soundstage where we'd been shooting, and I was glad to give him a lift. When we reached his apartment, we sat talking for a while, but I kept my car motor idling. I'd been in an itchy ape suit all day, and I was looking forward to taking a long soak in the tub before Lee got home from work.

"Would you come in and read some of my poetry?" the technician asked as he opened the passenger door. "It won't take long, and I'd like your opinion."

I parked at the curb, followed my new friend to his upstairs apartment, then read and carefully reread his disjointed verse. I was totally unable to follow the wildly meandering meter.

"Some parts of this I find a bit confusing," I ventured. I was being kind. I didn't understand any of it.

Before I realized what had happened, I was roughly thrown onto his daybed. Over me now stood a madman, holding a knife to my throat.

"If you move one muscle, I'll kill you, bitch," he snarled.

In moments of great danger, something extraordinary overtakes me. I become chameleon-like. A self-protection mechanism is triggered, causing insignificant gestures, movements, and objects to become crystalline images. In short, I subconsciously start searching for something that will save my precious ass. Now, tranquility washed over me. I was watching the scene from somewhere above the grip's daybed. Quietly, gently, I tried to persuade my attacker to let me go. That didn't work. I tried to bluff; I tried controlled anger. I wearily gave way to tears. There were moments when I acted as though his threats were a titillating game. I cajoled; I reasoned. Nothing dissuaded him. All night I lay on my captor's daybed, with his razor-sharp blade at my throat. I knew I was going to be raped, and feared I might die. Unreasonably, I focused on a small planter hanging above the bed. The madman's ivy was well tended.

Shortly after dawn, the *Bigfoot* grip threw me out of his apartment. He literally hurled me onto the porch, tossed my purse after me, called me a whore one final time, and locked his door. I had escaped physical rape. The ordeal was over.

I did not file charges. I had not been sexually assaulted, and should I accuse my attacker, a strong possibility existed that the police would discover my transsexual identity. Even genetically born female victims of physical rape are required to defend themselves in court. I feared the police more than I hated my assailant. They might consider my attacker's actions reasonable. With my history, I didn't dare take the risk. The crazed grip had threatened my life *because* I was a woman— the source of his loathing had been clear during that long night. I did not, however, trust the LAPD to make this subtle distinction. Instead of risking further humiliation, I plastered a sickly smile on my face, accepted the blame, and unhappily realized that my transgendered past was still haunting me. The worst part of the experience might have been understanding that I was still being marginalized. I was still on the outside looking in.

Lee's reaction was an additional attack. "You had no business being in a man's apartment," he said. "You got what you deserved."

My lucky stars were jerking me around in 1969. The next stiff shake came from Tennessee.

During my *Love God* tour, the *Nashville Banner* ran a front-page article picturing me vampishly posed by my hotel's swimming pool. The headline read, "Starlet Returns Home." I was shocked when a reporter called me in California.

"We've gotten an anonymous tip that you are a transsexual. Is there any truth in that, and if so, would you care to comment?" My feet took root in the carpet as I saw my fledgling film career flying out the window. Discovery had long been my greatest fear. By daring to follow my dreams into a high-profile profession, I'd opened myself to public exposure. I feared the same deadly tabloid catastrophe that had greeted Christine Jorgensen's gender transition. I cringed thinking that, as with Christine, people would send rusty razor blades in the mail, suggesting that I slit my wrist. Granted, I wasn't the world's first transsexual, but I was the first to have become a Hollywood actress—some Americans would find that even more distressing.

"There is nothing to discuss," I replied coldly. "It's malicious gossip, and if you print it you'll see me in court."

My indignant performance did not intimidate the *Nashville Banner*. The reporter followed his tip to my hometown. It was a wasted trip. The same community that lined the sidewalk to gape at me on my first visit home now defended their local transsexual starlet. The townspeople insisted they had no idea what the *Banner* reporter was talking about. The newspaper dropped the story.

Fast on the heels of the *Nashville Banner* scare came a call from Shelly, one of *The Love God* Pussycats.

"Did you know there's a billboard of us on Sunset Strip?" Shelly asked. "We're standing on either side of Don. It's the big sign across the street from the Playboy Club. I can get you an interview at the club if you're interested."

Shelly was a tall, gorgeous blonde and former Playboy "Bunny of the Year."

"It's a great place for an actress to work," she added. "It leaves you free to audition during the day. With your picture bigger than life across the street, there couldn't be a better time to ask Playboy for a job."

Hugh Hefner's club policy was to put a Bunny applicant in the famous costume, complete with ears and tail, and take a Polaroid shot of her. The photo was graded on a one to ten scale, ten being the highest, and if the applicant passed muster in the revealing costume, she was rewarded with a personal interview. On the strength of my photograph's score, a nine, I was seen by both the "Bunny Mother" and the managing director. From the offset, the Bunny Mother was not in my corner of the hutch.

"The image of the 'Playboy Bunny' is that of the girl next door . . . and Aleshia just isn't," twittered the sanctimonious mama rabbit.

"Depends on who you're living next door to," I blurted. "If you live next door to a whorehouse—I'm your typical girl next door!"

The managing director guffawed and pounded on his desk; the Bunny Mother turned sickly pale. I'd met overripe hothouse bimbos like this woman before. The arrogant Playboy matron was like an ex-Cotton Queen, trying to pass haughtiness off as good breeding. She didn't want me in her rabbit patch. It was clear I wouldn't be wearing a fuzzy tail pinned to French-cut satin.

To my bewildered amazement, I was hired. My training was at the Los Angeles club on Sunset Boulevard. Being a Playboy Bunny was serious business. It was like the army—except that these recruits wore spike heels, cinched their waists, and hoisted bar trays in the air. Boot camp was hell. Those trays were heavy, Honey! You carried glasses, ice, alcoholic shots, plus mixes—all on one little tray gracefully suspended above your well-coiffured head. After getting her cargo to a table, a Bunny was required to do a backbend called the Bunny-dip, introduce herself, and smile fetchingly while still balancing that damn tray. This job was not intended for pansies. Not only was the work far from glamorous, it was also intimidating. Before going on the floor, you had to stand inspection by the dreaded Bunny Mother. She checked your fingernails, your makeup, your ears, and your tail.

We used our snagged black silk hosiery to stuff the bra cups of the famous abbreviated uniforms. Be it Mother Nature's gift or the work of a Beverly Hills plastic surgeon, all thorax endowment rested uncomfortably on a padding of black silk. The glamorized Bunny presentation was based on male wish fulfillment more than on any reality concerning female anatomy. I'd worked long enough as a drag queen to understand the painful distortions that can be achieved with heavy corseting and boning.

"Hef's" Playboy Bunny captured the erotic imagination of men around the world, and I was convinced that my Bunny stint would wipe away any possible doubt about my assigned gender. This should prove, even to me, that I was 100 percent woman. Farm boys did not become the prevailing American male fantasy. I welcomed an opportunity to be part of the sensual hype. I tried to remain upbeat and merely focus on my lovely lavender costume. It was like trying to concentrate on my pale lip gloss another lifetime ago. The ploy no longer worked. I left the glamorous sweatshop.

If, as I suspect, life is truly a Fellini masterpiece, I was living *La Dolce Vita.* In Hollywood, the party was sometimes a little too fast and the music always a little too loud, but I convinced myself that I was lucky. I traded what was left of my tattered innocence for what I thought was the high life. I was not as cosmopolitan as I believed myself to be.

When Marve Atkins called, inviting me to a party for Anthony Newley's new film *Can Hieronymous Merkin Ever Forget Mercy Humppe and Find True Happiness,* I agreed at once. I'd maintained a valuable working relationship with Marve and the studio's publicity department since my Universal film tour. I realized that I was just another starlet used to decorate the set, but being seen at Hollywood events is almost as important as having an agent. It's a Hollywood ritual.

At the party, I spent the first part of the evening in the women's room talking with Ann Francis. I was a huge Ann Francis fan, and she'd been Don's co-star in *The Love God.* I admired her. To me, Ann Francis was the most underrated actor in Hollywood, and her tour de force performance in *Girl of the Night* only underscored my appreciation of her gifts. I cornered her in the bathroom and told her so.

The party had picked up steam by the time I left the bathroom. I found a table in the corner, sat down, and waited to be discovered. Andy Griffith joined me. We spent the evening having a polite discussion about the Old South, the old plantation system, and old-time gentility in general—as we both professed to remember it. Mr. Griffith's charm was unflagging until a member of that evening's entertainment group, The Orange Colored Sky, stopped by our table and said hello to me. "Get lost," Andy belched. The genteel mood broken, "Cousin Andy" cut to the chase. I declined, and Andy left looking for greener pastures. I went looking for Marve Atkins. I wanted to thank him for inviting me.

"Don't go yet, Aleshia," Marve smiled. "I'll see that you get home."

Flattered, I smiled and took a seat. Gosh, it had never occurred to me that Universal's publicity guru might be interested in me.

"Aleshia," Marve beamed a few moments later, taking my arm and leading me toward the door, "Mr. Newley will see you home."

Before I could think of an acceptable, witty way out, I'd been swept through the doors to a long black limousine. Still trying to think of an excuse, I automatically aimed my rear toward the back seat, missed, and fell at Anthony Newley's feet. We weren't out of the studio gate before the star made his move.

"Mr. Newley," I glowered, "I realize the party was given in your honor, but you need to realize that I do not come as a door prize." Without a word, the actor, director, and creator of "What Kind of Fool Am I?" scooted back to his side of the limousine.

"Did you have to be so hostile?" I silently berated myself.

"I loved you in *Sweet November*," I ventured. I couldn't afford to be taking potshots at the Anthony Newleys of this world. "I thought you and Sandy Dennis were wonderful together."

No longer was my accidental escort staring out the limousine window—his beady little British eyes were boring a hole right through me. It turned out he loathed *Sweet November* almost as much as he detested

Sandy Dennis. He got red in the face just talking about his eccentric co-star. I decided not to mention his wife, Joan Collins.

"Wait here," the songwriter extraordinaire told his driver when we pulled in front of my apartment building.

As the now-gentlemanly celebrity walked me to my door, the possibility of joining him for lunch at some smart, highly visible bistro popped into my head.

When we reached my apartment, Anthony Newley did not wait for an invitation to come inside. He pushed past me, entered my apartment, and unzipped his pants.

He exposed himself; I screamed.

"You're either the most naive person I've ever met, or you're the best actress I know!" With that, Anthony Newley rearranged, rezipped, and exited my life before I could say, "Thank you for the ride."

CHAPTER 12

That Female Bunch

ON THE twentieth of July, 1969, Americans sat glued to their television sets, cheering the Apollo 11 space mission. Neil Armstrong, astronaut, was walking on the moon. Aleshia Brevard, actress, was fanning herself on planet Earth. On a location shoot in the hot, arid, if picturesque Great Basin Desert that surrounds Hanksville, Utah, I might as well have been stranded on the moon.

After weeks in the wasteland, our cast and crew for *The Female Bunch* were thrilled to hear that the Mormon community was throwing a party. The fete was to honor a hometown boy, soon off to fight the Vietcong. The support Hollywood had shown for World War II was not present during the Vietnam fiasco, but still we were delighted with the news. The celebration would give us somewhere to go. Our bunch could hardly wait for the cameras to stop rolling.

When our glittering horde crashed the party at the town's house of worship, the Mormons moved their celebration outside. Some members of our cast were insulted, thinking the community considered us a dressed-up, godless bunch.

"We're lucky no one thought of lynching us," I giggled as I swayed back and forth in a churchyard swing.

In many ways my isolationist Appalachian ancestors had resembled these desert-dwelling Mormons. My people had loved their land, their God, and their independence. The similarity did not make me any more comfortable. Growing up, I'd choked on fundamentalist religious indoctrination. It was crammed down my throat. In the Tennessee mountains, a heathen was hated almost as much as a "revenuer"! Back home, however, the *really* righteous carried a rope.

It was Brenda Vaccaro's success in *Rosemary's Baby* that had landed me in this desert community. Originally, Ms. Vaccaro had been slated to play Sadie, the tough, drug-running misfit, but when her critically acclaimed performance as Rosemary's hapless neighbor propelled her into the spotlight, Brenda backed out of *The Female Bunch* at the last minute. She was headed for *Midnight Cowboy.*

"Can you ride?" Al Adamson, director of the film, asked during my interview. He was looking for a replacement with horse sense.

"I used to show!" I beamed. "I grew up with a five-gaited gelding named Fiddle-foot."

Within a week I was dozing fitfully in the back seat of a car headed for Utah. Up front, blocking the air-conditioning vent, rode an actress named Jenifer Bishop. She preferred her name without the double *n*— no matter how you spelled it, Jenifer had commandeered that front seat.

"I hope you don't mind, dear," she purred when the driver picked me up. "I get carsick in the back seat." What could I say? She was the film's female lead.

"You're the only actress," she assured me as we sped across the desert, "who wasn't taken to the stables and put through paces on a horse." Jenifer modestly added, "I have a magnificent seat."

In the back seat, I sweated and regretted coloring the truth about my skill astride a horse. Granted, my white lie had earned me featured co-star billing, but the truth was I hadn't seen a horse since childhood. Jenifer Bishop, with her excellent seat, was going to make me look like a rank amateur.

Once in Utah, the first day of shooting focused on our wayward bunch of women riding, hell-bent for saddle sores, up and down picturesque canyons. Burnt sienna gorges sheared away to blue nothingness far below. Up and down those beautiful gorges I galloped . . . Jenifer forever edging me closer to treacherous chasm rims. Staying alive meant staying out of our star's way.

It was a tedious, grueling first day of shooting. The desert was merciless. The desert dust mixed with the sweat of our horses and encrusted us all. I'd ridden for eight hours in a miniskirt—bringing new meaning to the term *saddle sore.* We were a saddle-weary, sunburned, woebegone group by the time our first filming day ended.

The next morning, we were sheepishly informed that the cinematographer had failed to put film in his camera. Sometimes, stupidity can be an omen.

Our film-savvy cow ponies soon grasped that slating a take is signaled by clacking the clapboard. "Cut!" the assistant director yelled during early filming. This was our signal to stop riding. Ms. Bishop's cow pony got the director's message. The horse quit running; Jenifer kept riding. The beautiful leader of *The Female Bunch* sailed over the head of her stationary mount and landed hard on her *magnificent* seat.

I had a real respect for our mounts. A cow pony is a very agile, bright spotted horse used to cut cattle from the herd— or in our case, to transport vapid actresses across a picturesque mesa. Our horses, having mastered the filming routine, were soon strewing thespians about like so many grass seeds on a barren landscape. Once a Hollywood starlet sat aboard a horse powdering her nose; after the signaling clapboard clack, she sat dusting the ground where only moments before her cow pony had stood, ears alert and listening. I never tired of seeing actresses momentarily suspended in air—their painted lips puckered in an unbelieving oval—before they hit the ground.

Had *The Female Bunch* been an Olympic event, I could have been riding for the gold. I never once lost my seat.

Off camera, Jenifer and I shared a motel room. We passed our time rehearsing lines and bitching about the film's stilted dialogue. Often our concentration was broken by an ardent lothario tiptoeing past our window on his way to some welcoming starlet's motel room. Seemingly, our fellow actresses had already given up on the script.

In such passionately impressive company, Jenifer and I ran the risk of appearing frigid. That wouldn't do. Nothing kills a Hollywood career faster than being considered "sexless"—we needed a way to focus on the film and still save face. We found it.

"Jenifer," I'd say after dinner as I ran my finger down her arm, "are you ready to go back to *our* room?" We'd hold our steamy gaze, making sure our message was clear to everyone, then head for our shared quarters. Behind closed doors, we'd fall across our respective beds, laughing uproariously. The crew was convinced that off screen, as well as on, the female star and her sidekick, Sadie, were lovers. The film soon developed its own lesbian overtones. The flavor of the piece was developing as we shot it.

Heat, horses, faux lesbians, and hedonistic prima donnas do not mix well. Even Russ Tamblyn, our male lead, seemed dispirited and tired of the film. He was always in place, ready with his lines, polite and comfortable in front of the camera—but our star's heart was not in the low-budget venture. He'd passed his classic *West Side Story* and *Seven Brides for Seven Brothers* glory days. Our third-rate western would not be launching a comeback.

The wrangler for our horses was perhaps the only member of our crew who was enjoying the filming experience. He was always extremely cordial. He kept his place in the film's pecking order and seemed to preferred his animals to people. At home in Los Angeles, he slept in a cave on Spahn Ranch. The ranch was an old western film set where the "Charlie" Manson Family now made their home. It was due to this questionable association that the beautiful young cowboy would soon be thrust into a spotlight of mayhem and madness. One month after our final "wrap," his face would be flashing across television screens.

On a hot morning in August 1969, five people were slaughtered at 10050 Cielo Drive, the estate of actress Sharon Tate and director Roman Polanski. Manson Family members were the perpetrators of this atrocity. Abigail Folger, a guest, was stabbed twenty-one times; Voityck Frykowski was shot once and stabbed fifty-one times. Hair stylist Jay Seebring was shot twice and stabbed six times. Steve Parex was shot three times. Members of the murderously insane Manson Family then left a message scrawled across the door of pregnant actress Sharon Tate. She'd been stabbed fifteen times, and the message was written in her blood. It read, "Pigs."

The gruesome, seemingly random murders took place mere blocks from where my friend Kathy, who years earlier had met "Charlie" Manson before starting North Beach Leather, was now living with her second husband. Kathy was terrified. The entire world was shocked by the Tate murders. As a nation, we were numbed by such brutality; yet after the shock and intense media coverage subsided, life quickly returned to normal. *The Female Bunch* was in the can; our cast had gone their separate ways; and I needed a job.

I'd wanted to be an actress since, with my head draped in a cotton towel, I'd first peeked at my reflection in the bathroom mirror. Nothing—not assigned gender, not involvement with domineering men, not even the depravity of Hollywood—had been able to stop me. As with many "natural" women, I learned what was expected of a woman while staring at the screen in a darkened movie theater on Saturday afternoons. I looked to the sirens of the screen to see myself. Rita, Lana, and Hedy were larger-than-life representations of the person I wanted to be. The masculine heroes of our day meant nothing to me. My life was shaped by the vixens, vamps, and goddesses of the cinema. Playing a Pussycat, a mother Sasquatch, or a Sadie in a western debacle did not make me another Veronica Lake—I knew that—but working in the film industry signified that I was on my way. The dream kept me moving forward. Only when I was working a "real job" in order to pay the rent did reality slap me in the face.

Shortly after leaving Utah, I started working at the Ambassador Hotel, home of the famous Coconut Grove. Less than a year before, on June 4, 1968, Robert Kennedy finished his victory speech at the California primary, left the podium, and took a shortcut through the Ambassador Hotel's kitchen. There he was gunned down by Sirhan Sirhan. The celebrated hotel would thereafter be associated with the tragedy. My job was far removed from the infamous kitchen. I was well behind the hotel's elegant facade, helping my friend Kathy run a health spa. It was hard work. We were merely doing the owners a favor so they could have a vacation, but it was hands-on management. While Kathy sweltered over the hot grill flipping hamburgers, I served food and drinks poolside.

I'm too fair for work in the noonday sun. I burn. Yet there I was, slinging drinks beside a sun-drenched pool, catering to a gaggle of well-heeled club members. Hell, if I was going to broil, I intended to look extraordinary on the spit. I began wearing a flattering black bathing suit, long black gloves, sunglasses, heels, and a huge floppy sun hat. I was merely trying to enjoy my drudgery, but sometimes if you're off-kilter enough, you're considered amusing. The brother of 1940s film star Claudette Colbert thought I was hilarious.

In Hollywood, *who* you know determines *what* you become.

My unexpected poolside benefactor's wife worked for *The Red Skelton Show*. In short order, I had an important audition with Skelton's CBS casting director, Marilyn Howard. She was a charming lady from North Carolina, and we hit it off immediately. Before I could grasp my good fortune, I was at an early-morning read-through for *The Red Skelton Show*. I'd gone directly from poolside drag to national television.

Because Mr. Skelton preferred working with known entities, I kept being invited back for stints on his hour-long broadcast. I was informed that on one of those early episodes, guest star Audrey Meadows voiced her objection to working with me. She wanted my lines cut. The production staff said Miss Meadows felt my vocal quality was too similar to her celebrated delivery.

Transsexuals are always concerned that their deeper vocal timbre will give them away. Many go through ridiculous vocal placements looking for a "more feminine" sound. I now believe the resulting falsetto merely draws attention to an unnatural delivery. Early in my transition, I took my vocal placement from the chest, supported by the diaphragm, and opted for wispy "head tones." I was trying to mask a delivery I considered "too male."

The first time I appeared in public dressed as a woman, my escort at one point excused himself and went to the men's room. To my horror, our waiter approached and asked how I was enjoying the meal. I was terrified. We were dining at San Francisco's Top of the Mark, and I was convinced that any answer would broadcast the true nature of my embarrassing gender. All conversation would stop, forks would clatter to the floor, and I'd be cast out. Of course, when I answered the waiter's simple question, nothing untoward transpired.

Vocal placement is one of the transsexual's major hurdles. It wasn't until I relaxed my surveillance and started *considering myself* female that the telephone ceased being an instrument of torture. For years, if an operator addressed me as "sir," it would ruin my entire day. By 1968, six years after transitional surgery, I'd gained enough confidence to appreciate my "whiskey sour" delivery. Professionally, my voice was an asset. On the Skelton show, it seemed clear to me that my lines had been cut from the scene with Miss Meadows not because I sounded like a man but because I sounded too much like a woman famous for her voice.

Jane Powell's guest-star appearance was entirely another matter. For reasons known only to the diminutive Miss Powell, "America's Sweetheart" flatly refused to work with me—but it wasn't because of my voice. I was in a skit that revolved around Miss Powell as a hobo-clad society matron hosting a fashionable costume party. Freddie the Freeloader, Red's famous bum character, stumbles uninvited into the gala costume event, and the skit humorously accelerates from that point. In the script, Freddie's wardrobe caused Miss Powell's character a problem. In real life, my glamorous décolleté gown seemed to be the cause of Miss Powell's problem.

The gown and my cleavage were important to the scene. They set up Miss Powell's punch line. Part of the dialogue ran:

Jane Powell: My, what a lovely dress you're almost wearing.

Aleshia: This is my coming-out dress.

Jane Powell: It looks like you're still coming out.

For the scene, the costumer had put me in a stunning beaded gown originally worn by sex kitten Corinne Calvet. I was as delighted to fill the voluptuous star's dress as I was to wear it on national television. The scene was equally important because I had more than five lines on the show. In our actors' union, AFTRA, "five lines or over" means that an actor's base pay goes up considerably. Miss Powell did not appear concerned with the number of my scripted lines. She simply refused to do the scene.

By the time we broke for lunch, a serious discussion was underway on the Skelton set. There was a distinct possibility that my beaded gown was going to be cut from the scene, thanks, as I saw it, to Miss Jane Powell. For me, the effervescent songbird had turned into a one-woman plague. Upset and desperate, I spent my lunch break crying on the shoulder of Duke Vincent, producer of *The Jim Nabors Show.*

Duke was too sympathetic, and I was late getting back from lunch. A stand-in was onstage rehearsing my role when I returned to the Skelton set. When the assistant director spotted me standing in the wings, he expectantly looked skyward toward the director's booth. He was seeking permission for a public reprimand. He got it. My severe dressing down was delivered in front of cast, crew, *and* Jane Powell. If you ask me, where that woman spit, no grass would ever grow again.

With each step toward airtime I lost more confidence. By the time we reached our final dress rehearsal, I was an emotional wreck. I still didn't know what I was supposed to wear for the taping, and the wardrobe crew seemed to be studiously avoiding the situation. No one wanted to get sucked into my downward spiral.

At the final run-through, I appeared onstage in my CBS terry-cloth robe. It was a mistake. *Everyone* looked toward the director's booth this time. In the end, the executive decision was made that I'd wear the beautiful décolleté beaded gown for the taping of the show—while standing behind a large crowd of extras. Neither the dress nor the actress would be seen. I prayed for Miss Powell. I begged God to let that heartless woman end her career doing false-teeth commercials.

My day had not gone well.

Before airtime, I timidly approached Red Skelton. I was convinced I'd never work on his wonderful show again, but it was not the comic star's fault. I'd let him down. I wanted to apologize to Mr. Skelton for the trouble I'd caused.

"Mr. Skelton," I gasped, trying to control my voice. "I'm sorry for all the confusion I've caused here today." I couldn't manage another word without crying.

"My dear," the comic genius said, taking my hand in his, "that's why it's called a *rehearsal*."

After the evening show wrapped, I noticed Mr. Skelton talking with his producers. When I left CBS Studios that evening, it was as the newly employed Moon Maiden for *The Red Skelton Show* prologue. My leading men were midgets, the Moon Men, who weekly cavorted on their lunar set as a lead-in to Red Skelton. For my new role, I was painted leafy green, stuck in tight-fitting silver lamé, and bejeweled with rhinestone droplets that sprouted from my bright-red coif. My nation was spellbound by American astronauts on the moon; I was starstruck by Red Skelton.

In the firmament that is Hollywood, I wasn't even a wrinkle on a star's silicone-rounded behind, but I was earning my living in an industry notorious for devouring its artists. I was also becoming ambitious. When Duke Vincent, who'd become second-in-command to Aaron Spelling, asked me to dinner, I jumped at his offer. Then I picked up the phone and called my film manager to ask his permission.

"Of course, you'll go," John prompted. "You need to be seen publicly with important people. Duke is important people. But," he added, almost as an afterthought, "Darling Child, be sure to take your own car."

During the 1960s, it was impossible to live in America without being affected by Vietnam. The era of Woodstock totally dissolved into chaos when, in April 1970, National Guardsmen went to Ohio's Kent State University. They were called to restore order on campus after several days of student anti-Nixon protest. Instead, four students were killed. One American mother, during a televised interview, cried out, "Not only are they killing our kids over there, they're killing them here, too." I totally agreed.

In spite of maturing political convictions, professional progress, and financial security, I was an eight-year-old transwoman who still believed that life was meaningless without a man to guide it. I was sitting on a bar stool when I found him. He walked through the front door; I turned to my girlfriend and said, "The new man in my life just entered the room."

James Melton was every man I'd ever dated—he'd merely shown up at the right time, wearing a different pair of pants. On June 13, 1970, I followed the Schlitz Brewery teamster down the aisle to my second marriage.

I woke from my wedding night to discover that my new husband had just sold my car. Jim wanted a stay-at-home wife. I didn't realize the full implications of having fallen into a traditional heterosexual marriage. Jim was a good, solid man, but the reins were firmly in his hands. Jim made the money and therefore held the power. The life I'd thought I wanted so badly slowly became oppressive as the romantic newness wore off. To keep the peace, I gave up more and more of my own identity. All through my first marriage to a gay man I'd constantly whined "I want to belong to a real man." The Fates had heard me, not knowing that I did not mean it literally.

By the time Jim married me, his three sons had been through a progression of surrogate mothers. All three boys had real needs, but my belated maternal instincts were deeply stirred by Mark, reputedly the family's budding juvenile delinquent.

Soon after marrying his father, I attended Mark's junior high school graduation. I was the only family member in attendance. The boy, fearing I would be late, had reserved me a seat down front, put aside a cup of watery punch, and saved a few crumbled cookies in his lint-lined pocket. I was deeply touched. Seemingly, my stepson and I shared fears of rejection.

After the graduation, I drove Mark to his father's favorite clothier.

"Who's the handsome fella you're with, Aleshia?" asked the salesman.

"This is my stepson, Mark," I said, introducing the shy young graduate. "We're looking for a suit that's as good-looking as he is."

Mark was deep in thought when we left the store, but he said little on the ride home. When he finally spoke, there were tears in his eyes.

"Do we have to say I'm your stepson?" he asked. "Why can't we just say I'm your son?" I loved the idea. This marriage would have its perks, after all.

In the 1970s, for the first time, I heard professional, thoroughly modern young women referring to children as the "bane of womanhood." I didn't believe they meant what they were saying. In fact, I found their harsh sentiments shocking. In the last twenty years, I've met many women who consciously embraced life's challenges and lived their lives joyfully while forsaking motherhood. Not every woman wants children. A desire to nurture may not be the best yardstick by which society can measure femininity. I certainly would prefer a world in which the raising of children is a privilege for all rather than the obligation of any one gender. Growing to adulthood as I did, with a nonresponsive father, I still long for a world where all children are raised in love by both parents. I find it difficult to believe, however, that love is gender based.

I've never known a transsexual who would not gladly risk everything for the privilege of creating life. One transsexual friend from those very early days, when the surgery itself was in its infancy, recently shared with me her feelings about having raised stepchildren. In the early 1970s, she married, buried her gender-dysphoric past, and devoted her new life to nurturing stepchildren. When she divorced the abusive father, her children cried, "That doesn't mean you're divorcing us, does it?" It did not. The three children became her life's work; grandchildren are now her reason for living.

Unfortunately, my friend's maternal experience is not the norm for the transsexuals I have known. For the transgendered, too often, successful parenting no longer remains an option. This is especially true for those who transition from a heterosexual lifestyle. Their parental role is often terminated. Social and family reactions to a gender transition are generally overpowering, even without children in the mix. Add outside family pressures, coupled with a desire to bring no confusion or shame to the offspring, and the result often proves overwhelming for a biological parent in gender transition. These transsexuals sacrifice more than an assigned gender in their attempt to feel emotionally and physically complete.

My personal transsexual history, emerging as it did from a gay-identified adolescence, eliminated the issue of parenting from my early life. I regretted that I'd never be a mother—but I certainly felt no inclination for fatherhood. Kathy and I often joked that our surgically induced womanhood had spared us much more than the pain of childbirth.

"Honey, it's a good thing you didn't have a baby with every man you've loved," Kathy quipped. "There isn't enough welfare in this world to feed *that* many little bastards."

Because of not having children, some early transsexuals feared their barren state might provide a tip-off to a transgendered sexual history.

"Do you have children, Aleshia?" was an invariable first-date question. I didn't always meet it head on. The minute my boyfriend asked about children, I pulled out a tear-stained portrait of my mythical late son, Jason. I carried a picture of a beautiful four-year-old boy in my wallet. "Jason" was my protection. I shared the lie of his drowning so often that I started to wonder if it wasn't true.

A bereaved-mother status works wonders. It instantly removes any nagging questions that might exist. As deceitful and bizarre as my behavior may appear, it is not unique in transsexual, gay, or lesbian society. Just as for Edward Albee's famous couple, George and Martha, in *Who's Afraid of Virginia Woolf?*, the invention of an imaginary offspring can sometimes offer a secure corner in a potentially hostile environment. Even in these liberal times, I know lesbian women who still discuss nonexistent children when dealing professionally with heterosexual customers. It's a homosexual minority's attempt to survive in a heterosexual business world. Telling the truth can cost a sale, advancement, or a job. I have met no one who wants to lie about an imaginary family, but I know many who still feel it to be necessary. I created and subsequently murdered my four-year-old son, Jason, for those same reasons.

By 1972, I no longer had to invent children. I had three of my own. My halcyon days in Hollywood, however, seemed to have passed. I was ready to play a woman of substance, displaying wifely charm, and no one cared. Donna Reed was out of style. I'd started another apple pie when my agent handed me three episodes of *The Dean Martin Show*. Dean's dancers, The Gold Diggers, were doing a show in Las Vegas, and NBC needed a tall, leggy "straight woman" for Dean's skits.

My favorite spot on *The Dean Martin Show* was coming out of the crooner's famous closet with his guest star Mickey Rooney. The irrepressible Mickey was playing Dean's agent, and I was playing Mr. Rooney's newest discovery. In the skit, Mickey was bringing me, his protégée, so Dean Martin could witness my *remarkable* expertise at blowing up a paper bag—while wearing a very skimpy corselet! Naturally, filling the bag with air required much inhaling, heaving, and undulating. It wasn't Emmy-winning material, but I was again on national television.

My husband didn't like any of it. He didn't like the bond I'd formed with his son, that I'd started back to college, or my choice of theater as a career. It seemed wise that I not share the whole truth about *The Dean Martin Show* rehearsals.

"Is that a wedding ring I see on your finger?" asked Greg Garrison, the powerful producer of the show.

It was indeed that precious little band of gold.

"That's a shame," commented the producer. "I was going to make you a star."

"Can't I be married and be a star?" I laughed.

"Yes, but you'd have to be available to fuck a lot." With that, Mr. Garrison turned on his well-shod heel and left the set. Our little verbal exchange occurred early on my first day of rehearsal, but I wasn't shocked. I'd witnessed the famous Garrison technique before.

For the 1972 Dean Martin shows, I'd interviewed with another tall redhead, named Teri. Because of our similar physical type, Teri and I kept bumping into each other at auditions. We were serious competitors, and in true starlet fashion, we never developed more than a nodding acquaintance. For the Martin audition, we were called into Greg Garrison's office together. Teri left me standing at the gate. I couldn't get a word in edgewise. I'd been weeding in the vegetable garden far too long. Now, when I finally had an important audition, Teri flipped her personality switch and left me standing in the theatrical dark. Mr. Garrison excused me from the interview and told me to leave my number with his secretary.

"Shame on you!" I chided myself. "You sat there like Marcel Marceau and let that bigmouth waltz away with your job. You used to be better than this, Aleshia."

I decided to return to his office and thank Mr. Garrison for his time and consideration. "That's being gracious and still making your presence known," I assured myself. I went down the hall and knocked on Greg Garrison's door. As it slowly swung open, a startled starlet with both arms elevated and a sweater pulled over her red head turned to look at me.

Two tall redheads were hired for *The Dean Martin Show.*

CHAPTER 13

Fashion's Guru

LIVING ON the banks of Old Man River is not as easy as those antebellum songs would lead you to believe. I was again in Memphis, and this trip the city truly was "The Home of the Blues." How could the riverfront community have changed so drastically since I'd lived there happily as a student? Granted, in those fourteen years I, too, had changed. No longer was I a boy away from home for the first time. No longer was I a boy!

I was in Memphis because my Mississippi-born husband dragged me, kicking and screaming, back to the South. He returned for a job with Schlitz Brewing Company, and I made the pilgrimage out of wifely duty. Our children stayed in California with their maternal grandparents. Mr. and Mrs. Milton were starting over, but marriage was not the same for me as it had been for Myrna Loy in those 1940s movies. I did not feel cherished, witty, or urbane. I felt trapped.

"London House Models, Int'l. is interviewing for in-house sales representatives. Will train." I grabbed the classifieds section of the Memphis newspaper and sprinted for the phone.

The Kansas City-based modeling agency had expanded south and overpowered the fourteenth floor of a towering Memphis complex. The offices were decorated in an outrageously theatrical style, with a lot of pink, red, and gilt. The staff was even more dramatic in their designer knockoff after-five fashions. London House Models, Int'l., was as close as I'd be getting to heaven in Tennessee.

I grabbed an entry-level job the moment it was offered. Not only did I accept the company's party line; I espoused it. To be the best woman one can be, one needs a little *finishing!* For my entire life, in one gender or another, I'd been concentrating on walk, posture, and presentation. I believed in my modeling agency's product, and therefore my students believed in me.

I was in high cotton, indeed, when a student-disciple entered a local division of the Miss Universe Pageant and asked for my help. If she won, my closing sales presentation would receive a tremendous boost, but my excitement was more vicarious than financial. In one of my boyhood dreams, the crowning moment had been a beauty pageant winner's parade, complete with tiara, roses, and scepter. Perhaps I could make my dream a reality for someone else.

My student was a guileless knockout, but as with all beauties, there were imperfections. This would-be queen had stubbornly ample thighs. Our Miss Universe bathing-suit competition had me worried.

On the night of the competition I was backstage, down on my knees, attacking those problem thighs with three separate shades of pancake makeup. To the inside and outside of her thigh I applied a darker makeup. Lighter shades of pancake graduated toward the center of her leg. To maximize the effect of my artistic contouring, I directed our contestant to work the ramp in a stunning black one-piece swimsuit, cut high on the thigh. Magic sometimes happens for a woman with a small waist, a partisan trainer, and some cleverly placed Max Factor pancake. Yet my stately beauty did not become Miss Tennessee Universe of 1974. She did, however, place first in the bathing-suit competition.

Tearoom assignments started coming my way, and soon I was modeling tall-girl fashions and picking up engagements to show glamorous furs. I liked being the mannequin even more than I enjoyed training others for runway work. Life became one long T-ramp fashion parade. The euphoria lasted until Schlitz Brewery handed my husband his pink slip. I was terrified of having to give up modeling to follow my husband on his quest for employment. I couldn't do that—yet I didn't believe I could survive on my own. I'd never lived without some man in control of my life, and the prospect of being totally responsible for myself filled me with dread. With the kind of inspiration often stimulated by desperation, I persuaded my husband to join the modeling agency staff.

Six months after Jim and I began working together, London House Models, Int'l., announced the opening of their sixth agency. The owner flew his top sales representative from each existing office to Denver, Colorado. I represented the Memphis shop. Our elitist staff would launch the Mile High City's operation, and the most successful group member would become the newest company manager.

"Aleshia, you've handled yourself well in Denver," my boss drawled, "and your agency track record speaks for itself. I want you to take over my Memphis operation." I beamed. "You'll run the entire operation, but Jim is being named agency director. Men make better authority figures, you know."

"My husband?" I squeaked in dismay. "What about all the work I've done?"

"You'll be running the agency, don't worry about that," my boss snorted patronizingly, "but I want your husband behind the agency director's desk."

My love affair with business died on the spot—I wasn't sure what I felt toward my husband. It didn't take me long to find out. Jim took his new position seriously, and soon I was too angry to see any humor in my husband's pomposity. We fought over everything—hiring practices, advertising, commission percentages. He almost fired me when I insisted that teaching be our school's primary concern. Since I was the Melton team member without a penis, my leadership position had been usurped. This was not amusing.

I'd made money for my company, joyfully shared my expertise by training others, and then my prize was snatched away and handed to a less deserving male. *Thump.* My head rammed into the much maligned "glass ceiling." It hurt—and I *hated* the experience. So this was what my friends in the women's movement were fighting! I was a bit late arriving at the fair. I'd never cared about business—never even understood women who were interested in having a career. My lifelong apathy toward enterprise had always been applauded by the men in my life. They thought it properly feminine. Then, lo and behold, I developed a communion with commerce and proved my proficiency in the workplace, only to have inequality come to roost on my doorstep. It was a wake-up call.

In the long run, the infighting with my husband was of no importance. The owner, having skimmed the lucrative cream from his Memphis operation, sold our agency right out from under us. The Meltons were auctioned off, right along with the "ol' plantation." We moved to Nashville as soon as another offer came our way.

I went through the motions of opening our Music City agency but couldn't get excited about it. I was dead to business, marriage, and normalcy. I'd survived adolescence, gone through gender-altering surgery, and married into mediocrity—all in an attempt to be exactly like everyone else. I was ready for what I thought theater to be—a "degenderized" zone.

Not Now, Darling was my first professional dinner-theater experience, and it slammed the door on my marriage. While I was at Chaffin's Barn Dinner Theatre following my heart, my husband was at home following his penis. I was working nights, so he seized the opportunity and took a pubescent modeling student to our marriage bed. To make matters worse, he took Polaroid pictures.

My mother refused to understand why I left my husband.

"Aleshia, you can't divorce that man," Mother argued. "Just because you're having a little success onstage, don't be foolish enough to throw away your marriage. Jim loves you."

"Mother," I tried to explain, "The point is that *my* husband has been sleeping with *my* student."

"Just remember, Missy, you played a big role in your husband's cheating." It upset Mozelle that I refused to accept responsibility for Jim's infidelity. "Because he's a man," Mother spelled it out carefully, "Jim has sexual cravings that are beyond his control."

"Oh! Get real, Ma!" I screeched. "I grew up falling for that 'blue balls' theory, and I'm not buying it anymore."

Even if my mother could forgive Jim's irresponsible coupling, I could not. There was no excuse. Not even southern, male-biased religious dogma could explain away my husband's actions. Every southern boy grows up knowing that men have dominion over their women. Fathers, husbands, and boyfriends all know that theirs is a divine right. If pushed, they'll quote you biblical chapter and verse to prove male superiority. Nowhere, however, was it written that James Melton could cheat on his wife.

I grew up a sissy, a transbeing, believing I had no rights. Only after surgery and growing into womanhood did I begin to grasp the absolute absurdity of "machismo" propaganda. Now, with each passing year, it became more difficult for me to abide by gender-biased rules. I was becoming my own person—a person for whom my gender history held little sway over my daily life. I had yet to understand, however, that a power struggle was at the heart of my unhappiness in marriage. In theory, I accepted that a husband should have the final word in any family disagreement. In practice, I had difficulty accepting my husband's dictates. I knuckled under to his wishes on every topic from sex to shopping—but I carried a serious grudge.

Were such a process possible, I'd freeze-dry the 1970s. Touring in dinner theater was an exciting, popular, and lucrative craft. It was "on the road" after leaving my second husband that I found myself. Not every experience was joyous, but each one offered its own reward.

My leading man in *Seven Year Itch* couldn't stand the ground I walked on, but despite our personal differences, the show received glowing notices:

". . . the beautiful, brainless, buxom, and bouncy red-head upstairs who begins their romance with a fallen tomato plant.

"Aleshia Melton, who is brilliantly cast in the role of the girl, is a bundle of talent, versatility and comedy.

"One can hardly believe Ms. Melton is anyone but the girl. Her portrayal is just that real. Melton's talent is limitless and she had 35 TV credits to her name." This one was from Samantha Blackburn, special correspondent.

My flashy interpretation of the role captured the attention of the press and the audience, but it consistently irked my leading man.

"Don't you ever pull something like that on *my* stage again," he screamed as our automatic stage ascended into the theater's ceiling. The actor was furious about an acting choice I'd made that evening. He accused me of upstaging him. Probably I had.

"*Your* stage?" I exploded. "I've toured this show four times; how many runs have you had with it?"

"I don't care how many times you've done the show, Bitch," he shrieked. "I have a master's degree in theater, and I know what I'm talking about."

I spewed and sputtered on my way to my dressing room, but the heart was gone from my argument. My co-star's postgraduate degree intimidated me.

The next week I was at Marshall University applying for a graduate teaching assistantship. No sawed-off runt of an actor would ever again throw his education in my face. I'd earn my own damn master's in theater.

My acceptance to the graduate program didn't come until after our show closed in West Virginia. By the time it arrived, I was in Louisiana enjoying a tour of *Come Blow Your Horn*. My intimidating leading man had been left behind, and I no longer wanted to go back to school. I was, however, playing another bubble-brained character called "the Girl Upstairs." Standing in the shadow of my fortieth birthday, I knew the vampish, youthful roles would not be mine much longer. They sharply decline with the fading of a woman's first blush. I wasn't blushing anymore.

I accepted Marshall University's assistantship offer twenty-four hours before my estranged husband showed up in Shreveport to court forgiveness.

"It's only two years," Jim rationalized when informed of my decision to return to school for an advanced degree. "We'll make it, Aleshia. I think you should take this opportunity. Give me another chance, and you can still go back to school. You have no idea how scared I get for you sometimes. Driving to work, Sweetheart, I've gotten so nervous that I'd have to pull off the road. 'Jim,' I'd say to myself, 'if something happened to you, Aleshia would have to get married the next day.' Darlin', you simply don't know how to take care of yourself."

I was a sucker for sweet words; always had been. Jim reminded me that I needed his help to survive; I believed him and forgave him everything. In the church of my youth, the preacher used to say that a sinner was "backslidin'." Well, I was certainly right back where I'd started.

I had let Jim convince me that no one is perfect. It made sense. I hadn't, for example, mentioned my transgendered past to my husband. The knowledge of my own deceit made me somewhat more willing to forgive his fall from grace. Sometimes love is better when it's blind, deaf, and dumb. I was never even tempted to share my transgendered history with Jim. I knew better. He made cutting remarks about my gay friends; he ranted about the "queers" in theater; he even resented my having a gay hairdresser. Without a doubt, I knew he would have a violent reaction to my own hidden past. There was no need to test his reaction. I'd married a strongly homophobic man, mainly to prove my womanly worth.

My husband loved me. Hadn't he come to Louisiana in order to save our marriage and to make amends for his infidelity? I'd go to West Virginia, get an education, and then dutifully return to my husband in California. My intentions were good—and I had two years before I had to report for duty.

My responsibility as a graduate teaching assistant was to introduce bright-eyed Marshall University students to the creative arts. I savored the honor but was shocked at how campus life had changed since my days as an undergraduate.

My first day on campus, outside the department chair's office, two undergraduate students entered the waiting area. The young man stopped, looked me up and down, and was promptly dragged from the room by his female associate. I thought it was cute. The boy's girlfriend was jealous of an older woman.

"You try something with her, and you're dead," the female student said once they were in the hallway. "I saw her first and she's mine."

When I was an undergraduate only eight years earlier, such a statement would have been unthinkable. No coed in the early 1960s, not even a confirmed lesbian, would have dared make that statement. The Stonewall Riots of 1969 had done a lot to free the homosexual subculture. I found it disconcerting. Being queer wasn't supposed to be easy. This was my first encounter with the sexual freedom and gender bending that was beginning to take place in America. After thirteen years as a woman, I was no longer on the cutting edge of the gender movement. At thirty-seven, I felt like a relic, a dysphoric dinosaur.

The attention I got from women at Marshall further served to complicate my life. Women had always liked me, and as a boy I flattered myself that some found me attractive. Physically, however, women

scared me to death. Until after transsexual surgery, no female had ever
sexually caught my attention.

I met Nancy in 1968, a time when many gay men believed that
appearing at a mandatory function with an attractive, understanding
female would divert attention from their homosexuality. Being about as
understanding as a woman could get, I attended many formal func-
tions. I'd get all dressed up, and we'd go hobnob with real-life heterosexual men and their wives.

"Don't I know you?" a blonde beauty piped up from across the table
at one formal dance. "I think I recognize you from that whorehouse
down the street."

Shocked, I looked up from my plate. Other guests at our table sat
with salad forks poised in midair.

"Yes," I sweetly smiled. "I have the towel concession—you're one of
the girls."

The next morning a dozen roses were delivered to my apartment.
The note read, "I truly enjoyed last evening. Let's do it again . . . soon."
The card was simply signed "N."

Nancy became the heart and stability I'd always sought in a man. We
were soon inseparable. When my grandfather Gillentine died, it was
Nancy who took over, helping me deal with my first major family loss
and seeing me through my grief. She was always comforting, caring,
and considerate. I truly loved her. Sexually, however, I knew only how
to respond to a male aggressor. Nancy's gentle attentions confused me.
I had no idea what she expected of me and refused to believe her when
she insisted her needs were neither mysterious nor magical. I couldn't
get past my fear of being a disappointment to her. After all I'd gone
through to become a heterosexual woman, how could I opt for yet
another sexual classification? Certainly, I'd always preferred the company of women, and I'd never been emotionally honest with men, but I
knew my smoke-and-mirrors routine would be an affront to Nancy.

Until meeting Nancy, sexually speaking, life had been quite simple.
I was available to those who found me sexually appealing. That hadn't
changed since I was four or five years old. If someone desired me, I
thought I owed him something. I didn't always understand what that

something was, not exactly; but in the past, men had always known to take advantage of my confusion. Now there was a woman in my life who wanted me sexually, and I had no idea what to do about that. I doubted that I could be a lesbian even if I wanted to. Some feminist separatists were saying, loudly and in print, that transsexuals shouldn't even be considered women. What would these separatists say if I was attracted to a lesbian lifestyle? It was easier to stay with men. With men, it was easy. I didn't have to do anything. Sexual aggression was part of their manhood, and with assault I knew how to deal. I was accustomed to being hunted, conquered, and mounted as a trophy.

Nancy and I finally had a showdown because of my tenuous grip on sexuality. We were parked in front of her rooming house at the time. It was a former hotel, just down the street from the Hollywood police station, now catering exclusively to young career women. I was smoking a cigarette and gazing off at the Hollywood sign.

"You want a man!" Nancy fired in exasperation. "Then that's what I'll be."

Her outburst caused me to smile. One transsexual per family was more than enough, in my estimation. Good-naturedly, I stopped staring off into space and turned to address my piqued friend. Nancy was sitting in my passenger seat with her jeans fly unzipped. A huge dildo protruded from the denim opening.

I shrieked and dropped my cigarette! The dildo was a shocking—if not frightening—sight to behold. It pointed heavenward, gleaming in all its glory. That massive phallic piece was a masterpiece of prosthetic engineering—a testimony to man in his finest hour. It was a monumental latex weapon, complete with bulging blue veins. My cigarette lay smoldering under the car seat, burning a hole in my carpet.

CHAPTER 14

Off-Broadway Baby

A master's degree was hanging on my wall before I grasped that male producers and casting directors respect the healthy chest of an artiste more than they do her education. I'd been in Manhattan for over six months but couldn't get an audition without an agent—and no agent was interested unless I was in a show. It was the actor's catch-22. In the Big Apple, as the saying goes, I couldn't get arrested.

Kathy, understanding the commercial ways of life, saved my career by giving me a boob job. She said to think of it as a graduation gift. Extreme feminist and physical purists of my acquaintance have since sniffed that bust augmentation is gilding an educated woman's lily, but Kathy knew what she was doing. In show business, there is no such thing as an oversized bosom.

Bedazzling boobs, however, did not diminish my desire to escape Manhattan. I was intent on leaving my theatrical failure behind and returning to Jim Melton in Los Angeles. My husband and I had an agreement, after all. I'd merely taken a little side trip through New York on my way west. Still, before throwing in the towel, I wanted at least to witness an Actors' Equity audition. It was a matter of pride. After living in New York City, I needed to truthfully say I'd attended an audition on the Great White Way. Let Hollywood incorrectly assume that the tryout was mine.

An Actors' Equity Association member and old friend took pity on me and invited me to tag along on her upcoming audition. As I followed my meagerly endowed colleague into the Forty-second Street audition hall, someone started shouting. "There's Julie!" they cried. My friend and I both turned around, but the role of Julie, the tall, buxom secretary in *Divorce Me, Darling*, was mine. My bodacious ta-tas were cast on the spot. I attended my friend's audition—and my twin thirty-eights landed the job.

It didn't matter to me that the show was off-off-*off*-Broadway . . . in Albuquerque, New Mexico. Nothing mattered except being cast in a

union production. The role of Julie made me eligible to join the Actors'
Equity Association. I called my husband to say I was "working" my
way west.

The Albuquerque Barn Dinner Theatre's new resident director liked
neither my whim-whams nor the actress sporting them. Not every male
director is impressed with "Tits and Ass." In Stephen Leery's estimation, his boss had flown to New York and offered an equity contract to
the first big-boobed bimbo he saw on Forty-second Street. It would be a
difficult rehearsal process.

"My director," I wrote to Kathy, "is an example of testosterone poi-
soning. He's like a primal man, and his only social rule of thumb is 'if
you couldn't fuck it—kill it.'"

Divorce Me, Darling opened on April 8, 1977. Millie Dew with the *Village Press* covered the premiere. She enjoyed the show, praised the cast,
and singled out the newest Actors' Equity Association member.

"As the sexiest of secretaries, Aleshia Brevard as Julie is an entice-
ment to all men who enter her office. . . . Aleshia is a very interesting
actress to watch. Being tall and pretty, she does wonderful things with
a part that could have been rather dull. She has grasped at small things
and created a very funny role."

Still, I was shocked when Stephen Leery offered me a pivotal role in
his next production. The director and I had not gotten along well. In fact,
I'd come to despise Stephen and his hateful equity cast—but I wanted to
play Sunny in *The Lady Who Cried Fox*. I placed another call to my waiting
husband. I was going to be a little longer getting to Los Angeles.

June 24, 1977, I received greetings from the State of Nevada. My husband, now known as the plaintiff, divorced me.

My mother was furious. "You never know when you're well off," she
screamed over the phone. Daddy thought she was having a nervous
breakdown. So much for running home to mama—that was obviously
not the answer to this problem. Instead, I grabbed the title role in *Move
Over, Mrs. Markham*, went on tour, and started putting together a grub-
stake. I'd just wait and see where life took me.

After twelve months on the road, I'd reached a decision. I would
return to Hollywood. Before making that fateful move, however, I

bowed to the inevitable reality of every maturing actress. I accepted a character actress role. I played an elderly bitch in Jules Tosca's *Subject to Change*.

I'd dreaded this aging transition for years. Without youth and glamour to back me up, people might find I was nothing but a talentless hack. Instead, I found my niche. As an ugly, selfish, grumpy old woman, the audiences and critics loved me. Of that show, the *Tampa Tribune's* performing arts writer Bruce Jones said:

"But most of all, 'Subject To Change' is funny because of Aleshia Brevard in the lead role. She's the one who's going to be left behind. Her rantings and ravings make a powerful characterization, and her way with the words of Tosca makes them even funnier than he did."

By the time I returned to Hollywood, I was forty-two years old—prehistoric for an actress. Employment, however, did come quickly. My success was because of Erika Wain, a great new theatrical agent. First, she landed me a role as Gigantia in Hanna-Barbera's *Legends of the Superheroes*, parts one and two. I thrived on being a villainess, pursued by Batman and Robin and engaged to Atom Man. Before the show aired on January 18, 1979, Erika had me cast as the bubble-brained Hedy La Rue in an equity production of *How to Succeed in Business without Really Trying*. By far, however, my weirdest job during the late 1970s was *Hollywood Diamond Jubilee*. It was a television special in which I played actress Tallulah Bankhead and introduced the Master of Shock Rock, Alice Cooper. Tallulah should have known Alice. What a couple they would have been!

Success as Aleshia Brevard was much more satisfying than it had ever been as Lee or Melton. Stupidly, I'd professionally changed my name with each marriage. I thought I was sharing film credit with the current husband. With hindsight, I was trying to ensure support by giving him bragging rights.

My agent called me after a film for which I had held high hopes had failed to materialize. I was sulking.

"Aleshia, do you have a really ugly picture of yourself?" Erika asked.

"Blackmail photographs are immediately shredded," I snapped. I was getting paranoid.

"Ugly yourself up," my brisk agent continued. "I submitted your head shots for *The Man with Bogart's Face*, but Marvin Paige at MGM casting says you're too pretty for the role of Mother. You can act the hell out of this role, Aleshia—we just have to get you in to see the producer. We'll try getting around Marvin another way. Get somebody to take some ugly pictures of you."

For the impromptu photo shoot, I stuffed bath towels in a panty girdle and crammed pillowcases into my largest bra. Over that bumpy, bulging figure, I wore a muumuu. The shapeless sack was made of furniture material. Still not satisfied with my look, I stained my front teeth with spirit gum, cut hair from a wig, and glued the stubble on my upper lip. After frizzing my hair and creating dark shadows under my eyes, my look was truly gruesome. For good measure, I added four-inch heels. I was a photogenic nightmare, but as Erika had suggested, the pictures got me past Marvin Paige.

The creator and producer of *The Man with Bogart's Face*, Andrew Fenady, wrote a publicity release that covered our meeting.

"You've sent out word to all the agents—you're looking for a woman between 40 and 50, must weigh a minimum of 225 pounds 'with a face like a suit of armor.'

"You, along with the director Robert Day and the casting director Marvin Paige, interview over eighty-eight candidates. They all look like fugitives from the fat farm, but somehow none of them is quite what you put down on paper and had in mind.

"Then one day Paige says there's a person outside. Her name is Aleshia Brevard. She just might fit the bill. 'Shoo her in' you say. Through the door with hardly any room to spare strides something that would make any football coach in the market for an offensive tackle sit up and take notice. Except this tackle is wearing a muu-muu.

"She's built along the lines of a factory smoke stack, only wider. She's got eyebrows like two caterpillars, a hairdo made out of spun steel, a less than elegant mustache and rusted teeth. You're afraid to go too close because her breath has to be worse than a grizzly bear's.

"She towers over you, as you stand up your six feet worth and try a pleasant 'hello.' She talks. Not exactly. Her response is more like the sound of a cement mixer. You ask her to read a scene. She does. She's a combination earth quake and blast furnace. Dynamite. You're sorry somebody has to go through life looking like that but you're happy because it looks like you've found MOTHER."

After five callbacks to MGM, I officially landed the role. Once the contract was signed, I couldn't wait to throw off "Mother's muumuu." I was going to work at the legendary MGM Studios, where once resided "more stars than there are in heaven." This hallowed ground had been home to Garland, Garbo, Hepburn, Crawford, and Taylor. I wanted to add Brevard to that list. After shucking the muumuu, I made my next visit to Metro-Goldwyn-Mayer in clothing more befitting the star I wanted to become. Mr. Fenady's publicity release, aptly titled "She Pulled a Fast One on You, Fenady," also had a few words to say about that persona.

"A week later on the set you notice a gorgeous girl in her mid-twenties talking to the wardrobe lady. Gorgeous is wearing a halter top and shorts revealing a body that would've had Ziegfield waving a contract at her. Gorgeous smiles a perfect pearly smile through a pair of luscious lips. You nod perfunctorily and keep going. You're a happily married man.

"A few minutes later the wardrobe lady comes over and says Aleshia wants to know if you want her to wear her own muu-muu in the picture. 'Oh, is she on the phone?' you ask. 'What do you mean, on the phone?' Wardrobe responds, 'you just said hello to her,' and points at gorgeous."

Deception had landed me a plum job. Mr. Fenady frankly admitted that had I auditioned without padding, stained teeth, and bushy brows, I would never have been cast as Mother. As a tag line he added, "My imagination is not that good." If I hadn't looked the part, it wouldn't have mattered how well I interpreted the role.

"Aleshia plays the hell out of MOTHER," Mr. Fenady wrote at the conclusion of his piece. "The cast and crew can't believe the 'before and after' transformation that takes place each day she works.

"When the picture is over, she writes you a short note, 'Mr. Fenady, sorry I had to pull a fast one.'

"You send her a shorter one.

"'I'm not.'"

Flush from *The Man with Bogart's Face*, I was soon reeling with frightening news from home. Mother had awakened in the middle of the night with a monstrous, throbbing headache. She ended her night in Johnson City Memorial Hospital's emergency room. The visit saved her life. Mother's diagnosis was arteritis, an infection of the arteries. Equally terrifying was the news that had she waited forty-five minutes longer to seek help, she would have suffered a fatal hemorrhage.

Mother was already on elevated doses of cortisone and her life-threatening illness was being closely monitored by the time she called to say how close we'd come to losing her. Even after the fact, I panicked.

In spite of my mother's upbeat assurance that there was no need to worry, I had major concerns about her health. For the first time, I acknowledged my mother's mortality. I'd come within minutes of losing my best friend—and I had not even suspected she was in danger. I'd always assumed that I'd know when she was in danger. I'd had no inkling. The person I held closest and dearest in the world was a temporal being. Mozelle might not always be a mere phone call away, and that realization frightened me. I was afraid for my mother; petrified for myself. I couldn't imagine a life without Mother in it.

Mother's physical disorder underscored my growing frustration with Hollywood and with the men responsible for feeding the industry's talent machine. Show business is a notoriously high-stakes game—and I was no longer sure I held winning cards. Film work kept coming my way, but my transsexual history was a growing source of anxiety. There was no one with whom I dared share my secret. Financially, I was dependent on the goodwill of the casting directors, producers, and directors. I was weaving an elaborate lie and increasingly fearful of getting caught in my own web. After ten years as a professional actress and seventeen years as a female, I was lost in the Hollywood labyrinth. My life was a sham, I knew it—and on the other side of the continent, my mother was seriously ill.

I fought the impulse to run to Mother's side. I feared I'd be using her illness as an excuse to flee California. Instead, I managed emotionally to tie my profession to my mother's future happiness. If I became a star, Mozelle would again become well. I even convinced myself that my success would give my mother's life more meaning.

Like so many starlets who move from the farm to the movie capital, I saw Hollywood as the fulfillment of my every dream. Films of the 1930s and 1940s offered an apprehensive nation a welcome escape. I was an impressionable child who believed filmland's hype that utopia is always accessible to a beautiful woman. My mother had believed it, too.

In the late 1970s my fascination with Pip's, a chic, private club in Beverly Hills, exemplified the sad fact that I still saw myself as a glorified object. The club was the newest happening place in town, and many starlets considered it a social coup to frequent the private club. Finding a member who'd sign them into the upscale pub was part of the game. Because the club was expensively exclusive, the playground seemed all the more appealing. This game differed only slightly, if at all, from the gay scene I'd known eighteen years earlier. As a boy, I'd mistakenly assumed that only drag queens needed to parlay looks, charm, and charisma into personal security. They had no alternative path to power. It shocked me to find beautiful women playing the same dead-end game in Beverly Hills. It didn't stop me from doing the same.

"Pardon me, Miss. How tall are you?" The unimposing little man asked the one question that anywhere other than Pip's would have prompted a scathing retort.

Politely I lied, added an inch, and said I was six feet, one inch tall. Who knew—he might be somebody important!

"Oh, stay right here, there's someone you have to meet," he called over his shoulder as he scurried off into the crowd. The little man soon returned with a very dapper older gentleman.

"Aleshia . . . ," the nondescript chap began.

"I'm Herb Ruskin," the polished gray-haired cavalier interrupted.

My first date with Herb began at the Beverly Hills Hotel's Polo Lounge, where the maître d'hôtel seated us in "Mr. Ruskin's booth." From that impressive beginning we progressed to Chasen's, the world-famous restaurant on Sunset Strip. On our way up the steps, two husky waiters passed carrying a soused Alfred Hitchcock. The virtual inventor of the thriller genre was carted from the eatery, unceremoniously dumped into his waiting limousine, and driven away. The award-winning director of *Psycho, Vertigo,* and *The Birds* had been ordering the same item from Chasen's menu, seated in the same booth, every Thursday night for many years. I guess they knew him well.

"Aleshia," Herb confided as he took my arm and steered me into the restaurant, "there are three seating divisions here at Chasen's. A, B, and C sections—you're seated according to your importance. I don't mind you dining here with another man—I do mind you being seated in the wrong section."

"If I were not on your arm, I wouldn't be in any section," I murmured. Herb took my hand and corrected me, "You are a beautiful woman, Aleshia. You're not expected to be important."

Like Leslie Caron in *Gigi*, I was too easily convinced of my feminine right to be a concubine. I thought I'd met Maurice Chevalier.

When we arrived at Pip's for an after-dinner drink, Herb introduced me to the bartender, instructed him to take care of me, and scooted off to into the social whirl.

"If you were with me," said a husky voice at my left elbow, "I'd never leave you alone for a minute."

I turned to face a buffed and polished Farley Granger look-alike—the type that often frequents Beverly Hills watering holes. Immediately, the tanned Don Juan worked into his conversation the news that he was the nephew of actress-dancer Mitzi Gaynor.

"Really?" I said. "How fascinating . . . " I meant it. Then I remembered an adage about a bird in hand, bit my lip, and informed the adorable playboy that I was the guest of Mr. Ruskin.

"Well," he smiled, flashing perfectly capped teeth, "if a time comes when you are no longer *with* 'Mr. Ruskin,' you give me a call. I'm Steve Barber—spelled just like the pole. I'm in the book." With that, Mitzi's nephew returned to his drink, and Herb reappeared at my side.

It was over a year before Herb openly bragged of my highly prized fidelity. We were in Las Vegas, in a Caesar's Palace suite, with my sponsor's investment partner and wife. Herb crowed proudly that he'd tested me when we first met.

"On our first date," Herb glowed, "I made a phone call from Chasen's, to Steve Barber, and asked him to hit on Aleshia."

Mr. Barber, spelled just like the pole, was the first person I called when I returned to Los Angeles. The men in my life had become interchangeable. I was desperately seeking something on which to base my life but had misplaced the code on which I'd been weaned. My intention had been to alter gender, not ethics. Hollywood had become a trap.

CHAPTER 15

A Faceless Intruder

IN THE spring of 1980, I gave up on Hollywood. Eighteen years had passed since my transsexual transformation at Westlake Clinic, but in all that time I had not stopped running long enough to reflect on the woman I'd become. Using Hollywood's famous femmes as archetypes, I'd squandered valuable years in an attempt to create someone worthy of love. Fear and low self-esteem remained my major problems. At age forty-three, I was going home to Appalachia, hoping to find myself. Like a dispirited reject from *The Grapes of Wrath*, I loaded my furniture, plus every last plant I owned, and headed across the desert. My prized vegetation committed suicide as I retraced my steps toward Tennessee.

The remainder of that spring and the entire lazy summer were idled away with my mother, rummaging through consignment shops, giggling on the telephone, or working on my new mobile home by Boone Lake. We were like girlfriends. Often, Mother would drive the few miles to my place just so we could meander between the huge chestnut trees that lined each side of my road. We called that lazy amble "goin' for our walk." Some days, when we'd had enough exercise, we'd sit on my dock that jutted into the lake. No matter what our activity, we were talking. We overlapped each other in our excitement to share everything from the important to the mundane. It wasn't unusual for us, legs dangling from the dock, to while away an afternoon discussing the summer shadings of a maple leaf that floated beneath our feet.

Our favorite outing, however, was to The Laurels, a beautiful mountain cove in the Cherokee National Forest. Our "special spot" was filled with wild, flowering bay and sat comfortably nestled between the mountains that separate Erwin and Johnson City. We loved it. We spent many summer afternoons strolling beside the cold mountain stream that bubbled, crooked, and tumbled its way through the shaded woods toward the lowlands. In a more perfect world, or an MGM musical, that summer would slowly dissolve into a rosy glow. It did not.

As the season changed, so did our idyllic time.

After a visit to The Laurels one afternoon in the early fall, my mother and I returned to my lakeside home. The moment we opened the door I knew something was wrong. I sensed it. Hand in hand, with our hearts in our throats, Mother and I made a nervous inspection of every room. Nothing was out of place. A hundred dollars in cash still lay on my kitchen table, where I'd left it.

"Aleshia, burglars don't leave behind money that's out as an invitation for them to take," Mother finally said, breaking the tension. I laughed, locked the door behind me, and drove my mother back to Johnson City.

It was almost midnight before my panic returned. After cleaning my face in preparation for bed, I went into the bedroom to put away my clothes. I opened the lingerie drawer—it was empty. My brassieres were missing. Dumbfounded, it took me several seconds to realize that someone had broken into my house, stuffed my lingerie in a pillowcase, and left the way he'd come. I didn't bother to lock the door as I ran from my home.

"Did you recently break up with a boyfriend?" the Johnson City patrolman drawled as he took notes in my parent's living room. Since coming home, I hadn't dated anyone in East Tennessee, and this wasn't some childish prank played by a spurned lover. This was more sinister. I tried to explain that, but the policeman agreed with my dad—there was no real danger. The patrolmen shook my father's hand, shared a laugh about the nervousness of women, and sauntered out the door. To both men this looked like a prank. Some madman had merely stolen my brassieres as a display of his affection.

Within a week the faceless intruder again stealthily entered my home. There was no sign of forced entry. On this visit he took a black dress from my closet, spread it across my bed, and placed a wig above the dress where my head would normally be. It took little imagination to visualize the rest of his ritualistic act.

Mother, shocked by a second constabulary dismissal, bought a gun and became a vigilante. With her pistol bulging in a jacket pocket, she'd leap from my deck to question any suspicious-looking man walking past my secluded home. Things had gotten out of hand. If my stalker didn't kill someone, my mother might.

The moment I was offered a role in *Big Bad Burlesque*, I packed my bags, padlocked my doors, and fled for the safety of West Virginia. The extraordinary summer on Boone Lake had come to an end.

When I'd left California in 1980, I was already disillusioned with men. I'd suffered through long-term relationships with gay men, straight men, and one strongly male-identified woman. After the stalker incident, I swore off anything remotely resembling a man. The Fates, however, taking this anti-male stance as a personal challenge, came flitting back into my life.

"Aleshia is scared to live alone," Clotho croaked to her spiteful sisters, "so let's send her a man who'll protect her."

"Watch her mismanage this situation," Atropos chortled.

I met Michael Lindin nine hours after his release from the West Virginia State Penitentiary. Regular theater patrons introduced us when they brought Michael to the Mountaineer Dinner Theater for a celebration. He didn't take his eyes off me all evening. Since I was seated in the audience rather than performing in the play, I found his attention especially titillating. The Fates had picked me a French-Cherokee hunk who hadn't seen a woman for nine years.

"Great Scott," I reasoned, blindly smitten, "you don't have to marry the guy. Sleep with the boy, get him out of your system, put your mind back on rehearsals, and open your play." Behind me, the three Fates started to bump and grind in a lascivious parody of "The Wedding March." The overseers of my destiny knew that Michael Lindin's downtrodden life would strongly appeal to my ridiculously liberal nature. They also knew that once I'd slept with someone, I thought I was in love. Not even those three bitchy hags suspected how deeply I'd be touched by Michael Lindin.

I thought I'd met Oliver Twist. As a child, his life had been a nightmare—so bad, in fact, that neighbors had tried to adopt him. His mother refused, even though Michael's drunken stepfather put young Michael to bed with a shotgun pointed at the boy's head. He'd threaten to blow off his stepson's head if "the little bastard" didn't go to sleep.

At age twelve the boy rebelled, laid his stepfather's head open with a shovel, and sealed his own fate. Michael was kicked out of the Lindin home. He became a throwaway child. He lived on the streets of Charleston, West Virginia. By fifteen, Michael Lindin, incorrigible youth, had been sentenced to the state penitentiary.

Childhood misery was not the sole province of those marginalized by gender dysphoria, nor was suffering unique to the transgendered! My new boyfriend had the kind of childhood that made growing up transsexual seem like a Sunday walk in the park. Certainly, my own odyssey had presented me with a Cyclops or two, but nothing like the beasts that had terrorized Michael. His story taught me that one cannot allow a few monsters to negate the beauty of life's voyage. That realization caused me to soften my unilateral damnation of men. I phoned Mother to share the news of my epiphany. She was delighted.

By the time my sixth consecutive play, *I Ought to Be in Pictures*, opened in West Virginia, Michael and I were a serious item. I thought the live-in cast adored my ex-con Cherokee. Years later, a member of that cast said Michael's history had scared them to death. One sees what one wants to see, I guess.

When I left the Mountaineer, it was with my socially inept, curly-haired jailbird by my side. Aleshia, self-appointed theatrical guru, was going to teach her baby boy a trade. I was to star in and direct *The Owl and the Pussycat*. Michael would be my prop master. This time I'd be running the soup kitchen. Oh, I was so smug in my role as Michael Lindin's savior-therapist! I was not the most needy, insecure person in this relationship, therefore I assumed it must be a healthy coupling. My longtime friend Kathy, knowing better, dubbed me "the first transsexual squaw."

Our third stop with *The Owl and the Pussycat* tour was the Old West Theater near Johnson City, Tennessee. The forty-two-year-old Pussycat was bringing her twenty-four-year-old Owl home to roost. Daddy hated the idea. I never suspected that the Boone Lake stalker might be less thrilled than my father.

The faceless intruder displayed his anger by again breaking into my home. In spite of bars installed over the windows and locks changed on the doors, the interloper continued to come and go without signs of entry. This time it was Michael's underwear that disappeared. The shadowy invader removed my lover's briefs and replaced them with what we assumed were the interloper's underclothing. All we knew for sure was that strange, rather shabby undergarments were suddenly in the drawer where Michael kept his skivvies. This frightened me more than anything that had transpired before. The stalker's ongoing invasion had become an echo of a recurring nightmare that haunted me through puberty.

In my ongoing, distressing dream, I sat at the end of my family's breakfast table. Mother and Daddy were in their usual places, but I'd switched seats with my sister. From Jeanne's seat, I faced the back door. My family, as though in a trance, sat with their hands on the table. Suddenly, the shadowy figure of an unknown man appeared at the back door. He would rap three times. Slowly. Knock. Knock. Knock.

"Someone's at the door," I'd whisper tentatively. No one moved. My family stared straight ahead.

Knock. Knock. Knock.

I was drawn to the shadowy figure. I was terrified but compelled to open the door. Just as my hand touched the knob, I would wake up screaming. Always. Throughout adolescence the same dream returned, night after night. It lasted until I hitchhiked to California in the late 1950s. Now the shadowy man returned to haunt my life. This time he wasn't a dream.

The reality of my nightmare now overshadowed my life. In my fear, I insisted that we move to the actors housing provided by the theater. Even staying away from my lakeside home did not ease my anxiety. I felt I was being observed. Michael could not touch me without me stiffening or pulling away from his embrace. The intruder might be watching. Finally, Michael insisted that we return home and face the problem, head on.

With the shotgun that had become our constant companion riding in the back seat, we went home after a late Saturday performance. We drove into the yard shortly after midnight. I remained in the car while Michael took the gun and went to confirm that everything was secure.

I remained behind to appease my lover's machismo more than for reasons of safety.

Two loud, resounding shotgun blasts suddenly split the still, country night.

"Get going, get going," Michael roared as he hightailed it around the corner of our house, waving his arms. "He's inside! Aleshia, get out of here!"

I slid behind the wheel, started the engine, and plowed up the embankment toward the house. The car lights shone directly on a smashed back door. After a lifetime of avoiding confrontation, I was finally angry enough to fight back. I jumped from the car with extra shells, grabbed the shotgun from Michael, reloaded, and fell to a prone position on the ground. I was going to kill the faceless son of a bitch.

Neighbors, having heard the gunshots, started to arrive in our backyard. One had already called the police. I dispatched Michael to call Mother and Daddy—my ex-con boyfriend shouldn't be there when the police arrived. I then joined my armed neighbors, who were forming a wide circle around my house. It wasn't the smartest pattern for a shootout, but perhaps it would thwart the intruder's escape.

When the cops arrived, they confiscated my neighbors' firearms and sent everyone home. By the time policemen entered my house, the intruder had vanished. In the confusion, he'd escaped into the surrounding timberland. A search produced nothing but a walkie-talkie—left behind outside my rear window. It was the property of our local fire station. On this visit the nameless intruder smashed my back door and ransacked my home. He systematically destroyed my framed pictures of former leading men, scattered the contents of several theatrical trunks throughout my house, and wantonly destroyed my keepsakes. Without comment, the police finished their paperwork, drove away, and left me standing in my driveway holding the only weapon they had not confiscated. My ammunition they took with them.

Not only was the intruder into my life never caught, the case did not even generate a follow up. Early in my transsexual journey, I would have wrongly assumed this callous treatment was because of gender imperfection. I was not, however, being ignored because some "Bubba" cop viewed transsexuality as a transgression against nature. My gender history was not known in Johnson City. Standing alone in my driveway by Boone Lake, with a malevolent stalker possibly watching from the dark woods, I realized the danger of being a woman in an unsympathetic men's world. Since surgery, this scenario had played out too often for me to not recognize it now. In our society there are many males—gay, straight, married, and single—who hate women. Some of them wear uniforms.

My father despised Michael Lindin from the moment he heard there was a younger man in my life. Apart from his age, Daddy knew nothing about my lover. Partially because of Daddy's strong negative reaction, I think, Mother was firmly in Michael's camp of champions. She did, however, suggest it might be better to keep Michael's teenage incarceration a secret. It made no difference. My lover was still not allowed in Daddy's house. Michael's feelings were hurt and I felt sorry for him, but I wasn't surprised. I'd learned to expect nothing positive from my father. He seldom exceeded my expectations.

It was a relief when Mother and Daddy left Tennessee for their yearly wintering in Florida.

In April, Mother called, laughing as though she'd heard a great joke. It was no joke; she had drop foot. Without warning, the muscles of her right foot let go—and literally "dropped." Now she had no control over the appendage. Even when elevated, the offending foot dangled uselessly from the ankle. Mother assured me that in time she would be able to compensate for her useless foot, but for the time being, she walked with a halting lurch. Over and over she repeated the story of how she'd bitched and complained as she dragged her uncooperative extremity to see a Florida specialist. As she reached the clinic door, a man was exiting the doctor's office. He was missing a foot. Mother kept talking long after there was anything left to say. I understood the moral of her tale, but still Mother couldn't bring herself to hang up. There was no trace of panic in her upbeat, offhand delivery, but I realized that my mother was a better actress than I'd ever been.

"What is it, Mother?" I asked, holding my breath. "What are you not telling me?"

"I'm afraid for you to see me like this, Aleshia," she whispered softly. "I don't think I could stand seeing pity in your eyes."

Her quiet desperation devastated me.

"Get your ass home," I said, trying to bluff as bravely as my stoic mother. "While your foot gets better, we'll sit on the porch and talk about people as they walk past."

When my parents arrived home from Florida, Michael and I were both there to greet them. Michael was an invited guest. The spirit of reconciliation lasted only long enough for Daddy's Pekingese to growl.

"What's the matter, boy?" Daddy asked his contrary canine. "Don't you like him either?"

By the end of the day, both men were sitting silently, side by side, at the kitchen counter. They could barely tolerate each other, but in Mother's extreme moment of need, they sat united in their silence. They were waiting for me to make things right. I sat, holding my mother's hand and willing that she not read the panic in my eyes. I didn't have the comforting words she needed to hear. My entire life this woman had taken care of me. It was now my turn to be the caregiver, and I was painfully aware of my inadequacy.

For two years, daily doses of cortisone had magically controlled Mother's arteritis, the infection of her blood vessels. I feared drop foot was a result of the magic potion. One of cortisone's infamous side effects, a rounded, "moon-shaped" face, had long been a visible result of my mother's treatment. Mozelle was more than her beauty, but for her, that was merely an intellectual concept. Emotionally, her worth had long been tied to her appearance, and the drastic physical change was very difficult for her to accept. She never openly complained about the noticeable bloating of her body, however. Instead, she made self-deprecating jokes. I understand a fear that drives someone to belittle themselves before others have the opportunity. I remain awed by my mother's strength.

"Aleshia, I wish you could have seen your mother when I first met her," Daddy said one evening, shortly after their return from Florida. "She was the most beautiful woman I ever saw." His sweet recognition was touching. In spite of long-standing problems with my father, I wanted nothing more than for my parents to support each other in their declining years.

"Was?" Mother replied in good spirit. "What do you mean *was*, James? I think I'm just as good-looking now as I ever was."

"If you think you're the same woman you were, you ought to look in a mirror," Daddy countered spitefully.

I sat speechlessly glued to my chair, a child again, insignificant and powerless. The room took on the airless, heavily oppressive remembrance of childhood. I sat. Mother made an effort to laugh off Daddy's derisive remark, and her attempt only made the moment more devastating. Daddy sullenly retreated into his shell. The evening, like our family life, wore on.

As Mother's face continued to bloat in reaction to the cortisone, she stopped seeing old friends. She restricted her social life to church on Sunday and a few intimate family members. Still, she worked hard at keeping her image alive. She invested in long, flowing caftans and started putting additional emphasis on her silver hair. We worked together to master cosmetic contouring techniques. Mother never lost her flair for presentation, but she was no longer her old vivacious self.

Looking for a positive reflection in my father's eyes became of paramount importance to Mother.

"Bless his heart," my mother would say. Daddy had begun to give Mother more attention and was constantly, gently massaging her damaged foot. That my father loved her was never a question. In some self-destructive way, my parents always needed each other. I never understood the true nature of their relationship. Perhaps Daddy loved his wife too much. Maybe he'd never found a security in her love that would allow him to share her. It has even been suggested by well-meaning friends that Daddy's moratorium on fatherly bonding was the result of an obsession with his wife. A psychological explanation of their conflict no longer matters; the effect remains the same. I grew up with an emotionally absentee father, a mother who tried too hard to compensate, and parents who were constantly enmeshed in battle. I blamed myself for the war.

Often, mothers like mine are accused of consciously training their male offspring, from childhood, to magnify the faults of the father.

Because of fault-finding articles she'd read, my mother went through a difficult period of soul-searching at the time of my transsexual surgery. She was terrified that she'd been the cause of my gender confusion. Mozelle cannot be blamed for my identity crisis. Nor can I blame my father. There is no blame. Instead, I believe my mother was intuitively sensitive to my gender dysphoria and spent a lifetime trying to compensate for my difference. It was that unspoken bond that made us especially close.

It is true, however, that I grew up focused on the pain inflicted by my father, rather than on my mother's own shrewish exasperation and rage. I thought her anger was justified. As a child, I believed it was my failure to be the son he wanted that caused my father's disapproval of me. Perhaps, however, Daddy treated me as fathers have always treated their sons. My gender dysphoria could be what caused me to internalize my father's every action as personal disregard and disdain. I needed more affection than a boy generally receives from his father. Not getting it made me angry. I was also angry that my daddy was not Robert Young of *Father Knows Best*. Most of my life, I fantasized that I was the child of some other man. My hostility, added to my innate femininity, only pushed my father further away. Living with me must have been very difficult for my father.

Daddy added fuel to my early fantasy when he heard about my need for transsexual surgery.

"I never thought that boy was mine," he exploded in a rage. Mother sealed that escape route for us both. She reminded Daddy that only his blood had matched mine when, as a baby, I'd needed a transfusion to survive.

"If you have any doubts about who fathered your children, it should be Jeanne you're worried about," Mother jabbed.

Because of the special bond I shared with my mother, my sister, Jeanne, must often have felt less than visible. Surprisingly, my "little sister" never held me responsible for pushing her aside. We grew up in the same household, with Jeanne receiving little more fatherly attention than her older sibling. Yet my sister reacted quite differently to our shared environment. She loved her daddy. Jeanne recalls an incident when our father, coming back from working in the farm's bottomland, stopped his horse, dismounted, and picked Mother a black-eyed Susan bouquet. His hands were greasy when he presented his offering to his wife. My sister tells how Mother tossed the wildflowers aside without so much as an appreciative nod. Mother's careless gesture deeply affected Jeanne. She was embarrassed for Daddy. In many ways she sided with her emotionally distant father and blamed our mother for the family's dysfunction. Despite our differences, however, Jeanne and I were allies. We remain the closest of friends.

It was to my sister that I first turned with my plans for transsexual surgery. Her response was typical of Jeanne. "I've always wanted to have a sister," she wrote. "Now I have one."

In 1981, I had yet to realize that the majority of children grow up in dysfunctional families—and that most beautifully survive the experience. I did know that with my mother distended by cortisone, my father pampering a weak heart, my sister devoting her life to an overpowering husband, and me towing a socially unacceptable ex-convict through life, my family was troubled. It was into this hubbub that Mrs. Katherine de Fallio, née Taylor, O'Brian, and Stormy Lee, came to scope out my Native American lover. Kathy's instinct for disaster had always been superb.

Kathy arrived in Tennessee full of mischief and ready for a good time.

"When's the baby due, James?" Kathy asked, patting Daddy on his protruding belly. My father laughed along with everyone else. I think he actually thrived on Kathy's disrespectful attention.

My live-in Cherokee took to Kathy immediately. The positive appraisal seemed mutual. This time she did not suggest that my man might be gay.

"That man's a fine young thing, Girlfriend—why are you holding out? You've got to marry him," Kathy enthused. "Your mother adores him . . . I know because I asked her. She thinks Michael is good for you, Girl, and so do I. He loves you, Hon."

"I think that maybe he does, too," I blushed.

"So what's your problem, Sister Woman? Keep jerking Michael around and you'll end up alone. A lot of younger women would be happy to jump the broom with that baby boy."

I hemmed and hawed.

"So are you going to marry him or not?" she kept pestering. "If you aren't going to marry Michael that's your business . . . but we both know that you are! Why not do it while I'm here?"

"I want my daddy's blessing," I said. "Daddy has to approve."

CHAPTER 16

Mother's Final Gift

"I'M GOING to marry your daughter whether you like it or not!" Michael snarled through clenched teeth. Finally, someone other than my mother was confronting my father. I married my liberator on October 18, 1982. The bride was an old forty-five—Michael Lindin, the groom, clocked in on the younger side of twenty-four. Kathy and Mozelle were thrilled to be in attendance. Daddy refused to attend the nuptials. The bride was barely there.

"Here, Honey, take this," Kathy started cooing after Michael approached my father to ask for his blessings. I opened my mouth, closed my eyes, and, like a greedy little bird, swallowed anything she poked into my mouth. I stayed sedated from the moment I accepted Michael's proposal until I slurred, "I do."

Mother was delighted to see me remarried. My third marriage was the first wedding—of either daughter—she'd been invited to attend. For her, the intimate exchange of vows was a grand occasion. She adored Michael. I, however, was nervous to be marrying anyone. Legally, I'd been a woman for only twenty years, but I'd started to suspect that perhaps I was an alien in the state of matrimony. I should have listened to my inner voice. Instead, I opted for the social safe haven of marriage. The romantic dream was enough to rekindle my desire for a successful commitment.

After two months of being Mrs. Lindin, I told Daddy of Michael's teenage incarceration. Hopefully, this heartbreaking tale of social injustice would soften my father's attitude toward my husband. It did not. In James Crenshaw's estimation, West Virginia had not been heartlessly bureaucratic when they banished a homeless youth to a state mental institution. Their irresponsibility was in allowing Michael to escape. The state had merely corrected their mistake by apprehending the runaway and sticking him in a penitentiary. State rights, to Daddy, was a political godsend.

"There has never been a criminal in the Crenshaw family, and there's not going to be one now!" Daddy seethed.

"But, Daddy," I pressed, "Michael studied law in prison and got himself pardoned."

"That only makes a stronger argument for capital punishment," Daddy sneered. As was his usual reaction to moments of family confrontation, he turned up the volume on the television set.

Michael now became Daddy's number-one suspect for every crime committed in the tri-county area. If scheduled programming was interrupted by a televised news bulletin announcing a crime, Daddy would immediately ask, "Where was Michael?"

For over forty years I'd tried not to care that my father and I were at loggerheads, but I'd always desperately needed Daddy's love and acceptance. Now it was too late. My third marriage was a family disaster. I'd overplayed my hand by trying to force my father to accept that I was lovable. I wanted nothing more than to please my father—but I'd never known how.

Although some fathers have interpreted their child's gender transformation as a personal vendetta directed against them, I never felt my father was part of that angry group. He didn't approve of me, but it was not because of gender-altering surgery. He had never considered me a proper son. On that issue we were in agreement—it didn't help us find peace. Daddy and I had never been close. After surgery, the only noticeable change was that I went from being a disappointing son to being an equally disappointing daughter. Still, I believe my father did the best he knew how. I am convinced of that. He raised me in much the same manner in which he'd been raised. It was a hands-off approach that must have left him feeling unloved. The emotional distancing certainly had that effect on me. I still do not believe my father ever loved me. Now, however, I feel that Daddy's inability to communicate caused him as much pain as it caused his family.

My unhappy early years resulted from my inability to please both myself and a society that saw me as male. My father was merely part of that external pressure. From childhood, Mother had tried to explain away my father's irrational reaction to my softness. Daddy had endured his own childhood taunts. Suffering from tuberculosis as a youngster, my father had also preferred playing with the neighborhood girls. He wanted only to spare his son the experience of his own early pain. To him, there was nothing more shameful than being a "sissy."

He, unlike his offspring, grew into an athlete. My father wanted the same for me. Daddy embraced his masculinity with the same fervor with which I would later cherish my femininity. If it was true, as Mother suggested, that my father always had my best interests at heart, I never realized it. His anger and disapproval wounded me more deeply than any hurt inflicted by the town's bullies.

All through my formative years I had sung for every beauty pageant, PTA meeting, and Ladies' Aide Society in Trousdale County. My dad never saw me perform. He always had a "nicotine fit" just before my performance. I'd cry all the way home. I needed his praise.

"Buddy, your daddy thinks you have the most beautiful voice he's ever heard," Mother would soothe. "He's afraid. He thinks that hearing your voice will cause him to cry in public. That's why he goes outside to smoke." I didn't believe her. I thought my father was ashamed of me—that he hated having a soprano for a son. As a result, and in an attempt to solicit Daddy's favor, I spent my youth passing on to him every compliment or piece of outside praise that I received. He always sniffed disdainfully, as a reminder that one does not bring attention to oneself. By the time I became a young adult, I was afraid to tell a stranger my name, even when asked. Now, after finally realizing that I do have talents and that I am loved for myself, Daddy is no longer here to appreciate me.

This same man, the man I so feared, was respected and liked by members of the community. The nickname Cutie stuck with Daddy from childhood, and he was considered a jovial and congenial man. Unfortunately, I did not know that man. I still wish we could have been friends. He was never able to give me his approval, and I never learned to live graciously with not having it. Daddy and I, in the years after my mother's death, found only an uneasy peace. I could never rid myself of the pain from having disappointed him.

During my third marriage, I didn't know I could feel anything other than animosity for Daddy. After a year, my husband and I finally stopped seeking my father's approval. Trying to win favor was too painful. I shut down, believing my father had finally succeeded in driving me away from the family. Michael and I would leave our Boone Lake home and start over in Nashville. Our decision made, I had to face the more painful responsibility of telling my mother.

Mother and I drove to our favorite spot in the Cherokee National Forest. It was winter in the Appalachian Mountains; woodland animals had burrowed in for the icy interval, and mountain songbirds had fled south for the season. The Laurels were appropriately dark and quiet. Mother was also subdued, as though she anticipated my announcement. Forlornly, we sat in the car as the windows frosted over. The delight my mother and I found in this spot was part of a spent summer. We sat together, silently, in the heart of the frigid national forest.

"Michael and I are . . . we're thinking . . . maybe we'll move to Nashville," I finally began. Mother looked at me, stricken.

"We . . . Well, Mother, we don't know any other way to make it," I blurted in a rush. Mother started to cry. Huge tears welled up in her eyes and brimmed down the side of her cortisone-swollen face. I ached, seeing how tired her eyes looked. Mother rummaged for a handkerchief. I was breaking my mother's heart. My ally and confidant sat dabbing at her eyes with a crumpled tissue. Mother looked frail and hurt and weak. She sat nervously searching her pockets for another tissue.

"We're . . . Mother . . . I mean, well, . . . we're only talking about it," I said, stumbling over my words.

I wanted to take back everything I'd said, to retrace a lifetime of ill-timed steps. I did not want my mother to be old and sick at age sixty-four. I didn't want her left behind, sitting alone at a kitchen counter while Daddy mutely sat staring at another ball game or reading another western paperback novel. At that moment, I would have willed my entire life to be different. It was not possible. No more possible than for me to grow up proudly, marry a nice young woman, and produce children who would continue the Crenshaw line. There had been no choices. That was my truth.

"We don't have to go to Nashville," I choked.

"You've got to go!" Mother whispered, still dabbing at her eyes with the disintegrating tissue. "Your Daddy will never accept Michael, and we both know I'm telling the truth. Give Michael a chance, Aleshia. You have to go."

With those words, my mother set me free.

I know how much the gift cost her. Mother's pain was palpable. We sat there in the gathering twilight, holding each other tightly. That parting was the single most painful moment of my life.

In Nashville, my husband and I stayed with friends. It was not easy for any of us. I resented Michael for having made life with my father more difficult. I blamed him for not fixing the unfixable.

When I got the news that Mother was in Johnson City Memorial Hospital's intensive care unit, none of that mattered any longer.

"There's no need for you to come home," Daddy assured me when I called home, sensing that something was wrong, and accidentally uncovered the truth of her condition. "Mozelle will be out of intensive care tomorrow." He did not understand. I had to be there.

Daddy picked me up at the Trailways bus station, and we drove directly to the hospital. When we arrived, there were only minutes left in the day's final visiting hour. I followed my father into Mother's curtained ICU space. Mother looked up, saw Daddy, then caught sight of me and noticeably brightened. She jerked off her oxygen mask and launched into a dialogue. We overlapped each other in our enthusiasm. This was exactly as it had always been; we had to tell each other anything and everything. Daddy, excluded, stood aside and watched the two of us.

Daddy never actually had a chance, caught as he was between his wife and their firstborn. From the beginning, Mother and I radiated with a life force that differed from my father's. Mother and child fed off each other's gaiety. We'd always operated that way—generally to the exclusion of others. It wasn't something we'd planned, but long ago Mother and I had accepted the intuitive bond that existed between us. We'd never felt a need to sever it. I, in fact, believed that I could not exist without it.

Too soon, Daddy and I were asked to leave Mother's bedside, but having seen her, I was filled with relief. I'd overreacted to my mother's illness. Everything was going to be fine.

"Put that oxygen mask back on, Mother, and get some rest," I admonished. "I'll be here at nine before they move you out of ICU and into your room. We'll talk tomorrow."

As we left, Daddy affectionately wiggled Mother's big toe under the sheet. It was a sweet gesture. Maybe their relationship had improved since Michael and I had been pruned from their lives. Perhaps, after all, things could work out for all of us. Daddy and I rode home in silence. We weren't angry—this was simply as things had always been. Without Mozelle, my father and I had nothing to say to each other. Tonight, that did not matter; tomorrow morning we would both be with her, shortly before nine.

Mozelle Gillentine Crenshaw suffered a massive stroke moments before her family arrived.

Bewildered, Daddy and I were led into the visitor's room. I was numb. Life in the hospital waiting room was surreal as visitors slept, cried, and waited for news of their loved ones. They were like silent celluloid images played against a blank screen. Nothing registered. I was present at an important event but totally removed from it. It was as though I'd been spliced into a muted newsreel that then suddenly switched to slow motion. The only sound was music piped into the waiting room. That was soft, distinct, and deafening. Ronnie Milsap was singing "There's a Stranger in My House."

Mother never came out of her coma. First, last, and always, she had been my mother, and she'd remained consistent until the end. By sending me away, she'd sacrificed her emotional well-being in order to save her firstborn. By insisting that I look out for myself, she'd kept me from being there for her. I'd lost her. Mozelle dabbing at swollen eyes with a disintegrating old Kleenex, telling me to save myself, would remain my last clear image of her.

The doctors assured us that Mother's brain stem was dead, but I still insisted on reading her the poems of Edna St. Vincent Millay. Over and over I read "Pennies." It seemed important that Mozelle should hear those words of parting. I wanted Mother to know I was by her side. I still needed to talk to her.

"It's okay, Mother," I lied. "You can let go now. Take care of yourself. I'll be fine. I will. It's time for you to take care of yourself."

Mozelle held on tenaciously.

When Michael arrived from Nashville, he went into his mother-in-law's room and spoke to her softly. Mozelle bolted upright in bed, her arms stretched forward, as though trying to reach something far in front of her. Like a blind woman, my mother lunged forward, straining, reaching toward Michael. She clawed the air in front of her and gurgled. That was her last physical outreach to anyone.

Before leaving Nashville, my husband told friends that Mother's death would end our marriage. In the end, he made this a self-fulfilling prophecy. Emotionally, he was not there for me. At a time when, more than anything, I needed someone by my side, there was no one there. I was alone. Michael would promise to pick me up at the hospital, then fail to show up. When any small consideration would have meant so much, my husband had nothing left to give.

I was plagued by doubts. Had we made the correct decision by removing Mother's life-support system? Did Mozelle realize her family was there holding her hand? Was she in pain?

Shortly before my mother decided to let go of life, I sat alone under a shady poplar tree on hospital grounds, trying to deal with her imminent death. I was disturbed that Mother kept holding onto life, even when we were assured that she was technically dead. I sat, deep in thought, reliving the years Mother and I had shared together. Then, cutting through all that bittersweet memory, came a sharp, clear vision of my husband. I could see Michael. He sat drinking beer in a seedy, downtown bar. Johnson City has many shabby beer taverns—but I'd never been inside them. Yet I got in Daddy's car and drove directly to the exact bar where my husband sat drowning his sorrows.

"You son of a bitch!" I spat. "My mother believes in you, Michael. Now she's dying, and you choose this time to sink to the bottom of the barrel. You're scum!" I never stopped to question how or why I knew where my husband sat drinking. I merely knew. In my deepest grief, I had a clarity of sight that eluded me in day-to-day living.

Later that week, I again left the hospital to drive to town. I had no idea where I was going. As I rounded a corner, I saw Michael walking two women to their parked car. Then, pulling my car to the curb, I watched my husband make a drug transaction. He concluded the deal by kissing both women. At long last I understood. A duck among swans will yearn to return to the mud from which it came.

On Tuesday, July 12, 1983, my mother knew she was free to leave me. She was sixty-five years old. Her transsexual daughter, Aleshia, had just turned twenty-one. The woman I was not born to be had come of age.

CHAPTER 17

The Finished Product

RECENTLY, A friend shared her personal view of me. She sees me as one who walks through a storm but between the drops of rain. It is interesting how we are perceived by others. In this instance, it is a far cry from my vision of self. Events, large and small, in our lives impact who we are and what we become. They shape us. It is an ongoing process. There are times, however, when one merely plays to the demands of the moment. That's how I spent my youth. The difficulty in writing this autobiography has been remembering, honestly, my life before the transitioning. I feel as though, until the moment of surgical rebirth, I was in a perpetual stage of quiet pretense. Even as I lived those early years, I was consciously attempting to blur my gender image. I believed that acceptance depended on distorting the me that others saw. From earliest childhood I lived two lives. There was me and there was the public boy. They were both an embarrassment. From that stand-point, the years before surgery are not a happy period to recall.

My life began in Los Angeles, at Westlake Clinic, in 1962.

After surgery, fearful that the world, friends, and family could never fathom my journey, I denied my transgendered history. I believed some might acknowledge my right to exist, but unless a person had lived my twofold existence, no one would ever understand what had driven me to have gender-altering surgery. No one would ever understand *me*. I accepted that as a fact—and tried to forget my past. My only chance for happiness, or so I believed, was carefully to conform to societal standards established for women and methodically to eliminate any hint of my pre-vious gender bewilderment. Everything I'd been taught, accepted, or learned as a male was rejected. Life had taught that androgyny in any form was not acceptable. You must be either a *masculine* man or a *feminine* woman. I had never been comfortable on the masculine end of the gen-der scale. I knew where I belonged. Now, due to a painful and invasive surgery, I could accept my feminine place in society—would society *accept* me?

It remains beyond my comprehension that others may be threatened by my gender alteration. It was a personal fulfillment. Psychiatrists, surgeons, and the U.S. government agreed that I should legally be considered female. All records of name and gender were legally changed after surgery. I was as free to live and to marry as any natural woman. Yet, each passing year brings an increase in the horrific incidents of violence, brutalization, and death for my transsexual brothers and sisters. Why? I do not understand the source of such anger.

Granted, fearing such rejection, I could not initially bring myself to acknowledge my transsexuality publicly. Emotional isolation remained my reality, but I tried to invent a life that appeared exciting, complete, and appropriate to my new identity. Often, that was enough. For the first time in my life, I liked myself. People were attracted to my personality and enjoyed my tongue-in-cheek assessment of the world around me. I made good friends and some true aficionados along the way. What I failed to realize was that in many important ways, little had changed. I was still a second-class citizen. As a woman, I was still the brunt of the boys' jokes. It was socially acceptable to tease me, pointing at any shortcomings as being charmingly indicative of my female inferiority. I laughed at gender jokes along with my boyfriends, husbands, and father. They all made cracks at the expense of my hair color, weight, cooking, driving, sexual expertise, and financial acumen. At least they weren't laughing at a faggot. They were men making fun of a woman. Out of gratitude and relief, I laughed louder than anyone. I was afraid of forfeiting what affection I'd found. I couldn't endure that, so I immersed myself in an age-old feminine mystique. In my desire to please, I scripted a role of subservience, inferiority, and anxiety.

A nagging question remained, however: Was I truly loved? I was never ashamed of my need for love, but I turned my self-doubt inward where it could fester and taint. If I could not acknowledge the woman I was, including her transgendered history, was I worthy of love? Instead of living life openly and honestly, I chose not to risk being perceived as anything less than the perfect woman. After having come so far, my courage now failed me. My need for love and acceptance, when coupled with an overwhelming lack of self-esteem, made me a willing victim. As a self-perceived innocent, I believed that to feel pain passionately was to know love; therefore, if love hurts, please hurt me more.

Every transsexual I knew in those early years faced life with a determined smile on her lips. We'd learned to mask our anguish with a laugh and a quick quip. Being entertaining at all cost, making light of one's bruises, is a familiar technique for survival. I learned that lesson early on the elementary school playground. Those who bully and despise you prefer to see you cry. Turn torment into laughter, and you have a defense. It is short-sighted, however, to believe that one bounces back quickly from ill treatment. Those who survive do so because they learn to get up off the playground. Stay down—you die.

Over the years, I became so anxious to please everyone, so afraid of being a disappointment to anyone, that I failed to please myself. I forfeited the spirit of the very woman I'd hoped to become. In spite of some cleverly contrived rhetoric to the contrary, I still viewed my gender transformation as something shameful. At the time of my surgery, the prevailing professional and personal advice for a transsexual was for her to totally turn her back on the past. As in a witness-protection program, to create a new life, everything and everyone you'd known must cease to exist. At this I failed miserably. I could not give up my friends or family. Rather, I swore everyone to secrecy and tried to create a new life through wit and verve. Few people knew how frightened I was of receiving a negative review. Judging myself by a nation's homophobic standard and distancing myself from the queer community, I went underground to become part of heterosexual society. This translated into a denial of my transgendered history. I was still uncomfortable being the person I was born to be.

Now, at sixty-three, I fully realize that to deny one's history is to deny one's self. This gender truth wasn't mine, however, until after I awoke one morning in my mid-fifties to discover that, overnight, men had stopped turning around in the street to watch me sashay past. No longer being a sexual object leaves a woman a lot of time to think.

Eureka! My startling discovery was that I could be a complete woman, even without a partner. I'd spent my life as a prospector, searching for love, but finding that I'd become my own person came as a complete surprise. Domination by husbands, boyfriends, and my own irrational fears had become increasingly intolerable with each passing year, but no remarkable revelations, no great insight, changed me into a self-sufficient woman. Rather, as with all developed beings, I'd quietly become the sum of my experiences. I became a woman, but the cultivation of personal character and spiritual power was my true bonanza. Over the years I've discovered that the gender casing is secondary to the spirit it houses. That said, it is still impossible for me to imagine my life other than as a woman. I have grown into a self-sufficient woman. Finding that I can exist, happily, without a man has also been a tedious, ongoing process. It was, however, as important to my life as a woman as was the physical reconstruction of my body. It took much longer.

When I reached a point in life when I could publicly acknowledge my gender history, people immediately started telling me that I had a story to tell the world. I believed them. Autobiographies have always fascinated me, and I have long joked that my particular yarn reads like a B-grade movie script. The life has certainly been melodramatic. Naively believing that I'd make a fistful of dollars by sharing my early transsexual history, so long hidden behind lies and illusions, I started looking for a ghostwriter. If I was afraid of exposing myself, I was terrified of doing it in my own words. The first professional ghostwriter I contacted was in New York. He questioned being able to handle the issue of my self-castration—he was uncomfortable with my "mutilation." This was not the writer for me. My second choice was an Emmy Award–winning television writer and friend. He died before we began work on my Homeric adventure. After a half dozen misguided attempts to find someone who would write my book, I realized that the voice behind the story must be mine. I had a lot to learn about publishing. I'd never read a transsexual's memoir and was not even aware that many existed. One of my first and hardest lessons was finding that, during my thirty-five years of hiding my past, many vocal transgendered sisters had been telling their own versions of the transsexual experience. My story might be different, but it was no longer unique. I would not be buying a villa in southern France by making my life story public. My decision to continue the project was based on my desire to revisit my past honestly—

and due to the encouragement from friends active in the transgendered community. I'd lived long enough as a transsexual to start feeling like an icon. The major difficulty in writing this book has been the editing of anecdotes. I've loved living every moment of my life. It hasn't always been easy, but it has always been rewarding. My objective in the writing has been to counter the popular concept and general talk-show notion that all transsexuals are dishonest, amoral social rejects.

When one's existence and self-image have been dependent on the affection and attention of men, the presence of a man in the plot development becomes mandatory. That does not, however, make all the men in my life interesting, vital, or glorious characters. That I, at one time, considered male input necessary for my life, however, makes the autobiography impossible without their presence. Most women of my day thought themselves incomplete without men.

It has been seventeen years since the death of my mother, Mozelle. My transsexual journey ended with my realization that, as a complete woman, I could live on alone. When I wrote the final words surrounding her death, I knew I'd told my story. No longer am I in a state of gender transition. I am the woman I was not born to be—the spiritual essence that Mozelle nourished. Mother engendered me. My style, my sense of humor, my strength come directly from her. She loved me unconditionally.

I only wish I'd found a more mature voice before I lost my father, James, on January 15, 1996. I did not. Instead, I continued my life pattern of acquiescing in the face of rejection and then later feeling I had let myself down. Our past hurts and fears stymied our relationship. In no way, however, do I feel that my father was the catalyst for my surgical transformation. I believe my gender destiny was programmed from birth.

Life isn't perfect, and in reality, the product is never finished—it's a work in progress. For me, there will probably always remain dark shadows from a transgendered past to haunt me. Still, I'm more at peace with my total person than I ever thought possible. Over the years it has become less important that I be considered 150 percent female. I am what I am. It is more important that I accept and value that person. Universal acceptance would be nice, but it is not necessary—and will never happen! Rejection does still hurt. These days, it just doesn't hurt as much, or for as long.

Age has also brought a sense of "oneness" that I never before experienced. As we mature, the genders physically tend to become more akin. Waists are less defined, features tend to blur, and a once-firm chin comes to rest on the chest. Now, as a senior citizen, I sometimes even hear myself, vocally, sounding exactly like my father. "Where is your precious femininity now?" I ask myself. These moments cause me to laugh. I know that I am complete, no matter how disheveled I may look on any given day or how bass the voice may sound when I first arise. I have found my place in the world. Now, if it exists, rejection is less threatening. A friend, in passing, might acknowledge that members of the transgendered community are not welcomed by some individuals within his or her immediate circle. Occasionally, I have been ostracized by someone based solely on my gender history. That is an unusual occurrence in my life. Perhaps my life as an acknowledged transsexual is so sweet because I live on the refreshingly liberal central coast of California. When a slight does occur, I am always taken aback. Thinking of myself as different is no longer part of my everyday social consciousness. My greatest joy comes with the freedom to be myself. A trip to the local market without makeup and devoid of any fear that my gender might suddenly become an issue is one of the rewards of my transsexual choice. A twilight's pleasant chat with a passerby as I water my roses is one of life's greatest pleasures. Being accepted, respected, and appreciated was all I ever wanted. Because I now enjoy a peaceful place in the world, small gender-based slights become disproportionately jarring. I've too much enjoyed my years of being just another one of the old "girls" on my block.

For every transsexual woman and man who will follow my path in the future, I wish for all of you the luxury of love, support, and understanding that I have found along my own road. I was given a real and extended family of supportive women.

The two most important people in my life, Kathy and my mother, Mozelle, did not live to share my success as a mature woman. Mother concluded her life journey in Johnson City, Tennessee, on July 12, 1983. Six years later, Kathy died. She had a glass of champagne to celebrate her Christmas Eve birthday, took a sleeping pill, and went to bed. She did not wake up. Although my proud friend would never have admitted it, she was fifty-eight years old. Kathy had lived her life as she saw fit. She lived with a vengeance, and as a woman of extremes. I'm not sure that she was always happy or content, but my friend was always true to her own spirit. Before she met me at Finocchio's in the late 1950s, she'd already made many of the mistakes I later seemed intent on making. I believe my friend saw much of her younger being in me, and that she worked diligently during our years together to nurture my sensitivity and innate love of life. She never failed to offer me love and encouragement. Today, I am an extension of her soul. I both loved and admired her.

The memory and spiritual presence of Kathy and Mozelle have remained with me. There is never a day that I do not think of them and wish that they were here to share my joy in life.

In the fourteen years since Mozelle's death, I have worked in repertory theater in Princeton, New Jersey; created the character Tex on the soap opera *One Life to Live;* worked in the early 1990s as an associate professor of theater at East Tennessee State University; appeared in the original cast of Chicago's hit run of *Ruthless!;* been featured in numerous commercials; and, lately, collaborated with a partner in writing eight full-length plays. The major and minor successes represent the fulfilling culmination of the life that my mother and my friend Kathy both wished for me. It is because of the love of these two women and the support of many loyal friends that I am able to tell my story honestly. Because of their support, I am now proud of the woman I have become. I did not survive on my own. My sister, Jeanne, remains a consistently supportive force in my life. Many others continue to shape my life. I am fortunate to be surrounded by supportive women, such as my longtime friend Joyce Nordquist, who has been a steady comrade on my journey. Joyce continues to serve as the bright, nurturing, and loving female image to which I aspire. There are also exceptional men who help keep life meaningful. Many compatriots continue as both inspirations and as guiding lights. It is to all those women who have lovingly called me sister and to the men who have called me friend that I dedicate this book. First and foremost, however, there was always my mother, Mozelle.

Index